Game Programming Theory
in C++

Vic Broquard

Game Programming Theory in C++
2nd Edition
ISBN: 978-1-941415-60-3
Vic Broquard
Copyright 2006, 2007, 2014 by Vic Broquard

Broquard eBooks
103 Timberlane
East Peoria, IL 61611
author@Broquard-eBooks.com

Table of Contents

To all of my dedicated, persevering students,
and to L. Ron Hubbard, who taught me to "Simplify"

Preface

Writers of computer game programs face many common situations, no matter what type of game they are creating. This text is designed to illustrate many solutions to these common problems facing anyone who is programming a computer game. The solutions can be applied to quite different situations and game genres.

The solutions can be grouped into two major categories: the physics of motion behind the action and the requisite artificial intelligence to make the action believable and realistic. Yes, these often do require very complex mathematics. However, this text is not going to derive any of these equations nor any of the proofs behind the physics. Rather, it presents the needed mathematical equations necessary to solve the problem and then shows how those equations can be effectively programed.

In the author's opinion, games programming in C++ should be all object oriented, that is fully utilizing classes. However, the assumption behind this text is that the reader is concurrently taking their first course that presents OOP classes and perhaps data structures. The usage of classes is purposely kept to a minimal level, especially at the beginning of the text. However, by the end of the text, much more sophisticated usage of the language is needed. Feel free to review other C++ OOP programming texts if you find that you are having trouble grasping the C++ coding.

Download the samples that accompany this text from http://www.broquard-ebooks.com/pb/games, and take the appropriate link.

But above all, please enjoy the text and the insights it gives to you. Please put some of these techniques to work in your own games.

If you find any errors or have any suggestions or comments, please email me at author@Broquard-eBooks.com

Chapter 0 A Math Review and C++ Class Design

The starting point must be to define clearly what this book is and what it isn't. This is a beginning text that covers many of the basic algorithms, methods, and equations that are needed to add realism to games that you create. While a computer game should be fun and entertaining, the objects in the game world should follow natural laws of which we are familiar.

This is not to imply that in a game universe there cannot be some new aspect, some new physical law, that makes that universe unique. Rather, if one throws a ball or shoots a gun or turns the steering wheel of a car, one expects from our intimate familiarity with the physical universe around us that certain laws will be obeyed. For example, when throwing a ball from one player to another distant player, we expect the ball to follow an arc path, not to go half way to the other player and then shoot straight up five hundred feet only to land in the thrower's glove. When one player shoots a carefully aimed gun toward an enemy unit, the player does not expect to see the bullet fly part way there and then take a sharp ninety degree turn and fly away. When the player moves the steering wheel of a car to the right, the player expects the car to turn to the right, not suddenly break to a full stop.

In order to simulate the motions and behaviors of objects, the computer program must deal with the underlying physics of that object's motion. A good half of this text covers the physics of motion of various objects commonly needed for computer games.

The second aspect of a good computer game is how the computer handles and controls the opponents of the player. For example, Frodo, the hobbit, walks into a cavern entrance and discovers the cave is occupied by twenty goblins. As he stands there momentarily confused, the computer must control the goblins. It would be a very dumb game indeed if the computer just had the goblins do nothing but stay where they were located while Frodo and his sword valiantly fought them, one by one. Such would be highly unrealistic indeed. In such a case, the computer game program ought to have the goblins recognize that they were facing a lone, small opponent and have all of then charge directly toward Frodo, perhaps even with swords drawn.

Or perhaps Frodo is not alone, but has a company of fifty dwarven foot soldiers with him. Now a more realistic goblin reaction might be to flee as quickly as they could. These "intelligent actions" taken by the computer controlled objects are known collectively as Artificial Intelligence, or just AI for short. The second aspect of this text is then to cover the main, key AI elements and algorithms commonly needed for computer games.

Game Programming Theory

In summary then, this book is all about the physics of motion and the AI commonly found and needed in computer game programming.

What this book is not about is the mathematical derivations of equations, complex mathematical solutions for problems. It is not about deriving the laws of the physics of motion. You will find no derivations in this text. If you are interested in these aspects, I refer you to the many good texts currently available on the web, in libraries, and book stores.

The philosophy behind this text is that of a pragmatical games programmer. Suppose that you wish to realistically simulate the firing of an artillery piece in a war game. All the programmer really wants to have at hand are the equations needed to solve the problem along with the requisite numerical constants that might be involved, such as the force of gravity. Games programmers are seldom keenly interested in just how those equations are derived, only how to best use them, along with their restrictions and limitations. This is the direction the text is heading.

Of course, all of the various algorithms and methods must be illustrated in coding. The language used is C++. My assumption is that you have already taken the basic, beginning C++ course. Further, all well designed games, in my opinion, fully utilize object oriented programming methods, or classes. This course and text also makes the assumption that you have had or are taking concurrently the next C++ programming course which introduces you to classes and the principles of object oriented design.

(Note, if you find your exposure to C++ object oriented programming or classes is far too weak, please acquire a copy of my C++ Object Oriented Programming textbook or any other good C++ OOP text and catch up.)

However, since my assumption is that you are just concurrently learning about OOP programming, I will severely limit my usage of classes and that technology. That is, I will keep class complexity to a bare-bones minimum. Yes, this is rather unrealistic for production coding, but keeping the OOP to a minimum at this stage allows you to concentrate on the physics and AI and not on the language. In the sequel book, *Non-graphical Games Programming*, this will not be the case. In that book, I make full usage of the OOP language to maximize the programming ease. In that text, you will see nearly every aspect of OOP put to good use in games programming.

The sample programs covered in depth in this text are of two types: DOS programs with which you are familiar and actual Windows graphical applications which you are not familiar. Yes, some examples can only be shown using actual computer graphics and that requires what is known as a Windows application, not the black and white, character oriented DOS screen. I'll be honest with you. To write the Windows applications, you need two additional courses in C++ programming, C++ Object Oriented Programming and Windows Programming I. This is because Windows programming is inherently making full use of OOP coding and principles.

Game Programming Theory

Thus, while some of the examples in this text will use a Windows programming application shell, I do not expect you to be able to write them. Rather, I will expect that you can follow that portion of such programs that pertains to the physics model or AI algorithm. I have been careful to keep those aspects highly separated from the Windows graphical coding. Further, I have kept such Windows programming to a very simplistic, unrealistic level so as to keep the "magical coding" to a minimum. In the capstone course of our Games Programming degree program, you will learn how to code fancy DirectX 2D and 3D graphics. At that point in your education, you can delve into fancy graphics and methods.

The starting point must be a brief review of the key mathematical principles needed to understand and grasp the various equations and solutions presented in this text. Along the way, I will introduce the concepts of C++ classes and coding, showing you just how using classes simplifies your work as a programmer.

Basic Math Review

The formulas and principles presented in this text will be both 2D and 3D in nature. The most fundamental idea to grasp is that of the coordinate system used to locate a point within the 2D or 3D space. Any given point can be located by specifying its x and y axis coordinates as shown in Figure 0-1. In 3D space, a third coordinate, the location on the z axis, is also required. This is known as the Cartesian coordinate system. The origin point (0, 0) is that point where the x and y axis meet. Note that the axes are perpendicular to each other.

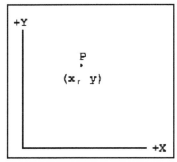

Figure 0-1 A Point in 2D

In the polar coordinate system, a point is specified by giving its angle and distance from the origin point, as shown in Figure 0-2.

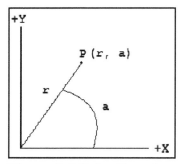

Figure 0-2 Polar Coords

Next, given a right triangle, that is a triangle with one of its angles ninety degrees, we get the basic trig functions, sin, cos, and tan. We also get the conversions between Cartesian and polar coordinates. These relationships are shown in Figure 0-3.

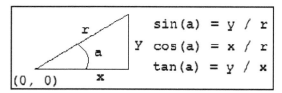

Figure 0-3 Basic Trig Functions

Game Programming Theory

We also know that the sum of the squares of the two sides equals the square of the hypotenuse.

$$r^2 = x^2 + y^2$$

Thus, the conversion functions are then these.

$x = r \cos (a)$
$y = r \sin (a)$
$r = sqrt (x^2 + y^2)$
$a = atan (y / x)$
$a = atan2 (y, x)$
$a = asin (y / r)$
$a = acos (x / r)$

Notice that three points make up that triangle. Each of these bounding points is called a **vertex**. The three lines forming the edges or outer boundary of the triangle are called **edges**. The surface of the triangle is called its **face**. These three definitions play an enormous role in 2D and 3D graphics programming.

Given a triangle, one extremely common action that's required in games programming is to rotate that triangle about an axis. This is shown in Figure 0-4.

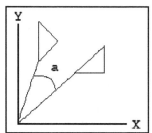

Figure 0-4 Rotation

Given the angle of rotation, a, the new location of the three points can be found. Given the coordinates of each of the three points, the rotated values are given by these equations.

$x_1 = x_0 \cos(a) - y_0 \sin(a)$
$y_1 = x_0 \sin(a) + y_0 \cos(a)$

where x_0, y_0 represent the original coordinates of a point and x_1, y_1 represent the new rotated values.

Another action that is often performed on an object is **scaling**. This means to alter the overall size of the object without changing its basic shape, just its size. To scale an object, one only needs to scale its dimension points. In the case of our triangle, altering the three vertices alters its size. Again, if x_0, y_0 represent the original coordinates of one of the vertex points of the triangle and x_1, y_1 represent the new scaled values, then to perform scaling apply this formula.

$x_1 = x_0 * ScaleFactor$
$y_1 = y_0 * ScaleFactor$

Game Programming Theory

Of course, the scaling must be done to each vertex that defines the object. A similar action that is often done to an object is to move it to another location. This is called **translation**. Again, you perform the translation calculations on each vertex that defines the object.

$x_1 = x_0 + \text{TranslationFactor}$

$y_1 = y_0 + \text{TranslationFactor}$

Now what about the edges? These are lines and lines are defined in a number of different ways. Figure 0-5 shows the general situation.

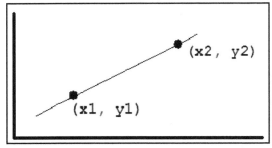

Figure 0-5 A Line

The slope of a non-vertical line, m, is given by this.

$m = \text{change in y / change in x} = (y_2 - y_1) / (x_2 - x_1)$

Any given point (x, y) on the line can be found from one of these equations of a line.

Point-slope form: $(y - y_1) = m (x - x_1)$

Slope-intercept form: $y = m x + b$, where b is the y value when x is zero

Horizontal line: $y = b$

Vertical line: $x = a$

The midpoint between two points on a line is given by this equation.

Midpoint coordinates $= ((x_2 + x_1) / 2, (y_2 + y_1) / 2)$

For the faces, the area is often needed. Here are some area formulas.

Square area $= \text{side}^2$

Rectangle area $= \text{length} * \text{width}$

Circle area $= \text{PI radius}^2$

where PI is given by acos (–1.)

Triangle area $= .5 * \text{base} * \text{height}$

Trapezoid area $= .5 * \text{height} * (\text{base}_1 \text{ length} + \text{base}_2 \text{ length})$

Game Programming Theory

In 3D, the volumes of objects are needed. Here are some common volumes.
Square volume = side^3
Rectangular solid volume = length * width * height
Sphere volume = 4. / 3. PI radius^3
Cylinder volume = base area * height
Cone volume = 1. / 3. * base area * height
Pyramid volume = 1. / 3. * base area * height

Vectors

Handling directions and movements, such as velocity, requires an additional property, the direction. A car's velocity has both a magnitude, the miles per hour, and the direction it is traveling. In common notation, vectors are shown in bold face. Hence, the velocity of a car will be annotated this way, **v**. In contrast to a vector, a scalar is just a number, the magnitude. Figure 0-6 shows the vector notation.

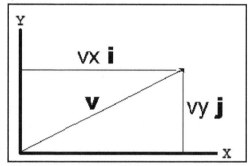

Figure 0-6 A Vector

The vector is often stored by giving it x and y axes projections. A unit vector is a vector whose magnitude is unity or one. Thus, vector **v** shown in the figure would be written this way. For a 2D vector, omit the z axis value. Here, **i**, **j**, and **k** are unit vectors along the x, y, and z axes.

$\mathbf{v} = v_x\mathbf{i} + v_y\mathbf{j} + v_z\mathbf{k}$

The magnitude of the vector is given by
sqrt $(v_x^2 + v_y^2 + v_{z2})$

Vectors are a powerful mathematical tool that has widespread use in games programming. So let's see how we are going to store them. Notice in the preceding section, I did not elaborate on how to store a point either. Yes, both need to store either 2 or 3 numbers depending upon whether it is a 2D or 3D representation. Things can get very messy very quickly unless we turn to Object Oriented Programming for a solution. Here is where classes really benefit our coding.

Before we dive into the details of vectors, let's see how OOP can make our programming task vastly easier.

C++ Object Oriented Programming, an Introduction to Classes

An object is "a thing," an entity. Consider a computer emulation of a car object. It has **properties** associated with it, the **data members**. Some car object properties might be the number of doors, its color, the engine size, its mpg, gas tank capacity, a flag representing whether or not the motor is running, and its current speed. A car object also has **member functions** or **methods** to perform actions on the car object, such as, start, stop, drive, speed up, slow down, and turn.

Similar to a structure template, a **class** is a model for the compiler to follow to create an object. A class usually has data members that define its various properties and has member functions that perform requested actions. When one creates a specific instance of the car class in memory, one has then a real object. This is called **instantiating an object**. The actions and nomenclature parallel that of a structure. Given an instance of a car, we can then request it to perform various actions, such as starting up and driving.

The data members and the functions to operate on those data are joined into an inseparable whole, this is called **encapsulation**. The outside world can utilize the object normally only through its provided member functions. How those actions are actually implemented is totally hidden from the outside world. With this black box approach, ideally one should be able to completely rework the internal algorithms and never touch the client's coding.

With the car, the user might invoke a **StartCar()** function. How the car is actually started is never known nor is it ever a concern to the user. The benefit of encapsulation is large with perhaps the biggest being code reusability.

The member data and functions have a user **access attribute**: **public**, **private**, and **protected**. Specifying **public** access on a data item or function allows the user to use and refer to it directly by name. Only **public** data and functions can be accessed by the user of the object. Sometimes we do not wish the user to be able to access some of the class data and function members; these are given either **protected** or **private** access; these are for our own internal use within our class.

For example, the manner in which we wish to keep track of whether the car is started or not is our own business. The user should not be given public access to that member; instead we give him a function **IsStarted()** which returns **true** or **false**. If we do not like the way we are internally storing the started state, we can change it without affecting the user's code. It is unwise to make data members public for that allows the user to be able to change object state directly; doing so removes a bit of the black box. For then we cannot change these public data members without impacting the users of our class. Member functions are often public so the user can perform actions with the object.

Class Syntax

A class is normally composed of two files: a definition file and an implementation file — that is, a header file and a cpp file. The definition of a class begins with the keyword **class** which is followed by the name of the class and the begin brace. Class names are usually capitalized while the data member names it contains are usually lowercase. An end brace and semicolon end the definition.

Here is the basic syntax of a class definition.

```
/*********************************************************/
/*                                                       */
/* name: purpose, etc.                                   */
/*                                                       */
/*********************************************************/

class name {

  /*********************************************************/
  /*                                                       */
  /* class data                                            */
  /*                                                       */
  /*********************************************************/

  public:
  protected:
  private:
    data definitions

  /*********************************************************/
  /*                                                       */
  /* class function                                        */
  /*                                                       */
  /*********************************************************/

  public:
  protected:
  private:
    function prototypes
};
```

Notice that I usually group all of the member data into one area and all of the member functions into another portion. This enables the reader to rapidly find things. If you intersperse data definitions and function prototypes, it becomes more difficult to rapidly find items of interest.

Suppose that we wanted to create a class to encapsulate a simple vehicle, such as a wagon or cart. We can code the following.

```
class Vehicle {
 // here the default access is private unless qualified
};
```

This definition is located in the file **Vehicle.h**; its implementation is in **Vehicle.cpp**.

The Three Access Qualifiers

Every data member and member function has an access qualifier associated with it: **public:** or **protected:** or **private:**.

Rule: By default, everything after the begin brace of the class definition is private.

Public items can be accessed directly by everyone, including the client programs. Certainly the class user interface (member functions) should be public. This represents the main user interface to the object. However, most all of the member data should not be given public access.

Private access is the most restrictive. No client program can ever access private items. Furthermore, if we derive a **Car** class from the **Vehicle** class, the **Car** class inherits all of the member data and functions of the **Vehicle** class. However, those items that are private cannot be accessed from the new derived **Car** class. In general this is way too restrictive. The whole idea of OOP is to create a good hierarchical collection of classes. Thus, one should really make private only those really critical items that even a derived class should not have access to.

The third access qualifier is **protected**. Protected items are not accessible by client programs. However, a derived class does have direct access to them.

Since you are perhaps only now beginning to learn about writing classes in your other programming courses, in this text, I will make bare bones use of classes. Our classes will have all data members public as well as member functions. In reality, this would not likely be the case.

For a **Vehicle**, what data members could be defined? Let's keep this simple and track whether or not the vehicle is in motion and how fast it is traveling. We have then the following.
vehicle.h

```
class Vehicle {
 public:
```

10

```
bool isMoving;
int  speed;
};
```

Now we need some functions. Function fall roughly into three broad categories: constructors/destructor functions, access functions, and operations functions.

Constructors and Destructors

Generally, a class has one or more **constructor** functions and one and only one **destructor** function. The constructor function is called by the compiler when the object is being created and its job is usually to give initial values to this instance's data members. Think of the constructor as getting the object all ready for operations. The destructor function is called by the compiler when the object is being destroyed. Its purpose is to provide clean up actions, such as removal of dynamically allocated memory items or reference count decrementing. Both functions have the same name as the class, except that the destructor has a ~ character before its name. For all of the classes used in this text, the destructor functions have nothing to do.

Neither a constructor nor a destructor function can ever return any value of any kind, not even **void**. A destructor function cannot ever be passed any parameters, ever, and thus cannot ever be overloaded with multiple versions. However, the constructor function can have as many parameters as desired and often is overloaded so that the class can be initialized in a variety of ways. Note that "constructor" is often abbreviated as "**ctor**." Likewise, "destructor" is often called "**dtor**."

> **Rule: All classes must have at least one constructor function whose job is to initialize this instance's member data. It can be overloaded and is always called by the compiler.**
>
> **Rule: All classes must have a destructor function whose job is to perform cleanup activities. It is called by the compiler when the object goes out of scope and must be deleted.**
>
> **Rule: If a class has either no constructor or destructor function, the compiler provides a default constructor or destructor function for you. The provided constructor and destructor do nothing but issue a return instruction.**

Overloaded functions are functions whose names are the same but differ in the number and types of parameters being passed to the function. Return data types do not count. Here in the **Vehicle** class the constructor function and destructor function prototypes could be

```
Vehicle ();
~Vehicle ();
```

When designing the constructor functions, give some thought to how the user might like to create instances of your class. With a **Vehicle**, the user might want to create a default vehicle or they might like to create a specific vehicle that is moving down the road at 42 miles an hour. Thus, we should provide two different constructor functions in this case. Here is the class definition with the new functions added.

vehicle.h

```
class Vehicle {

  public:
    bool isMoving;
    int  speed;

            // creates a default Vehicle
            Vehicle ();

            // creates a specific Vehicle
            Vehicle (bool move, int sped);
};
```

The **default constructor** is a constructor that takes no parameters.

Rule: A class should always provide a default constructor as a matter of good practice.

This default constructor is called when the user wishes to create a default instance. Hence, this is most likely to be the most frequently invoked function in a client program.

Notice the comment lines just above the function prototype. Any comments above the prototypes will be shown by Intellisense! This is a very nice feature of the new compilers!

The Implementation File

These functions are actually implemented in the **Vehicle.cpp** file; they are only defined in the header file. Think about the default constructor's implementation. What should it do? Suppose that in the **Vehicle.cpp** file we coded the following.

vehicle.cpp

```
#include "Vehicle.h"
Vehicle () {          // error
  isMoving = false;
  speed = 0;
}
```

How does the compiler know that this function **Vehicle()** is the constructor that is defined in the header file? As it is coded, it does not know this. The compiler thinks that this is an ordinary C function whose name is **Vehicle**! It does not know that this function actually belongs to the **Vehicle** class. Further, no return data type is coded, so it assumes it returns an **int**.

To show that a data member or a member function is part of a class, we use the **class qualifier** which is the name of the class followed by a double colon — **classname::** To notify the compiler that this function belongs to the **Vehicle** class, we code

```
Vehicle::Vehicle () {
...
}
```

Rule: When you define the member function body, include the classname::

```
returntype   classname::functionname (parameter list) {
....
}
```

Rule: any member function has complete access to all member data and functions.

This last rule is why classes are so vitally important in this text. All member functions have total access to the member data! This means that the member data **do not** need to be passed to these member functions! This is a tremendous benefit indeed!

Outside that class, only public members are available. Here is how we could implement the two constructor functions of the **Vehicle** class.

vehicle.cpp

```
#include "Vehicle.h"

Vehicle::Vehicle () {
 isMoving = false;
 speed = 0;
}

Vehicle::Vehicle (bool move, int sped) {
 isMoving = move;
 speed = sped;
}
```

Of course, the implementation in the second constructor function is a bit shaky. Suppose that the caller passed **false** and 42 miles per hour. We are then storing a vehicle that is not moving at 42 miles an hour. Or suppose that the user passed **true** and 0? Ok. We could check on the speed and override the user's request so that the object was not in some silly state. But for simplicity, I am overlooking this situation.

13

Game Programming Theory

Notice how that within the member functions, we have complete access to all of the member data.

One must be a bit careful of parameter variable names. Suppose that we had coded it this way. We run into a scope of names situation. Specifically, a parameter name hides member names of the same exact name.

```
Vehicle::Vehicle (bool isMoving, int speed) {
  isMoving = isMoving; // error
  speed = speed;       // error
}
```

What is happening is that the parameter variables hide the class member variables of the same name. These two lines are saying to copy the contents of the parameter **speed** and put it into the parameter **speed**. One way around this conflict is to use different names for the parameters as I originally did. However, you can also use the class qualifier to specify which variable is desired.

```
Vehicle::Vehicle (bool isMoving, int speed) {
  Vehicle::isMoving = isMoving;
  Vehicle::speed = speed;
}
```

Since this is a lot of extra coding, the simpler solution is to ensure the parameter names do not conflict with member names.

Adding Member Functions

Next, let's add some member functions. A user of a Vehicle object probably needs to access the isMoving state and the vehicle's speed. Thus, the definition is expanded to include four more functions.

vehicle.h

```
class Vehicle {

public:   protected:
  bool isMoving;
  int speed;


      Vehicle  ();
      Vehicle  (bool move, int sped);

  // the access functions
  bool IsMoving ();
  void SetMoving(bool move);
```

14

```
  int  GetSpeed ();
  void SetSpeed (int sped);
};
```

These four new functions are implemented as follows.
vehicle.cpp:

```
#include "Vehicle.h"

bool Vehicle::IsMoving () {
 return isMoving;
}

void Vehicle::SetMoving(bool move) {
 isMoving = move;
}

int Vehicle::GetSpeed () {
 return speed;
}

void Vehicle::SetSpeed (int sped) {
 speed = sped;
}
```

Again, the implementations are oversimplified with respect to the interrelationship between **isMoving** and **speed**. One could also overload the **SetSpeed()** and pass two parameters. The definition and implementation are as follows.

```
  void SetSpeed (bool move, int sped);

  void Vehicle::SetSpeed (bool move, int sped) {
   is_moving = move;
   speed = sped;
  }
```

Creating and Using Class Instances

How are instances of a class instantiated or created in client programs? An instance is defined just like any other data type — just like you would create an instance of a structure. Objects can be of automatic storage type, static, constant and even dynamically allocated. Arrays can be created as well.
main.cpp

```
#include "vehicle.h"
int main () {
```

```
Vehicle a;              // calls the default constructor
Vehicle b (true, 42);   // calls the overloaded version to create
                        // a vehicle that is moving at 42 mph

const Vehicle c (true, 55);    // a constant vehicle
static Vehicle d (true, 60);   // a static vehicle

Vehicle e[100];         // creates an array of 100 vehicles
```

The next action is to access public data members and call public member functions. The syntax parallels that of structures. How is a member of a structure accessed? By using the dot (.) operator. The same is true with classes. We use

```
    object_instance.function
```
or
```
    object_instance.data_item
```


The client program can now perform the following actions on its newly created vehicle **a** by coding the following.

```
    a.SetSpeed (100);       // get the car moving
    a.SetMoving (true);     // at 100 miles per hour
    cout << a.GetSpeed ();  // display a's speed
```

Or if using element j of the array of 100 vehicles, code the subscript as follows.

```
    e[j].SetSpeed (100);       // get the car moving
    e[j].SetMoving (true);     // at 100 miles per hour
    cout << e[j].GetSpeed ();  // display a's speed
```

Back to Vectors and the Creation of a Vector Class

To store a vector or a point in Cartesian space, we need to store the x, y, and z components. If only 2D space is needed, always use a value of 0 for the z component. This way, we can write one Vector class that can be used in either 2D or 3D situations. Here is the start of the Vector class definition file. Notice that I also defined two useful constants and a couple of ordinary C function prototypes to convert an angle to radians and to degrees. Remember that all the trig functions require the angle to be in radians, yet normally we store angles measured in degrees. The EPS constant, short for error precision, is used to handle floating point round-off errors.

Vector.h
```
#pragma once
#include <iostream>
#include <iomanip>
#include <cmath>
```

16

```
using namespace std;

const double PI = acos(-1.);
const double EPS = 0.000001;

double DegreesToRadians (double degrees);
double RadiansToDegrees (double radians);

class Vector {
public:
 double x;
 double y;
 double z;

 Vector ();
 Vector (double xx, double yy, double zz);
 ~Vector () {}

 double Magnitude () const;
```

Next, let's see how we implement these beginning functions. Here is the start of the Vector.cpp file.

```
#include "Vector.h"

double DegreesToRadians (double degrees) {
 return degrees * PI / 180.0;
}

double RadiansToDegrees (double radians) {
 return radians * 180.0 / PI;
}

Vector::Vector () : x(0), y(0), z(0) {}

Vector::Vector (double xx, double yy, double zz) :
              x(xx), y(yy), z(zz) {}

double Vector::Magnitude () const {
 return sqrt (x * x + y * y + z * z);
}
```

Finally, how do our client programs use this Vector class? Here is the start of a main() function.

```
#include "Vector.h"
```

```
int main () {
  Vector v;                          // a default vector (0,0,0)
  Vector u (10.5, 40.3, 0);     // a 2D vector
  Vector w (10.5, 40.3, 22.8); // a 3D vector
  cout << u.Magnitude ();       // outputs the magnitude of u
  Vector array[100];            // creates an array of 100
  array[0].x = 10.5;            // element 0 now has the same
  array[0].y = 40.3;            // values as vector u
  array[1] = u;                 // element 1 is also same as u
  v = u;                        // vector v is also same as u
```

Notice one clever action, the assignment of one vector to another. While we can individually assign values to the x, y, and z data members, it is faster and easier to just copy the whole thing in one line. The assignment operator, =, copies all data members of one instance into the corresponding data members of the other instance. It is a very fast block copy operation!

Additional Vector Operations

Sometimes, a vector must be **normalized**. A normalized vector has a magnitude of 1.0. Once in a while, a vector needs to be reversed in its direction. Let's add these two functions to the class.

```
void  Vector::Normalize () {
  double mag = Magnitude ();
  if(mag <= EPS) mag = EPS;/// not 1

  x /= mag;
  y /= mag;
  z /= mag;

  if (fabs(x) < EPS) x = 0;
  if (fabs(y) < EPS) y = 0;
  if (fabs(z) < EPS) z = 0;
}

void  Vector::Reverse () {
  x = -x;
  y = -y;
  z = -z;
}
```

Normalize() first finds the magnitude of the vector. However, small round-off errors can and do accumulate. Hence, I check to see if the current magnitude is less than the error precision value. If so, I re-assign the magnitude to this smallest allowable value. Then, each axis component is divided by the magnitude. Can you see what would happen if we allowed the magnitude to become zero? Finally, each new axis component is also checked to see if it is sufficiently close to zero to be zero.

To reverse the vector's direction, simply negate each axis component. We would use these two functions in our main() program this way.

```
u.Normalize ();
u.Reverse ();
```

However, what happens if main wrote this line of code?

```
v = - u;
```

Here, the operator is the minus or unary minus to be more accurate. In OOP, all of the various operators of the C++ language (with three exceptions only) can be overridden in the class to provide greater functionality of that class. These are called **operator overloaded functions**. The prototype for the unary minus operator is this.

```
Vector operator- () const;
```

In the above equation, if v and u were integers, we know that u remains unchanged. Thus, in the vector function, we must not change the stored values of u. The const qualifier on the end of the prototype is saying that this is a constant member function, one which does not change the stored values in any way. The function does return a new Vector which contains the reversed direction values. It is implemented this way.

```
Vector Vector::operator- () const {
  return Vector(-x, -y, -z);
}
```

This single line is saying to make up a new Vector instance whose three values are the negative of this object's three values and to return a copy of this new Vector back to the caller. Now we can write this.

```
v = - u;
```

Adding and Subtracting Vectors

Two vectors can be added or subtracted. Figure 0-7 shows both operations and what they mean.

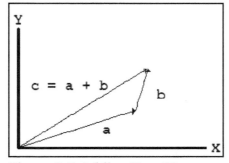 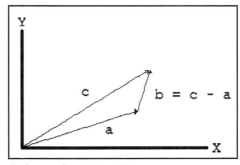

Figure 0-7 Adding Two Vectors   Subtracting Two Vectors

19

To add or subtract two vectors merely add or subtract the individual axis components. For example, let **a** represent the velocity of our car which is hit by another race car and given a collision velocity of **b**. Vector **c** then represents the new velocity of our car after the collision. The vectors are added by placing the tail of one vector against the tip of the other.

There are two ways that a client might desire to add two vectors.

U += V;

W = V + U;

In the first one, **U** is changed to hold the result, while in the second version, neither **U** nor **V** are altered, only **W**.

The two prototypes for the += and + functions are these.

```
Vector& operator+= (const Vector& v);
Vector  operator+  (const Vector& v) const;
```

These are known as binary operators because there are two operands, one on either side of the operator itself. The operand on the left will be the instance in which we find ourselves in the coding. The operand on the right side of the operator will be passed as the single parameter to the function. Notice that the second function, operator+, is a constant one, that is, no member data are altered.

The actual implementation is as follows. However, the function must return a reference to this object which is holding the result. This gets deeper into the complexity of OOP coding and is beyond the entrance level I wish to use in the normal coding of the examples in this text. So I will just say that the line that reads return *this; is returning a reference to the object which is holding the results.

```
Vector& Vector::operator+= (const Vector& v) {
     x += v.x;
     y += v.y;
     z += v.z;
     return *this;
}

Vector Vector::operator+ (const Vector& v) const {
     return Vector(x + v.x, y + v.y, z + v.z);
}
```

In contrast, operator+ creates a new Vector whose three values are the sum of the two.

Subtraction of two vectors is done by subtracting each component from the given vector, similar to the addition.

U −= V;

```
Vector& Vector::operator-= (const Vector& v) {
     x -= v.x;
     y -= v.y;
     z -= v.z;
     return *this;
```

```
}
```
As with addition of two vectors, sometimes the subtraction operator alone is needed.

W = **V** − **U**;

```
Vector Vector::operator- (const Vector& v) const {
    return Vector(x - v.x, y - v.y, z - v.z);
}
```

Multiplication and Division by a Scalar

Sometimes we need to multiply a vector by a scalar number, as when we are performing a scaling operation. Other times, we might need to divide a vector by a scalar number. These functions are also easily implemented this way. Each axis component is multiplied or divided by the scalar value.

```
Vector& Vector::operator*= (double s) {
  x *= s;
  y *= s;
  z *= s;
  return *this;
}

Vector& Vector::operator/= (double s) {
  x /= s;
  y /= s;
  z /= s;
  return *this;
}
```

The alternate forms are these.

```
Vector Vector::operator* (double s) const {
  return Vector (x * s, y * s, z * s);
}

Vector Vector::operator/ (double s) const {
  return Vector (x / s, y / s, z / s);
}
```

A client, or main program, can now do any of these operations.

U *= 42;

W = **V** * 42;

U /= 42;

W = **V** / 42;

The Vector Dot Product, Cross Product, and Triple Scalar Product

Now come the critical vector functions. The **cross product** between two vectors, here notated as an ^, returns a vector perpendicular to the plane of the two vectors. In collision detection, this is a workhorse function, since we often need know if an object hits or collides with another object, say a wall, for example. The object or wall will be defined by a series of one or more polygons. The four corners or vertices can be used to construct a pair of vectors. Taking the cross product of these two yields a vector that is perpendicular to the plane of the wall. Using this vector, we can then easily tell if our object hits the wall. The formula for **U** x **V** is given by

$$\mathbf{U} \times \mathbf{V} = (uy*vz - uz*vy)\mathbf{i} + (-ux*vz + uz*vx)\mathbf{j} + (ux*vy - uy*vx)\mathbf{k}$$

The resulting vector is perpendicular to the plane containing **u** and **v**. Use the right hand rule to find the direction. Curl your right hand fingers from **u** to **v** and the thumb points in the resultant direction. Notice that **v** x **u** gives a different result, in the opposite direction.

Corollary: if the result is 0, then the two vectors are parallel. This is useful when you need to find out if two objects are traveling parallel to each other. In the coding, vector **U** is the **this** parameter as is **U ^ V**.

```
Vector Vector::operator^ (const Vector& v) const {
  return Vector (y * v.z - z * v.y,
                -x * v.z + z * v.x,
                x * v.y - y * v.x );
}
```

The vector **dot product** of **U** . **V** gives the projection of the magnitude of **U** projected onto **V**, and is simply the length of that portion of **U**. The dot product is used in collision detection, where we need to find the closest distance between a point on one object to a polygon face on another object to see if the object is sufficiently close for a hit. Use the cross product to find the vector perpendicular to the polygon face and then use the dot operator on the vector made from the object point and a point on the polygon, such as a vertex. The formula for calculating the dot product is

$$u.v = ux * vx + uy * vy + uz * vz$$

In the coding, vector **U** is the **this** parameter as is **U * V**

```
double Vector::operator* (const Vector& v) const {
    return (x * v.x + y * v.y + z * v.z);
}
```

Another interesting use of the dot product is to find the angle between the two vectors. From the law of cosines, that angle, a, is given by this equation.

$$\cos(a) = (\mathbf{v} \text{ dot } \mathbf{u}) / (|\mathbf{v}| \, |\mathbf{u}|),$$ where the | | notation means the magnitude of the vector.

The last one is called the triple scalar product: u dot (v cross w) or just u*(v^w).

```
double TripleScalarProduct (const Vector& u, const Vector& v,
                            const Vector& w) {
    return (u.x * (v.y*w.z - v.z*w.y)) +
           (u.y * (-v.x*w.z + v.z*w.x)) +
           (u.z * (v.x*w.y - v.y*w.x));
}
```

Handling Rotations in 2D and the I/O of Vectors

Rotation about an axis is commonplace in game simulations. When your drive a race car, for example, your point of view is that of the driver, a local coordinate system. Yet to plot the location on the track, the local coordinates must be converted into the global coordinate system of the game. I added a GlobalToLocalCoords() rotation function that converts or rotates a vector from global coordinates back to local, and vice versa. It simply implements the rotation formula presented earlier.

```
Vector GlobalToLocalCoords_2D (double angle, const Vector& u) {
  double x, y;
  x =  u.x * cos (DegreesToRadians (-angle)) +
       u.y * sin (DegreesToRadians (-angle));
  y = -u.x * sin (DegreesToRadians (-angle)) +
       u.y * cos (DegreesToRadians (-angle));
  return Vector (x, y, 0);
}
```

Again, the exact syntax for handling the extraction and insertion operators in OOP classes is somewhat beyond the entrance level. Neither can be an actual member function because when the compiler sees

cin >> v;

the operand to the left of the >> operator is not a Vector, but an istream class instance. In such cases, the functions are normal C functions, not member functions. However, such functions must be made a friend of the Vector class so that they can access private or protected data, as the case may be.

To implement the extraction of a vector, the form of the input data must be three numbers separated as usual by whitespace. Notice that I input into automatic storage doubles. Only if the input stream is still in the good state are the inputted values then stored in the member variables.

```
istream& operator>> (istream& is, Vector& v) {
  double x, y, z;
  is >> x >> y >> z;
  if (!is) return is;
  v.x = x;
  v.y = y;
  v.z = z;
  return is;
}
```

For the insertion operator function, since we are dealing with doubles, I set the fixed point flag and arbitrarily set the precision to two decimal places. The format of the output will be the three numbers surrounded by () and separated by commas, a very readable format. For example, the output might appear this way.

```
    (10.50, 42.42, 0.00)
ostream& operator<< (ostream& os, const Vector& v) {
 os << fixed << setprecision(2) << "("
    << v.x << ", " << v.y << ", " << v.z << ")";
 return os;
}
```

Relational Operators and Conversion to Integers

Sometimes, one needs to compare to vectors to see if they are the same or not the same. If **v** and **w** are Vectors, one can write the following.

```
    if (v == w)
    if (v != w)
    if (v > w)
```

In the case of greater or less than, I am only going to compare the magnitudes of the vectors, ignoring their signs.

When implementing tile based games, coordinates are needed in integer form. ToIntegers() converts the doubles back to integers.

```
bool Vector::operator== (const Vector& v) const {
 if ( fabs (x - v.x) < EPS &&
      fabs (y - v.y) < EPS &&
      fabs (z - v.z) < EPS)
   return true;
 return false;
}

bool Vector::operator!= (const Vector& v) const {
 return !(*this == v);
}

bool Vector::operator>= (const Vector& v) const {
 return Magnitude () >= v.Magnitude ();
}

bool Vector::operator<= (const Vector& v) const {
 return Magnitude () <= v.Magnitude ();
}
```

```
bool Vector::operator>  (const Vector& v) const {
 return Magnitude () > v.Magnitude ();
}

bool Vector::operator<  (const Vector& v) const {
 return Magnitude () < v.Magnitude ();
}

void Vector::ToIntegers (int& xx, int& yy, int& zz) const {
 xx = (int) (x + .5);
 yy = (int) (y + .5);
 zz = (int) (z + .5);
}
```

The actual Vector class definition and implementation files are located in the Pgm01a sample program folder, as well as quite a number of other program folders. The Vector class is key to many physics and AI algorithms.

Chapter 1 Chasing, Evading, Intercepting, and Patterned Movement

No matter what type of game you are designing, sooner or later you will have one or more people, creatures, or things chasing after or running away from another. Your player character enters a cavern currently occupied by twenty foul orcs. As your character stands there taking in the situation, the orcs grab their swords and rush towards your character. Or perhaps you are flying a spaceship and have just entered enemy space where a dozen enemy fighter ships are located. At once, they turn their ships and fly towards your craft. Perhaps, you decide to flee and turn your ship around and attempt to fly away from the oncoming fleet. Or perhaps some enemy ground based force decides to launch a guided missile at your spaceship. Countless scenarios arise where one or more items are supposed to close or chase another, or conversely, evade the chase.

However, when a missile is launched at your ship, an interception is a better approach. That is, a course is plotted so that the missile will follow a trajectory designed to intercept your ship. Finally, any number of pre-planned patterns of movement are desirable to add realism to the game. An orc on patrol around their camp is an example. A fighter plane doing a barrel roll is another. Patterned movements are merely an extension of the basic principles involved in chasing.

Game systems fall into two broad categories, as far as chasing is concerned: **tile-based** games and **continuous environment** games. In a tile-based game, only discrete locations are allowed to be occupied, often squares or hexagons. If one considers the screen to be composed of an array of locations, often 80 columns by 24 rows in a DOS screen, then any person, creature or object is constrained to be in one of these locations. Hence, the location is designated by providing its row and column coordinates. If the game is three dimensional, then merely add a third coordinate. In a continuous environment type of game, the person, creature or object is permitted to move freely in all directions. Its location is given by x and y coordinates, relative to some universal coordinate axis. (Add a z coordinate, if three-dimensional space is used.)

The Sample Programs and Model Coding

In order to see how the various algorithms are implemented, sample C++ coding is given. The prerequisite for this course is only the beginning C++ course. Hence, all coding samples must attempt to not exceed this level of experience in programming. Once you have learned Object Oriented Programming, you will at once see much better ways to encapsulate these algorithms in your games. Also, presumably you are concurrently taking your next course in C++ programming. In later chapters, I will use somewhat more sophisticated coding than at the start.

Even here in the very first chapter of Game Programming Theory, demo programs are needed. For the level of experience in C++ programming dictated by the course prerequisites, tile-based demos are vastly easier to understand, write, and follow. This is because essentially you are dealing with nothing more complex than a two dimensional array, typically here 80 columns by 24 rows. To further ease the burden, I have included my DOS Screen class encapsulation which is thoroughly presented and discussed in the Non-graphical Games Programming text. Here, you are only expected to be a user of that Screen class and the functions are very simple to use, much like those for cin and cout.

However, continuous environments must be shown, since the algorithms are implemented differently in such situation. The only way such environments can be displayed in with a Windows application, which allows individual screen pixel access for drawing operations. Unfortunately, basic Windows programming cannot be effectively studied until you have learned well Object Oriented Programming. Again, I will present a working model for our use in the demos. I will keep the Windows programming specific coding completely separate from the algorithm coding that we are learning. That way, you can concentrate on learning the algorithms and not worry about the fancy graphics until you progress to that level in your training.

Chasing and Evading

Chasing/evading is one of the most fundamental aspects of nearly any game and is an easy entrance point into game design. Three factors govern chasing and evading.

1. The decision to chase or evade must be made. This, of course, depends upon the situation.

2. An effective algorithm must be part of the game engine to implement a chase or an evasion.

3. During the movement, obstacles must be avoided. It is unrealistic to have an orc smash through a table and a bed while chasing toward your player character.

This chapter handles only the second factor: the algorithms needed to implement either chasing or evading. Note that evading is merely going in the opposite direction from a chase. That is, if we get the logic down for handling a chase, to handle an evade, one merely negates the directions chosen.

Historically, what I call Basic Chasing is very simple to implement, but the observed results are far from satisfactory in terms of game realism as we will see.

The Basic Chasing algorithm consists of always changing the chaser's coordinates so as to decrease the distance between it and the chasee. Evading is the opposite, the chasee attempts to increase the distance between it and the chaser. The logic is very simple to implement. If we use an orc versus a player, then the algorithm is implemented in one of two ways, depending upon whether it is tile-based or continuous movement.

In a tile-based environment, it is done this way.
```
if (orcRow > playerRow)
     orcRow--;
else if (orcRow < playerRow)
     orcRow++;

if (orcCol > playerCol)
     orcCol--;
else if (orcCol < playerCol)
     orcCol++;
```

28

Game Programming Theory

In a continuous movement system, the code is done this way.
```
if (orcX > playerX)
    orcX--;
else if (orcX < playerX)
    orcX++;

if (orcY > playerY)
    orcY--;
else if (orcY < playerY)
    orcY++;
```

If implementing evading, just reverse the increments and decrements.
```
if (orcX > playerX)
    orcX++;
else if (orcX < playerX)
    orcX--;

if (orcY > playerY)
    orcY++;
else if (orcY < playerY)
    orcY--;
```

Using this algorithm, the orc will unrelentingly chase after the player. However, as beginning game programmers, we really need to see and study the visual effects that this and other algorithms produce. One could invent some graphical game engine in which you could program these algorithms and then run them to see the effects. However, doing so implies writing vastly more complex code than can be found at the beginning level of programming. Hence, I will use a very simple model adapted from the Non-graphical Games Programming course. This model, called Screen, encapsulates the old DOS screen of 80x24. In that course, you will study how this encapsulation works. For now, we are only going to be users of this simple object oriented class, treating it similar to the way that we use either cin or cout.

The Screen Class

To use this class in your programs, copy the two files, Screen.h and Screen.cpp, from the Samples folder and paste them into your project's folder. Right click on your project and add these existing two items to your project. In your main program, include the line

```
#include "Screen.h"
```

You **must** make two project settings or face numerous compile errors. Go to Project Settings and make two changes. C++ tab, General tab, set Detect 64bit portability to "No." General tab, set Character Set to "Not Set".

In your main function, add a line to define an instance of the Screen, such as:

```
Screen s (Screen::Blue, Screen::BrightYellow);
```

You are specifying the background color and the foreground color defaults to be used. The possible colors are:

```
Screen::Black       Screen::Blue        Screen::Green
Screen::Aqua        Screen::Red         Screen::Purple
Screen::Yellow      Screen::White       Screen::Gray
Screen::BrightBlue  Screen::BrightGreen Screen::BrightAqua
Screen::BrightRed   Screen::BrightPurple Screen::BrightYellow
Screen::BrightWhite
```

Next, you can provide a title to your DOS Console Window by using the function SetTitle(), which is passed a character string to be used as the caption or title.

```
s.SetTitle ("Tile-based Basic Chasing");
```

A nice, but not necessary effect, is to draw a box around the screen in a different color scheme. This is done using the DrawBox() function. The function is passed the coordinates (row and column) of the upper left corner of the desired box and the coordinates of the bottom right corner. Additionally, it is passed the background and foreground colors to be used.

```
s.DrawBox (0, 0, 24, 79, Screen::Gray, Screen::BrightYellow);
```

Output can be done in a number of ways. One way is to display a single character at a time. This is what we need in this chapter. The function is called OutputUCharWith(). It is passed the unsigned character to be displayed, the x and y coordinates at which to display the character, and the color scheme to be used, background and foreground. For example, one could display 'F' for Frodo this way.

```
s.OutputUCharWith ('F', PlayerAtY, PlayerAtX, Screen::Blue,
                   Screen::BrightRed);
```

Note that you can pass it a normal char character, because a char can be converted to an unsigned char. It is an unsigned char because this way some of the upper ASCII characters can also be displayed properly.

Game Programming Theory

At anytime, the screen can be cleared using the ClearScreen() function. It uses the installed default color scheme setup when the Screen instance was defined.

```
s.ClearScreen ();
```

At any time, the color scheme can be changed by using the SetColor() function, providing the background and foreground color desired.

```
s.SetColor (Screen::Red, Screen::Green);
```

The Screen supports a highlighting, alternate color scheme. To use it, call the SetHighlightColor() function to install the highlighting colors.

```
s.SetHighlightColor (Screen::Red, Screen::Green);
```

Normal outputting to the screen occurs at the current X-Y location, called the cursor position. The cursor position can be set at any time to any location within the 80-24 canvas using the SetCursorPosition() function, specifying the row (Y) and column (X) coordinates.

```
s.SetCursorPosition (row, col);
```

Alternately, the function GoToXY() does the same thing. Chose which version you prefer.

```
s.GoToXY (int x, int y) const;
```

To output at the current cursor position, several methods can be used. First, you can use the insertion operator to output a string, a character, or an integer.

```
s << "Tile-based Basic Chasing";
s << 'F' << 42;
```

These will be outputted at the current cursor position. The setw() and doubles are not supported, however.

Second, you can output a string at a specific location, independent of the cursor position using the OutputAt() function, specifying the string and the row and column desired.

```
s.OutputAt ("Tile-based Basic Chasing", row, col);
```

Alternatively, OutputWith() allows you to also specify the color scheme to use.

```
s.OutputWith ("Tile-based Basic Chasing", row, col,
              Screen::Black, Screen::White);
```

If you have set the highlight color scheme, then you can cause any area to be shown in the highlighted scheme by using HighlightArea(). You specify the starting row and column and the number of columns to highlight.

```
s.HighlightArea (startRow, startCol, numCols);
```

Calling the ClearHighlightArea() function returns that area back to the normal color scheme.

```
s.ClearHighlightArea (startRow, startCol, numCols);
```

Several different methods can be used to input data. Now you have access to the 101+ special keys as well, such as the arrow keys. GetAnyKey() gets any keystroke, but does not display or return it.

```
s.GetAnyKey ();
```

If you wish to accept special keystrokes, such as the up arrow, use the GetSpecialKey() function. However, just because you call it, the user might press a normal key, such as the letter 'a' key. Hence, the function returns the letter char or a 0. If 0 is returned, then the passed by reference unsigned character contains the special key code, the up arrow for example.

```
unsigned char specialKeyCode;
char letter;
letter = s.GetSpecialKey (specialKeyCode);
```

Normal extraction can also be used to input a char or an integer. GetString() can be used to input a string, without overwriting the array of characters. All of these input and show the characters on the screen at the current cursor position.

```
char c;
int x;
s >> c >> x;
char msg[50];
s.GetString (msg, sizeof(msg), '\n');
```

Note that the third parameter is the default delimiter for the string. It is a new line (enter key) by default. You can use a '\"' if the string ends with a double quote.

Finally, you can also use cin to extract data. However, if you wish to use cin, then include a first line in your main function:

```
cin.sync_with_stdio ();
```

Finally, you can flash an area on the screen briefly using the FlashArea() function. It works similar to the HighlightArea() function.

```
s.FlashArea (startRow, startCol, numCols);
```

Sample Pgm01a illustrates the use of these functions. Run it and observer the effects on the screen.

Implementing the Basic Chase Algorithm

We can use the Screen class to show an implementation of the Basic Chase Algorithm and see it in operation. Examine the first half of Pgm01b. The scenario is Frodo steps into a room that has eight orcs in it. While he stands there looking at them, they rush towards him.

The program creates an instance of the screen and gets it ready for action.
```
Screen s (Screen::Blue, Screen::BrightYellow);
s.SetTitle ("Tile-based Basic Chasing");
s.DrawBox (0, 0, 24, 79, Screen::Gray,
           Screen::BrightYellow);
```

Next, the player is defined and displayed on the screen. Note that in this sample, the player does not move at any time. Frodo remains frozen at the entrance way.
```
const int PlayerAtX = 40;
const int PlayerAtY = 2;
s.OutputUCharWith ('F', PlayerAtY, PlayerAtX, Screen::Blue,
                   Screen::BrightRed);
```

In this simulation, eight orcs are placed initially along the bottom area of the screen.
```
const int MAXORCS = 8;
const int OrcsStartX[MAXORCS] = {1, 5, 10, 20, 30,50,60,70};
const int OrcsStartY[MAXORCS] = {22, 21, 22,20,19,22,20,14};
```

The two arrays, orcAtX and orcAtY, hold the current position of orcs at each turn.
```
int orcAtX[MAXORCS];
int orcAtY[MAXORCS];
```

The initial position of all orcs is displayed with a simple loop that also installs the initial x, y location for each orc in the two arrays.
```
for (i=0; i<MAXORCS; i++) {
  s.OutputUCharWith ('O', OrcsStartY[i], OrcsStartX[i],
                     Screen::BrightYellow, Screen::BrightRed);
  orcAtX[i] = OrcsStartX[i];
  orcAtY[i] = OrcsStartY[i];
}
```

Now we are ready for the animation illustration of just how this Basic Closing Algorithm operates. The program loops through all the orcs, calculating their new positions and showing them at their new locations, over and over, until they reach Frodo's position. Different orcs will arrive at the final destination at different times, so the bool **done** controls when all of them have reached him, stopping the looping process.
```
bool done = false;
```

```
while (!done) {
  done = true;
  for (i=0; i<MAXORCS; i++) { // move each orc in turn

    // skip any orc who has arrived at the player's location
    if (orcAtX[i] == PlayerAtX && orcAtY[i] == PlayerAtY)
      continue;

    // here, at least one can still move toward player
    done = false;

    // basic closing algorithm
    if (orcAtX[i] > PlayerAtX)        // if x is > player, dec x
      orcAtX[i]--;
    else if (orcAtX[i] < PlayerAtX)  // if x is < player, inc x
      orcAtX[i]++;

    if (orcAtY[i] > PlayerAtY)        // if y is > player, dec y
      orcAtY[i]--;
    else if (orcAtY[i] < PlayerAtY)  // if y is < player, inc y
      orcAtY[i]++;

    // display new orc position on the screen
    s.OutputUCharWith ('O', orcAtY[i], orcAtX[i],
                  Screen::BrightYellow, Screen::BrightRed);
    Sleep (100); // pause for 100 milliseconds
  }
}
```

I slid a new function in there, Sleep(). This function delays any further processing for the passed number of milliseconds, 100, in this case. Without this delay, the orcs "fly" toward poor Frodo.

Run the sample and observe the algorithm in operation. Here is the final screen. I pasted Frodo's 'F' back onto the final image so that you can see the destination point of the eight orcs. Notice that all of them did reach the desired destination, some sooner than others.

However, examine the action once more and notice how poor the results actually are. Only for those orcs that are at a forty-five degree angle from Frodo take a path that leads straight at him. All others have a major unreal aspect to them. Those who are primarily a long Y distance from the destination point but are close with respect to the X coordinate end up quickly joining into an long vertical line, marching single file straight up to the end point. Others that have a large X coordinate disparity end up meeting along the destination row and then moving horizontally to the final location. Both of these are very undesirable movement actions, which is highly distracting to game play.

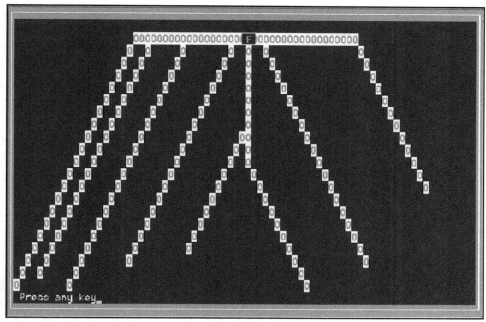

Figure 10 Basic Chasing Algorithm

The Line of Sight Algorithm

A better approach is the Line of Sight Algorithm. In a continuous movement environment, the algorithm forces the pursuer to always maintain its direction facing toward the prey. Thus, the pursuer is always traveling in a straight line toward the prey. However, if the prey is also moving, the path followed by the pursuer will not be a straight line, necessarily, but it always is moving toward the prey, wherever it moves. The results of this make for a more realistic pursuit.

The idea is to calculate based upon the pursuer's velocity how far it can travel in this unit of game time and then add that to its current position, redisplaying the pursuer at its new, hopefully closer, position. Usually, the pixel is the unit of measurement in continuous movement situation. For very smooth movement, the pursuer is moved only a pixel at a time. However, if faster action is desired, it can be moved several pixels at one time with good realism.

However, there are other considerations with which to deal. Suppose that the pursuer is a guided missile heading for a collision with a ship. What happens if the ship is faster than the missile? The missile may never actually be able to catch up with the ship! In such a scenario, interception course plotting would be a better choice, which we will discuss later on in this chapter.

Game Programming Theory

When we take the line of sight approach to a tile-based game, a new constraint is placed upon the pursuer's movement. It can only move in eight possible directions: up, down, left, right, and the four diagonals into the adjacent tiles. Please note that diagonal movement seems to be faster than up-down, left-right movement. This is because the length of a diagonal across a tile is the sqrt(2) times larger, or about 1.4 times larger. An additional constraint occurs because a tile often is fairly large, showing terrain and similar features, which require a number of pixels to render. Hence, a tile size might be twenty pixels or more square. Thus, to avoid ragged, jerky movement, movement must be constrained to one tile at a time.

This problem of line of sight movement in a tile-based environment has a good solution, one that forces the pursuer to take a straight line toward the prey. That solution is called the Bresenham algorithm. In the early days of crude CGA monitors, it was used by graphics engines to draw a line between two points on the screen.

The key to the algorithm lies in determining which axis requires the most tile movement. Then, forcing movement long that axis more so than along the shorter axis. Specifically, it guarantees that the movement will never traverse two tiles in a row along the shorter axis, rather forcing multiple tiles moved along the lengthier axis before taking one along the shorter axis.

The Bresenham algorithm is given the positions of the pursuer and prey. It then calculates the best straight line of sight path from the pursuer to the prey, filling an array with each move that must be made. Obviously, if the prey should move before the pursuer reaches the prey, the entire process must be redone, based upon the new, current positions of both. Figure 1.2 shows the eight orc's line of sight path to Frodo using the Bresenham algorithm, as shown in the second half of Pgm01b.

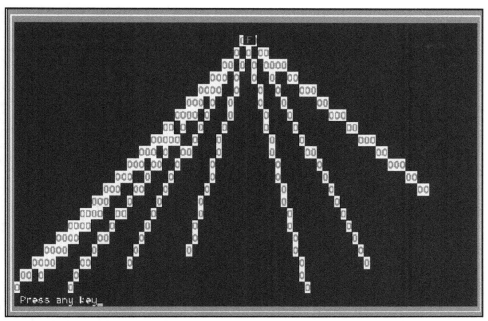

Figure 11 Bresenham Algorithm for Line of Sight Tile-based Chasing

The main program coding is relatively simple. A pair of arrays sufficiently large enough to hold all of the moves for an orc are defined.

```
const int MOVES = 200;
int orcPathX[MAXORCS][MOVES];
int orcPathY[MAXORCS][MOVES];
```

Next, the program loops through each orc in the array, calling Bresenham() to calculate its path.

```
for (i=0; i<MAXORCS; i++) {
 Bresenham (orcPathX[i], orcPathY[i], MOVES, OrcsStartX[i],
            OrcsStartY[i], PlayerAtX, PlayerAtY);
}
```

Finally, one by one, the path taken by each orc is shown on the screen.

```
for (i=0; i<MAXORCS; i++) {
 for (int j=0; j<MOVES; j++) {
  // if an orc has aleady arrived, skip that one
  if (orcPathX[i][j] == -1 || orcPathY[i][j] == -1)
   break;
  s.OutputUCharWith ('O', orcPathY[i][j], orcPathX[i][j],
                Screen::BrightYellow, Screen::BrightRed);
  Sleep (100); // delay 100 milliseconds
 }
}
```

Game Programming Theory

The actual coding for the line of sight is contained within the Bresenham() function. The starting point for the orc and player are passed to the function along with two arrays to be filled with the successive movements, assuming that the player has not moved during the entire time. It the player moves, the function must be recalled to calculate the new line of sight path.

```
void Bresenham (int orcPathX[], int orcPathY[], int max,
                int orcAtX, int orcAtY,
                int playerAtX, int playerAtY) {
// nextX and nextY hold the orc's next position
int nextX = orcAtX;
int nextY = orcAtY;

// deltaX and deltaY hold the difference between the locations
int deltaX = playerAtX - orcAtX;
int deltaY = playerAtY - orcAtY;

// stepX and stepY hold how much to inc or dec each time
int stepX = deltaX < 0 ? -1 : 1;
int stepY = deltaY < 0 ? -1 : 1;

// clear out the answer arrays, using invalid screen coord: -1
for (int i=0; i<max; i++) {
 orcPathX[i] = -1;
 orcPathY[i] = -1;
}
```

Notice that −1 is not allowed for a row-col location on the screen. Hence, a −1 can indicate an empty, unused element in the array.

```
// install the starting location in the answer arrays
orcPathX[0] = orcAtX;
orcPathY[0] = orcAtY;

// double the total difference between locations
// and take the absolute value to remove negative signs
deltaX = abs (deltaX * 2);
deltaY = abs (deltaY * 2);

// set the current step to 1, [0] holds the original location
int currentStep = 1;
int fraction;

// two cases: is the x length greater than the y length?
if (deltaX > deltaY) {
  // x > y, so constantly move x but control when to move y
  // fraction controls times to move in y
  fraction = deltaY * 2 - deltaX;
```

```
  // now fill in all steps the orc must take to reach player
  while (nextX != playerAtX && currentStep < max) {
   if (fraction >= 0) { // fraction is still > 0, must move in y
    nextY += stepY;      // add another y step to total y move
    fraction -= deltaX; // remove one column amount
   }
   // here, we have moved enough in y to justify moving in x
   nextX += stepX;
   // now add in another y move for next iteration
   fraction += deltaY;
   // store this move in the answer array
   orcPathX[currentStep] = nextX;
   orcPathY[currentStep++] = nextY;
  }
 }

 // here, y is greater than the x length
 else {
  // fraction controls times to move in x for each y move
  fraction = deltaX * 2 - deltaY;
  // fill in all steps the orc takes to get to the player
  while (nextY != playerAtY && currentStep < max) {
   if (fraction >= 0) { // fraction > 0, so must move in x
    nextX += stepX;      // add another x to total move
    fraction -= deltaY; // remove one row amount
   }
   // here we have moved enough in x to justify moving in y
   nextY += stepY;
   // add in the x move to fraction for next iteration
   fraction += deltaX;
   // store this move in the answer array
   orcPathX[currentStep] = nextX;
   orcPathY[currentStep++] = nextY;
  }
 }
}
```

The Bresenham algorithm is the standard for plotting a line of sight path in a tile-based game. What about implementing line of sight in a continuous environment?

The Complexity of Line of Sight in a Continuous Environment

Let's examine a two-dimensional typical situation. Suppose that we have a pair of space ships or bi-planes, one the attacker and the other the defender, where the attacker is pursuing the defender, hoping to engage it in combat. Now we are dealing with vectors that represent the current motion of each ship.

Remember that motion has two components, speed and direction. That is the definition of a vector quantity, a magnitude and a direction. When one wishes to deal with closing in a line of sight method in a continuous environment, he or she must deal with vectors and various coordinate systems. Let's see why.

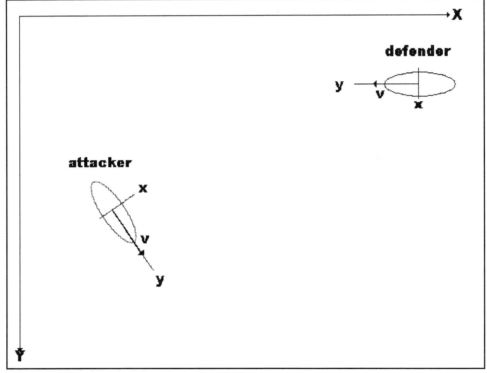

Figure 12 Attacker-defender Initial Situation

In Figure 3, the world X-Y coordinate system is shown along with the local x-y coordinate systems of both the attacker and defender. The attacker is currently traveling in one direction at some speed, v, while the defender is traveling in another direction at some other speed, v. That is, imagine you are the driver of the attacker vehicle. From your point of view, your local positive y-axis is straight ahead of you and your speed is in the forward direction you are facing. Now, having spotted the defender, you need to turn your craft so that your craft is facing the defender's craft and your speed is now directed toward the defender's craft. Using the available mechanical means, such as bow thrusters, steering wheel if this is a car, or whatever means is applicable, you must turn your vehicle to face the defender.

Immediately a number of physical problems arise. First, we are dealing with a two-dimensional solid body or rigid body situation. The actual turning is done around the center of gravity of the object, if this is a flying machine. Second, turning is not an instantaneous action unless the vehicle is traveling very slow indeed. Imagine driving your car and you desire to turn left. If you are traveling at one mile per hour, you can turn a very tight turn almost at once. However, if you are traveling at sixty miles per hour, the turn takes place over a considerable distance, compared to the slow speed turn, or the car overturns. The vehicle's momentum must be considered when making a turn. Third, the actual turning is accomplished by providing a varying acceleration to the vehicle so that it ends up facing the desired direction. In the case of a flying ship, thrusters would provide the steering accelerations along the positive and negative local x-axis. However, the amount of change applied varies over time. When entering a turn, you begin with a large motion of the steering wheel and then gradually lessen is as you come out of the turn. Fourth, each vehicle has a maximum speed of which it is capable of traveling.

In short, a lot of additional complexity arises very quickly. A study of physics is needed to totally describe the problem. During the semester, we will be examining all of the component parts of this problem in detail. By the end of our study, you should be able to deal with the complete situation posed by games such as these. However, at this point, let us only concentrate on how to deal with the line of sight chasing, leaving the remainder for later chapters.

So what do we know about the problem of line of sight? We know the two vectors of motion and the positions within the global game coordinates, the upper case X and Y axes in Figure 3 above. What do we need to know so that we can steer toward the defender? We need to know whether to turn our ship left or right, ignoring the unlikely possibility that we are already heading straight for it. If we subtract the two position vectors which locate the ships in global game coordinates, we can find its relative position to us in global coordinates. However, our viewpoint is not global coordinates, our thrusters or turning mechanism are related to our own local x-y axes, that is, our local x axis is perpendicular to our forward direction. Do we fire the port or starboard turning mechanisms? Do we turn the steering wheel to the left or right? Thus, we must convert the global coordinates of the resulting relative position back into our own local coordinates.

Finally, if we then normalize that resultant vector such that its magnitude is unity, we have the vector pointing directly from us to the defender. We do not need the y component, only the x. If the x component is 0, we are heading straight to the attacker. If the x component is positive, we must turn to our right or starboard. If the x component is negative, we must turn to port or left. Simple enough, if we review how to subtract vectors and how to convert from local to global coordinates.

Vectors

Figure 4 shows how we can store a vector in three-dimensional space. By using three-dimensional space, we can easily handle both two and three dimensional problems in vectors. If you are using only two dimensions, simply let the z-axis component be zero.

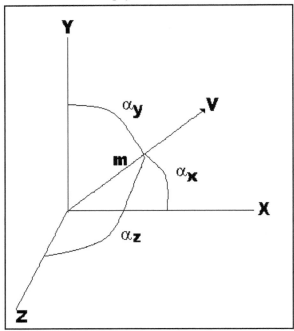

Figure 13 A Three-dimensional Vector

The vector **V** has its magnitude (total length from the origin point) and its direction stored as three components, its x, y, and z axis components. The magnitude or length of the vector is notated |**V**|. The projection of **V** onto each of the axes is given by

Vx = |**V**| cos (αx)
Vy = |**V**| cos (αy)
Vz = |**V**| cos (αz)

where the magnitude is given by

$$|\mathbf{V}| = \sqrt{x^2 + y^2 + z^2}$$

Along with the Screen class, I have also provided in Pgm01a a simple Vector class to aid our programming samples. The Vector class was discussed in depth in chapter 0. In the problem at hand, determining line of sight so that course corrections can be made, the resultant vector of the difference between the pursuer and prey needs to be normalized. That is, it needs to be scaled so that the magnitude is 1. Then, the x component can be used by the pursuer to make course corrections so that it continues to head towards the prey.

Conversion from Global Coordinates to Local Coordinates

From the viewpoint of the driver of the attacker ship, the positive y axis is directly in front of the ship. The local origin point is the center of gravity of the object, which will be covered later on in 2d solid body theory. For now, think of it as being the "center" of the attacking ship. The local x axis extends to the attacker's left and right. Think of the distinction between local and global coordinates as our ancestors once did here on earth. When the earth was considered the center of the universe, everything was measured from the earth as the origin point, local coordinates. It is, after all, how we view things. Yet the earth goes around the sun, and the sun goes around the galaxy. Thus, to study the large scale movements of earth, a more encompassing coordinate system is used, the global coordinates.

In games, we store the location of objects in the global coordinate system, such as an object's position, as a vector in two or three dimensional space. Yet, when it comes to operations, such as orienting or firing missiles at a target, local coordinates are used because it is more convenient and relates to the actual viewpoint of the craft. Figure 5 shows the geometry of the conversion situation.

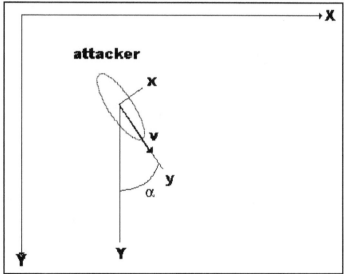

Figure 14 Local Coordinates from Global Coordinates

To project point X,Y of the attacker onto the local x,y system of the attacker, we must also know the angle alpha, or the orientation of the craft with respect to the Y global axis. From geometry, the formula to convert from global to local coordinates is given by the following.

$$x = X \cos \alpha + Y \sin \alpha$$
$$y = -X \sin \alpha + Y \cos \alpha$$

Of course, the angle in degrees must be converted to radians for the trig functions. The Vector class implements this conversion in the GlobalToLocalCooords() function. It was coded this way.

43

```
Vector GlobalToLocalCoords_2D (double angle, const Vector& u) {
    double    x, y;
    x = u.x * cos (DegreesToRadians (angle)) +
        u.y * sin (DegreesToRadians (angle));
    y = -u.x * sin (DegreesToRadians (angle)) +
        u.y * cos (DegreesToRadians (angle));
    return Vector (x, y, 0);
}
```

However, a complexity arises immediately concerning that angle alpha, in the figure above. Normal trig functions assume the positive Y is up; here it is **down**. If we wish to show the ship at a 45 degree angle, using the above coding, the ship will be pointing upwards and to the north west (to the left) not down and to the southeast as expected. To get the above function to work properly, when we want an angle of 45 degrees to the left of down, we would enter -135 degrees. This is just too confusing. Looking at the screen, we don't think of Y as being inverted, positive Y being downward. We naturally think of up as the positive direction. Thus, we would like to say that the angle is 135 degrees from the up position and to the right, to yield the ship oriented to the southeast. Let's call this the **orientation** angle. An orientation angle of 0 degrees points straight up. 180 degrees points straight down. 90 degrees points due east or to the right. If we wish to pass the orientation angle to the function, then in the function, let's simply negate the angle.

```
Vector GlobalToLocalCoords_2D (double angle, const Vector& u) {
    double    x, y;
    x = u.x * cos (DegreesToRadians (-angle)) +
        u.y * sin (DegreesToRadians (-angle));
    y = -u.x * sin (DegreesToRadians (-angle)) +
        u.y * cos (DegreesToRadians (-angle));
    return Vector (x, y, 0);
}
```

Again, this Vector class is part of the Pgm01a sample program as well as many other samples covered later on in the text.

Line of Sight in a Continuous Environment

Armed with vectors and coordinate conversion, we can now tackle the problem of line of sight closing upon the defender in a continuous environment. The objective: keep the defender right in front of the attacker as the attacker moves toward the defender. All that is known are the two vector locations (the attacker and defender) and the defender's orientation angle from the Y global axis. Further, assume that the attacker has some means of steering its vessel or ship by means of a function called TurnShip().

First, calculate the relative position vector between the attacker and the defender, which also gives the line of sight from the attacker to the defender. This is done by subtracting the defender's position vector from the attacker's position vector. However, this resultant vector is in global coordinates. In order to control the attacker's steering, it must be converted into local coordinates as viewed from the driver's seat, so that the craft can know whether to turn right or left or not at all. After the vector is converted to local coordinates, examine the x value. If its x value is positive, turn left or port. If negative, turn right or to the starboard. If zero, no turning is required.

The coding of the function is then very simple, assuming that we know how the attacker and defender are defined. They could be structures or object oriented classes. Let's keep it simple for now and assume that both the attacker and defender are instances of a structure called SHIP, whose partial definition is as follows.

```
struct SHIP {
 Vector position;
 double orientation;
 . . .
};
```

Further, assume that we also have defined an enum to indicate the type of turning required to keep the attacker moving toward the defender.

```
enum TurnType {None, Left, Right};
```

Our line of sight function then is passed two instances of the structure.

```
void LineOfSightChase (struct SHIP& attacker,
                        const struct SHIP& defender) {
 Vector lineOfSight = defender.position - attacker.position;
 Vector local = GlobalToLocalCoords_2D (-attacker.orientation,
                                lineOfSight);
 local.Normalize ();
 TurnType turn = None;
 if (local.x < EPS)
  turn = Left;
 else if (local.x > EPS)
  turn = Right;
```

```
if (turn != None)
  Steer (attacker, turn);
}
```

Again, remember that calculations involving floating point are subject to small roundoff errors. Hence, do not check against 0., but use the error precision value of EPS, which is 0.000001.

What will be the overall appearance of our algorithm? If the defender does not move, the attacker will follow a straight line to the defender. If the defender is moving and varying its position, the defender's path will be curved, continuously adjusting its orientation as it attempts to close the distance. The algorithm is relentless. Again, it is likely that eventually the attacker will end up behind the defender, following it and closing the distance, hopefully.

Ah, but this raises an immediate question. What happens if the velocity of the attacker is much larger than the defender's? It is very likely that the attacker will overshoot the defender's position and be forced to circle around and come at it again. This is not very realistic. If the game simulation has a way for the attacker to slow down, then you can add in another check. If the distance between the attacker and defender is less than a predetermined amount, begin to slow down or if the distance is too great, increase the defender's speed. To find the distance between the two simply subtract their position vectors and take the magnitude of that result.

Finally, if evading is required, then reverse the turn variable settings, go left when closing suggests going right.

Drawbacks to this algorithm become apparent. Having the attacker always heading directly toward the defender is not necessarily either the shortest path in distance or time. Usually, the attacker ends up behind the defender, closing in on it. If the attacker is much faster than the defender, the attacker often overshoots and has to circle around and come back. If the attacker is much slower than the defender, it may never actually catch the attacker. This last is highly unreasonable. Often by taking a different course, a slower vehicle can intercept a faster one. Similarly, some guided missiles have a limited range. Plotting an interception can yield a hit where as simply following it and closing may miss because too great a distance traveled is required.

Sample program Pgm01d is a Windows application that illustrates these principles. Essentially, Snoopy is flying the yellow biplane and is being chased by the Red Baron. The Action menu item Basic Chase, implements the coding we have just seen. Figure 6 shows the action in progress.

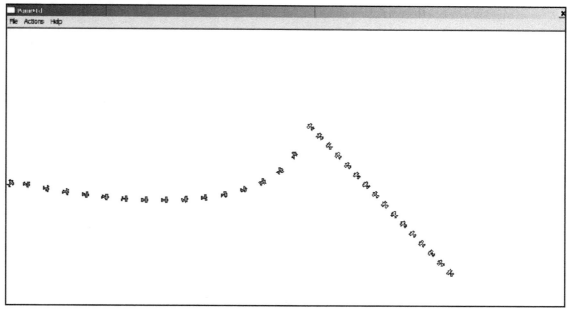

Figure 15 Chasing in a Continuous Environment

Run the demo and watch what happens when the red plane gets behind or ahead of the yellow one. Realistically, one needs to determine if this is the case and then revert back to a Basic Closing method for a short time doing a small circle or such before resuming the Line of Sight method. Doing so yields a better angle of approach to the target.

Intercepting

Intercepting an opponent requires knowing one additional property of the opponent, its velocity vector. The idea is to predict where the defender will be at some future time and then move the attacker to that position so as to arrive when the defender arrives there. Please note that the interception point is not the shortest distance to the attacker, because that is ignoring the relative speeds of the two ships. If the attacker has a shorter distance to travel to that location and moves much faster than the defender, the attacker will arrive at that location way ahead of the defender and must sit there waiting for the defender to arrive, very unrealistic.

To intercept, one calculates based upon the attacker's and defender's position and speed where they will intersect, and steer the defender to that location. Obviously, that location will have to be continuously updated as the attacker alters course or changes speed. The basic equation involved is

distance = velocity * time

or

time = distance to travel / velocity

We can calculate the closing velocity by subtracting the two velocities. By subtracting the two distance vectors, we can get the distance to close.

$$\mathbf{V}_{closing} = \mathbf{V}_{defender} - \mathbf{V}_{attacker}$$
$$\mathbf{D}_{closing} = \mathbf{D}_{defender} - \mathbf{D}_{attacker}$$

Thus the time to close is

$$T_{closing} = |\mathbf{D}_{closing}| / |\mathbf{V}_{closing}|$$

that is the magnitude of the closing distance divided by the magnitude of the closing velocity.

Finally, knowing the time to close, you can then calculate where the defender will be at that time in order to steer towards that location.

$$\mathbf{D}_{predicted} = \mathbf{D}_{defender} + \mathbf{V}_{defender} * T_{closing}$$

The changes from LineOfSightChase to do an interception are highlighted in bold face.

```
void LineOfSightIntercept (struct SHIP& attacker,
                    const struct SHIP& defender) {
  Vector vClosing = defender.velocity - attacker.velocity;
  Vector dClosing = defender.position - attacker.position;
  double tClosing = dClosing.Magnitude() / vClosing.Magnitude();
  Vector predicted = defender.position +
                    defender.velocity * tClosing;
  Vector lineOfSight = predicted - attacker.position;
  Vector local = GlobalToLocalCoords_2D (-attacker.orientation,
                                lineOfSight);
  local.Normalize ();
  TurnType turn = None;
  if (local.x < EPS)
    turn = Left;
  else if (local.x > EPS)
    turn = Right;
  if (turn != None)
    Steer (attacker, turn);
}
```

Rerun Pgm01d and chose the Action menu item Intercept. Figure 7 shows the interception point as a small circle, which is continually updated as needed. Also watch what happens when the attacker gets in front or behind the target.

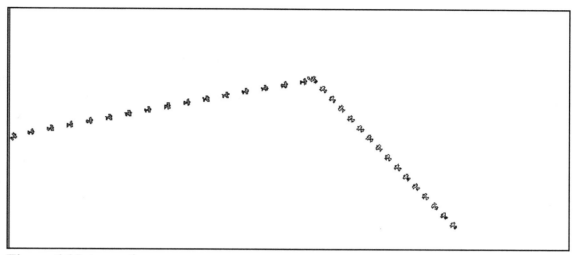

Figure 16 Interception

What are the drawbacks to this algorithm? Sometimes interceptions cannot be made. For example a slow attacker which ends up behind the defender might not be able to catch up. Another way it can fail is that the attacker gets way ahead of the defender, predicts a closing point that is so far ahead of both of them that neither reach it. You can determine whether the attacker is ahead of or behind the defender by looking at the normalized y resultant local variable. If y is negative, the defender is behind the attacker and a good move might be to circle around to get a better shot; to do this, use the pure LineOfSightChase and then revert back to the intercept version. If y is positive, the defender is ahead of the attacker.

Patterned Movement

Closely related is the patterned movement situation. The idea is to add realism by giving the computer controlled objects the illusion that they are doing something, such as patrolling the perimeter of their camp, performing barrel rolls while attacking, washing clothes, working in fields, and so on. The patterned movement does not have to be a rectangular path, but can be any path allowed in the game world, as complex as needed.

Patterned movement is implemented by constructing an array of control data that define the pattern of movement to be taken by the computer controlled object. For example, an NPC on guard duty might march in a rectangular pattern around the encampment. Workers in a field might move up and down long rows of crops. Enemy biplanes might perform a signature barrel roll as they sweep down to attack you.

Obviously, the precise form that the control data takes varies between a continuous environment and a tile-based one. In the continuous environment, the structure could contain members that specified an amount to turn left, turn right, speed up or slow down, a move to this location, fire weapons, drop depth charge here, cast a certain spell, and so on. In a tile-based game, locations are specified by providing row and column locations of the tiles to move to instead of angles of direction and positions in two or three dimensional space, x, y, z coordinates.

Suppose that the orc camp is located within the rectangle defined by (10, 10) and (15, 15) (x, y) values. An orc guard paces the perimeter of the camp. Thus, it begins at say (10, 10) and moves from there to (10, 15). From there, it moves to (15, 15); next, it goes to (15, 10); and finally it moves back to the starting point, (10, 10). This is the first step in creating a patterned movement, defining the locations of each segment of movement, forming the pattern. To actually compute the individual tiles to which to move, we ought to use Bresenham's algorithm to yield the best looking path between each of the points.

Thus, at first glance, it would seem that we only need to enter the four sets of data in the form of x, y from and x, y to: (10,10, 10, 15), (10, 15, 15, 15), (15, 15, 15, 10), (15, 10, 10, 10). However, and this is a big however, if we kept our data this specific, then if the orc camp moved to another location with the same size, our patterned movement would be invalid! Assuming that the camp size and shape remained the same no matter where it relocated, then we desire to enter the path in a normalized format such that it could be executed from any orc camp location!

To normalize a specific path, take the first coordinate pair, here 10, 10, and subtract those values from each x, y pair in the entire pattern, yielding a normalized path that looks like this: (0, 0, 0, 5), (0, 5, 5, 5), (5, 5, 5, 0), (5, 0, 0, 0). When the program is about to display the patterned movement for a specific orc camp, specify the upper left corner x, y indices and add them to each pair of values in the normalized pattern. For example, if the orc camp was now located at 6, 5 (the upper left corner of the camp), the display patterned movement of the orc guard would first add those values to the normalized path values, yielding: (6, 5, 6, 10), (6, 10, 11, 10), (11, 10, 11, 5), (11, 5, 6, 5).

One caution on normalization. By subtracting whatever is in the very first (x, y) pair in the patterned movement from all other coordinates, a potential problem arises when a subsequent point is above and left of the original one. Consider this path: (1, 1) to (0, 0). Normalization yields (0, 0, -1, -1)! The pair of -1's indicate the end of the path, not another point in the sequence. Thus, it is wisest to always begin tracing the patterned movement from the upper left corner of the sequence.

Programming-wise, we have several options. The original patterned path could be hard-coded into the program, necessitating a normalization function, and then a specific pattern created for the current camp. A normalized pattern could be built originally and hard-coded into the program, and then the specific pattern for the current camp created. Another approach is to store the patterned movement data in a file and load it into arrays when needed. The benefit of storing the patterned movements in a file is that they can be created independent of the program itself. In fact, one could create a file that stored all of the possible patterned movements for the entire game. One could store the data in binary format for fast input.

Let's use the file method, storing our patterned movement in a simple text file. In reality, one could create a helper program that would allow the designer to enter a pattern and then the program would normalize it before storing it into the file. In this chapter, let's assume that the inputted patterned movement has been normalized. That is, the first x, y pair are both zero. Then, the game engine only needs to input the pattern and create a specific instance of it based upon where the patterned movement should take place.

Here is the oasis.txt file I used for the orc guard patrolling the perimeter of the orc encampment.
0 0 6 0
6 0 7 3
7 3 4 6
4 6 0 6
0 6 0 0

Pgm01c illustrates how patterned movement is implemented. Figure 8 shows the final screen shot outlining the path taken by the guard. Notice that the path can be anything desired, it does not have to be a boring rectangle or square. The path can even be back and forth along a single line.

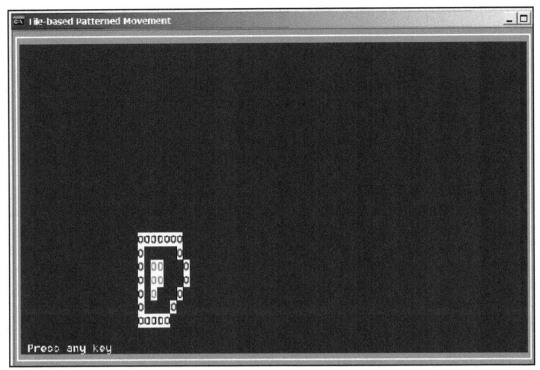

Figure 17 Orc Guard's Patterned Movement (Tile-based)

Implementation consists of three actions. First, the file containing the normalized pattern must be loaded and each line segment must be created using the Bresenham method for creating an optimum path. Once the normalized path has been created, it must be made specific for the current orc guard. Second, a modified Bresenham function is used to make the optimum path for each line segment. Third, the final resultant path must be displayed.

The main function is very straightforward. I define a series of orcs, the first one will be the guard and its starting coordinates will become the initial location for the patterned movement. An array to hold the patterned movement path, pathX and pathY, is defined and passed to the function LoadPatternMovement. Maximum flexibility is retained by passing the load function the name of the file, the answer arrays, and the specific initial location for the start of the patterned movement.

```
// define the orcs and set their initial coordinates
// the orc guard is index 0
const int MAXORCS = 6;
const int OrcsStartX[MAXORCS] = {19, 21, 22, 21, 22, 21};
const int OrcsStartY[MAXORCS] = {15, 17, 17, 18, 18, 19};

const int MAXPATH = 200;  // max number of pattern moves
int pathX[MAXPATH];       // pattern movement in X
int pathY[MAXPATH];       // pattern movement in Y
```

```
// load the patterned guard's path ready for display
int maxSteps = LoadPatternMovement ("oasis.txt", pathX, pathY,
                        MAXPATH, OrcsStartX[0], OrcsStartY[0]);
int i;
// display all orcs at their starting locations
for (i=0; i<MAXORCS; i++) {
  s.OutputUCharWith ('O', OrcsStartY[i], OrcsStartX[i],
                Screen::BrightYellow, Screen::BrightRed);
}
```

Showing the patterned movement of the orc guard is merely a matter of displaying the orc at each step in the array.

```
for (i=0; i<maxSteps; i++) {
  s.OutputUCharWith ('O', pathY[i], pathX[i],
                Screen::BrightYellow, Screen::BrightBlue);
  Sleep (100); // delay 100 milliseconds
}
```

The loading function opens the file. If it is successful, the answer arrays are initialized to a -1, indicating this element is not used, and the number of steps taken in the entire patterned movement, numSteps, is set to 0.

```
int LoadPatternMovement (const char* filename,
                        int pathX[], int pathY[], int maxPath,
                        int startX, int startY) {
 ifstream infile (filename);
 if (!infile) {
  cerr << "Error: cannot open patterned movement file: "
       << filename << endl;
  exit (1);
 }
 int i;
 // initialize whole path array to unused (-1)
 for (i=0; i<maxPath; i++)
  pathX[i] = pathY[i] = -1;

 int numSteps = 0;
 int xstart, ystart, xend, yend;
```

Next, the main primed loop begins, obtaining the first pair of start and end x y coordinates. If the four values are inputted successfully, the BuildPathSegment() function is called to append this line segment of the path onto the total path, using Bresenham's algorithm to form the line. The process is repeated until the end of file is reached.

```
 infile >> xstart >> ystart >> xend >> yend;
 while (infile && numSteps < maxPath) {
  // add this segment to the total path
```

```
BuildPathSegment (pathX, pathY, maxPath, xstart, ystart, xend,
                    yend, numSteps);
// get next pair of start and end x y coordinates
infile >> xstart >> ystart >> xend >> yend;
}
if (!infile.eof ()) {
  cerr << "Error: bad data in patterned movement file: "
      << filename << endl;
  infile.close ();
  exit (1);
}
infile.close ();
```

Finally, the normalized path must be made specific to a given actual starting location of the orc. The initial location for the orc is added to each x, y pair in the entire path to be followed. The total number of steps in the complete path is returned to the caller.

```
for (i=0; i<numSteps; i++) {
  pathX[i] += startX;
  pathY[i] += startY;
}
return numSteps;
}
```

BuildPathSegment() appends a new straight line path onto the existing path array. While the basic algorithm is not altered, provision must be made for the appending action. This means that the current starting index must be passed from the caller and updated by this function as it adds on more steps. Hence, the currentStep is now passed by reference into the function.

```
void BuildPathSegment (int pathX[], int pathY[], int max,
                int startAtX, int startAtY,
                int endAtX, int endAtY, int& currentStep) {
// nextX and nextY hold the orc's next position
int nextX = startAtX;
int nextY = startAtY;

// deltaX and deltaY hold the difference between the locations
int deltaX = endAtX - startAtX;
int deltaY = endAtY - startAtY;

// stepX and stepY hold how much to inc or dec each time
int stepX = deltaX < 0 ? -1 : 1;
int stepY = deltaY < 0 ? -1 : 1;
```

The original coding to initialize the resultant path array to -1's has been removed and replaced by installing the initial location, only if there is no points yet in the final path, currentStep being 0.

```
if (currentStep == 0) {
 pathX[currentStep] = startAtX;
 pathY[currentStep++] = startAtY;
}
```

The remainder of the Bresenham solution is exactly the same as before.

```
// double the total difference between locations
// and take the absolute value to remove negative signs
deltaX = abs (deltaX * 2);
deltaY = abs (deltaY * 2);

int fraction;

// two cases: is the x length greater than the y length?
if (deltaX > deltaY) {
 // x > y, so constantly move x but control when to move y
 // fraction controls times to move in y
 fraction = deltaY * 2 - deltaX;

 // now fill in all steps the orc must take to reach player
 while (nextX != endAtX && currentStep < max) {
  if (fraction >= 0) { // fraction is still > 0, must move in y
   nextY += stepY;    // add another y step to total y move
   fraction -= deltaX; // remove one column amount
  }
  // here, we have moved enough in y to justify moving in x
  nextX += stepX;
  // now add in another y move for next iteration
  fraction += deltaY;
  // store this move in the answer array
  pathX[currentStep] = nextX;
  pathY[currentStep++] = nextY;
 }
}

// here, y is greater than the x length
else {
 // fraction controls times to move in x for each y move
 fraction = deltaX * 2 - deltaY;
 // fill in all steps the orc takes to get to the player
 while (nextY != endAtY && currentStep < max) {
  if (fraction >= 0) { // fraction > 0, so must move in x
   nextX += stepX;    // add another x to total move
   fraction -= deltaY; // remove one row amount
  }
  // here we have moved enough in x to justify moving in y
```

```
    nextY += stepY;
    // add in the x move to fraction for next iteration
    fraction += deltaX;
    // store this move in the answer array
    pathX[currentStep] = nextX;
    pathY[currentStep++] = nextY;
   }
 }
}
```

Patterned Movement in a Continuous Environment

When in a continuous environment, totally new problems face game designers. They all stem from the fact that the simulation is based upon the physics of motion of the objects. Suppose that we are implementing an air combat game. Each plane has certain physical properties which impact the way the plane operates. Additionally, we are simulating the flying of airplanes. Thus, one cannot utilize the patterned movements of the tile based games as is. For example, you cannot have an airplane making instantaneous right turns. Doing so violates the physics of the flying plane, ruining the simulation for everyone. The computer cannot be allowed to break all the operational rules of physics while the player must follow them.

Nevertheless patterned movements can be implemented in such a way that they work with the physics of the simulation. The control structures now contain relative requests for an action, which the physics engine then carries out over as many turns as necessary to accomplish the requested action. With an airplane, the following might represent a control structure.

```
struct PATTERNMOVE {
        double altitudeChange;
        double turnToHeading; // in degrees + => to the right
        double alterSpeedTo;
        double travelThisDistance;
};
```

In other words, the control structure requests an altitude change, leaving the physics engine to accomplish that task in as many turns as is required to achieve the result. The main thing to keep in mind is not to use absolute values, but relative ones. Climb another hundred feet, not move to this x, y position. That way, the pattern can be utilized whenever it is needed. Patterns might describe a barrel roll, for example. If you keep the movements relative, then the barrel roll can be executed by any plane anywhere it is physically possible to do so.

In the implementation phase, since any pattern request may take several turns to accomplish, another control structure must be added to aid in carrying out the request. This structure would contain the initial settings and the accumulated changes thus far. Each turn, the implementation loop of the pattern can check to see if it has finally accomplished the request. If not, continue applying the changes. If so, end that pattern and do what is next in line.

Problems

Problem 1-1 Interception in a Tile-based Game

The text discussed implementation of interceptions in a continuous environment. They can also be done in a tile-based game. Using the sample programs provided, allow Frodo to move in some direction at some rate of speed. Have one orc at some other position move to intercept him.

When the program begins and before you create your Screen instance, prompt the user for the initial setup values. Allow the user to specify the initial position of Frodo and his direction of travel and likewise for the orc. Run the simulation until one of the two runs into the edge of the screen or they meet. The edge of the screen is row becoming 0 or at the bottom or column becomes 0 or 79. They meet when they are in the same location, row and column indexes are identical.

Use the Vector class as desired.

Problem 1-2 Guards on Patrol

Draw the outline of a castle's outer wall which occupies a rectangular area approximately half the height and width of the screen, that is 40x13, for example. Use Grey on Black for the color scheme to display the wall.

Next, create four guards who are to patrol the walls by marching designated paths along each side of the walls on the outside of the walls. Create a text file with the four patterned movements of the guards. Assume that the guards move one tile per turn. Show the guards position, sleep for 100 milliseconds and then move the guards to their next location, repeating the sequence 100 times before stopping. Invent a good symbol and color scheme for the guards.

Chapter 2 Basic Physics

We've gone about as far as we can go without diving into the underlying physics of motion of objects. Right here at the start, let's be very clear about our objectives. This is not a math or physics course. How the various formulae are derived is not important, only the resultant formula and how it is to be applied to solve our problems are vital.

The Units of Measurement

Inherent in any physical formula are the units of the various quantities.

Principle 1: The various properties and quantities must be entered in both the correct units and the same system.

For example, if the formula involves a distance and velocity, both must be in the same system and units. If the distance is in feet, then the velocity should be in feet per second. One of the NASA probes to Mars crashed instead of landing because the landing program and the inputted data were in different systems, metric and English. Sometimes conversions are necessary. If the speed is in miles per hour and the distance is needed in feet for the simulation, then one must convert from miles to feet.

Principle 1 applies most often during the data collection phase of game design. Here, one is obtaining the basic data about the objects to be simulated. Make sure that all of the quantities gathered are in the same system, English or metric, and that they are internally consistent, such as all distances are in feet. If you are vigilant at this stage, errors of this nature are not likely to creep into your program.

Table 2-1 shows the commonly used quantities, an example of their units in both English and Metric units, along with the commonly used symbols in the equations. One of these, the slug, is not so well know as a unit of mass in the English system. When one thinks of the mass of a ball, for example, one thinks of it in terms of its weight in pounds. However, weight is actually the object's mass times the force of gravity here on earth, 32.17 feet/sec/sec. Thus, a slug's definition is a mass that has an acceleration of 32.17 feet/sec/sec which is acted upon by a force of one pound. Confusing? In many of our equations that deal with the mass of an object, one mass will be divided by another mass. In these cases, one can simply use the object's weight in pounds for both masses, since in the division, the force of gravity will be canceled; it is in both the numerator and denominator.

Table 2-1 Physical Units and Quantities			
Quantity	Symbol	English Units	Metric Units
length	L (or x, y, z)	feet	meters
Mass	m	slug	kilogram
Time	t	seconds	seconds
Velocity	v	feet/sec	meters/sec
Force	F	pounds	newtons
Acceleration (linear)	a	feet/sec/sec	meters/sec/sec
Angular Acceleration	α	radians/sec/sec	radians/sec/sec
Density	ρ	slug/cubic feet	kg/cubic meter
Kinematic Viscosity	ν	square feet/sec	square meter/sec
Moment (torque)	M	foot-pounds	newton-meters
Moment of Inertia	I	foot-pounds/sec/sec	newton-meters/sec/sec
Angular Velocity	ω	radians/sec	radians/sec
Pressure	p	pounds/square foot	newton/square meter
Viscosity	M	pound-seconds/square foot	newton-seconds/sq meter

Closely tied to the quantities will be the coordinate system in use. Throughout these lectures, the right-handed Cartesian system is used. The positive Y axis is up, the positive X axis is to the right. If in 3D space, the positive Z axis comes up out of the page. One caution about the coordinate system. When displaying on the screen, the upper left corner of the monitor is the origin point with positive Y going down, the opposite of what one might expect.

Also intimately connected with quantities are vectors. The velocity of a vehicle is a vector quantity, that is it has a magnitude, usually called its speed, and a direction of travel. Often we will need to find a vector that is perpendicular to a plane or contacting surface and a cross product is used to find it. Finding the shortest distance between a point to a plane or parallelogram of a surface uses the dot product. Throughout all the example coding, I will make extensive use of the Vector class presented in Chapter 1.

Newton's Laws of Motion

About 1687, Sir Isaac Newton wrote his *Philosophiae Naturalis Principia Mathematica* describing his famous three laws of motion, summarized below.

Law 1: A body at rest tends to stay at rest; a body in motion tends to move in a straight line at a constant velocity unless acted upon by some external force.

Law 2: The acceleration of a body is proportional to the resultant force on the body and its direction is the same as that of the force.

Law 3: For every action there is an equal, but opposite reaction. For every force acting on a body, there is an equal and opposite reacting force.

These laws form the basis of the field of mechanics. Some of these formulae are very commonly known, such as:

Force = Mass * Acceleration
usually written as
F = ma

The mass of an object becomes a critical component in game simulations, because the mass of an object is found in many of the equations that define the motions of the object. Let's say that you wish to simulate a car race. You implement ways for the player to increase and decrease the racer's speed and ways for the player to turn the car, emulating the steering wheel. It is not enough to then just have the car speed away doing unrealistic actions in response to the player's controls. For instance, imagine you are driving your car at one mile per hour and desire to make a right turn. Certainly, you can turn the steering wheel sharply to the right to make that turn, because your velocity is very small. Now imagine you are going eighty miles an hour and make that same sharp pull to the right on the steering wheel. What will likely happen? The car now is going fast and tends to continue at that speed and direction. You have introduced a sharp turn to the right and the car will likely roll over in a fiery crash or spin out of control!

Suppose that a car collides with a semi that is fully loaded. Both are traveling at sixty miles per hour, but heading towards each other. What happens during the collision? The car becomes demolished. Why? The truck has a larger mass than the car, but more importantly, it has a far greater momentum, mass times velocity. Another example, suppose that you have two hunters who are suddenly attacked by a grizzly bear. Both hunter's guns shoot the same weight of bullet, say .50 caliber. Hunter One's rifle has a muzzle velocity, the velocity at the point of exit from the barrel, of say 3000 feet per second, while the other's gun's muzzle velocity is only 500 feet per second. From the bear's point of view, one delivers only an annoying sting, while the other is devastating. No matter the simulation, mass properties of the objects play a key role.

The properties of an object are: mass, center of mass (sometimes called the center of gravity), and the moment of inertia, collectively called the mass properties of a body.

The mass of an object is the measure of the amount of matter in it, but it is also a measure of the resistance to motion or a change of motion. The more mass an object has, the harder it will be to get that object into fast motion. Which would be easier to throw at a target: a pea or a fifty pound barbell?

A car racing down the road or an airplane flying in a straight line are examples of linear motion with which you are likely quite familiar. However, these to not consider any effect of rotation upon the body. Angular motion refers to the rotation of the object around its axis and which may have no linear motion connected with it. Imagine a tip spinning. It has no linear motion like the speeding car as it stays in one spot. Yet, its angular motion is quite large. Now how easy is it to take that spinning top and move it around? Try it, get a top spinning and then attempt to change its position.

The moment of inertia is a measure of radial distribution of the mass of a body around an axis. Take two cars, a tall sports utility wagon and a low to the ground racing car. Assume that the Y axis is in the forward direction, from the driver's point of view. The Z axis is straight up toward the sky, and the X axis is to the right. Have these two cars traveling eighty miles an hour down the road. Suddenly an obstacle appears blocking the road and both drivers pull hard to the right on the steering wheels. Which car is most likely to flip over? This is one of the problems that sports utility vehicles are prone to have, roll over. The moment of inertia of the sports utility vehicle about the X axis is quite large compared to that of the low to the road race car. The moment of inertia about the Z axis determines how easily the vehicle responds to turning requests.

Principle 2: The total mass of a body is the sum of all of the elemental particles making up the body, where the mass of the particle is its density times its volume.

mass of an object with n pieces $= \rho_1 * v_1 + \rho_2 * v_2 + \rho_3 * v_3 + \ldots + \rho_n * v_n$

If the density of all the pieces is the same, then the mass is just the density times the total volume.

When dealing with cars and airplanes, we can use this principle to calculate the object's total mass. With the car, we can add together the various pieces. Add the car's body, the driver, and the fuel. With an airplane, add the wings, plus fuselage, fuel, driver, wheels, for example. Take a complex object and break it down into its component parts. Find the mass of each part and then add them together to get the final object's mass.

Game Programming Theory

Principle 3: The center of gravity of an object is a vector given by
center of gravity $= (m_1 * d_1 + m_2 * d_2 + \ldots + m_n * d_n)$ / total mass
where **d** is a vector representing the center of gravity usually the center, of that piece.

Principle 4: To find the relative positions of each of these n pieces from the center of gravity
$$cg_n = d_n - cg$$

Let's say that you are simulating a race car. Figure 2-1 shows the initial setup. The driver is shown in yellow, the fuel tank is in blue, while the car is green. Since mass is being divided by mass, we can use normal weights in pounds, since the effect of gravity will be cancelled out by the division.

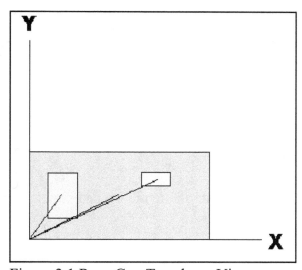

Figure 2.1 Race Car, Top-down View

Initially, the tank is full and ready to begin the race. The center of gravity must be calculated for this situation. The first step is to gather the basic data needed to do the calculations. Assume that each of the three objects is of uniform density and shape.

63

Table 2-2 Race Car Properties			
	Car	Seated Driver	Fuel
length	16 feet	3 feet	2 feet
width	6 feet	2 feet	3 feet
height	4 feet	3.5 feet	1 foot
weight	4000 lbs	150 lbs	
density			1.45 slugs/cubic foot
x center	length/2 = 8 feet	10 feet	2 feet
y center	width/2 = 3 feet	5 feet	3 feet

To calculate the weight in pounds of the fuel, we must use Principle 1, get all into the same units. We do the following.

Wfuel = density * volume * gravity
    = 1.45 * 1 * 2 * 3 * 32.174 = 279.91 pounds

Total Mass = (4000 + 150 + 279.91) / 32.174 = 137.69 slugs

Pgm02a shows how this can be implemented. First, define the needed structures and the functions needed.

```
RaceCar Structure

 1  #pragma once
 2  #include "Vector.h"
 3  const int MaxPieces = 3;
 4
 5  struct MASS_PROPERTIES {
 6    double mass;
 7    Vector designPosition;
 8    Vector correctedPosition;
 9  };
10
11  struct RACECAR {
12    MASS_PROPERTIES m[MaxPieces];
13    double totalMass;
14    Vector centerOfGravity;
15
16  };
17
```

```
18 void InitializeMassProperties (RACECAR& r);
19 void CalculateCG (RACECAR& r)
```

RaceCar Implementation

```
 1 #include "RaceCar.h"
 2
 3 const double g = 32.174;
 4
 5 void InitializeMassProperties (RACECAR& r) {
 6  r.m[0].mass = 4000 / g;
 7  r.m[1].mass = 150 / g;
 8  r.m[2].mass = 279.91 / g;
 9  r.m[0].designPosition = Vector (8, 3, 0);
10  r.m[1].designPosition = Vector (10, 5, 0);
11  r.m[2].designPosition = Vector (2, 3, 0);
12 }
13
14 void CalculateCG (RACECAR& r) {
15  int i;
16  r.totalMass = 0;
17  for (i=0; i<MaxPieces; i++) {
18   r.totalMass += r.m[i].mass;
19  }
20  Vector moments;
21  for (i=0; i<MaxPieces; i++) {
22   moments += r.m[i].designPosition * r.m[i].mass;
23  }
24  r.centerOfGravity = moments / r.totalMass;
25  for (i=0; i<MaxPieces; i++) {
26   r.m[i].correctedPosition = r.m[i].designPosition
27                             - r.centerOfGravity;
28  }
29 }
```

The main program allocates a RACECAR instance and calls the two functions.

The main Function

```
1 #include <iostream>
2 #include <iomanip>
3 using namespace std;
4 #include "RaceCar.h"
5
6 int main () {
7  cout << fixed << setprecision (2);
8
```

```
 9   RACECAR r;
10   InitializeMassProperties (r);
11   CalculateCG (r);
12
13   cout << "Total Mass: " << r.totalMass << "  Center of Gravity: "
14        << r.centerOfGravity << endl << endl;
15   for (int i=0; i<MaxPieces; i++) {
16    cout << "  Piece# " << i+1 << "  Mass: " << r.m[i].mass <<endl;
17    cout << "            Design Position:    "
18        << r.m[i].designPosition << endl;
19    cout << "            Corrected Position: "
20        << r.m[i].correctedPosition << endl << endl;
21   }
22
23   return 0;
24
```

Here are the results of the calculations.

```
The Results

 1 Total Mass: 137.69  Center of Gravity: (7.69, 3.07, 0.00)
 2
 3    Piece# 1  Mass: 124.32
 4            Design Position:    (8.00, 3.00, 0.00)
 5            Corrected Position: (0.31, -0.07, 0.00)
 6
 7    Piece# 2  Mass: 4.66
 8            Design Position:    (10.00, 5.00, 0.00)
 9            Corrected Position: (2.31, 1.93, 0.00)
10
11    Piece# 3  Mass: 8.70
12            Design Position:    (2.00, 3.00, 0.00)
13            Corrected Position: (-5.69, -0.07, 0.00)
```

Notice how the center of gravity has shifted from the basic car alone. The car should be (8, 3, 0), but is (7.69, 3.07, 0). The fuel has shifted the center of gravity toward the rear of the car nearly a half foot, while the person has made the car slightly lopsided to the left or in the positive Y direction. Have you ever seen a heavy set person sit in the driver's seat? The results make sense.

Game Programming Theory

Principle 5: Finding the Moment of Inertia requires you take the second moment of each piece about each coordinate axis.

$$I_{XX} = \int r_x^2 \, dm = \int (y^2 + z^2) \, dm$$

Ugh, notice that an integration must be done. For all but simple shapes, this computation becomes very complex indeed. However, a few simple shapes are easily done and often we can break the object down into a series of these simpler shapes, as we will shortly see.

Closely tied to this is the parallel axis theorem which allows us to find the moment of inertia about some axis distant from, but parallel to the object. You have calculated the moment of inertia around the center of gravity, this is called the **neutral** axis. However, you need the moment of inertia about another axis that is some distance from the neutral axis but parallel to it, use

$$I = I_0 + md^2$$

where Io is the neutral moment of inertia and m, the total mass and d the distance between the two parallel axes. For example, our race car is blazing down the track and needs to make a turn. Since we are in 2D space, the only rotation we must calculate is about the Z axis. Assuming that we know our Io moment of inertia about our own local center of gravity and we also know the radius of the curve, we can find our moment of inertia about the curve by adding m*r*r.

Here are some known formulas for specific shapes.

$$I_{yy} = \int r_y^2 \, dm = \int (x^2 + z^2) \, dm$$

$$I_{zz} = \int r_z^2 \, dm = \int (x^2 + y^2) \, dm$$

1. Rectangular solid whose dimensions are x, y, z in the three corresponding axes.
   Ixx = 1/12 m (y² + z²)
   Iyy = 1/12 m (x² + z²)
   Izz = 1/12 m (x² + y²)

2. Sphere of radius r.
   Ixx = Iyy = Izz = 2/5 m r²

3. Cylinder whose length is along the Z axis and of radius r.
   Ixx = Iyy = 1/4 m r² + 1/12 m l²
   Izz = ½ m r²

Applying this to our race car example, let's extend the program to calculate the moment of inertia. Notice this calculation comes after we find the center of gravity. Further, we only need to calculate the moment of inertia about the Z axis since we are dealing only with 2D space.

First, assume that each of the pieces is a rectangular solid and calculate each local moment of inertia for each piece. Since we are going to need the length and width of each piece, it makes sense to modify our structure and the initialization to include these two new members, xlength and ylength. Next, find the distance squared of design position minus the center of gravity position. Then, add mass times this distance squared to the local moment of inertia to get the center of gravity moment of inertia for this piece and accumulate them into the total moment of inertia. Here are the results; notice how significant the fuel component becomes in the simulation.

```
The Results

 1 Total Mass: 137.69  Center of Gravity: (7.69, 3.07, 0.00)
 2
 3   Piece# 1  Mass: 124.32
 4               Design Position:    (8.00, 3.00, 0.00)
 5               Corrected Position: (0.31, -0.07, 0.00)
 6
 7   Piece# 2  Mass: 4.66
 8               Design Position:    (10.00, 5.00, 0.00)
 9               Corrected Position: (2.31, 1.93, 0.00)
10
11   Piece# 3  Mass: 8.70
12               Design Position:    (2.00, 3.00, 0.00)
13               Corrected Position: (-5.69, -0.07, 0.00)
14
15 Moment of Inertia: 3376.20
16
17   Piece# 1  Local I: 3025.22
18               dist*dist: 0.10
19               I cg:      3037.84
20
21   Piece# 2  Local I: 5.05
22               dist*dist: 9.08
23               I cg:      47.37
24
25   Piece# 3  Local I: 9.42
26               dist*dist: 32.36
27               I cg:      290.9
```

Here is the revised RaceCar files.

```
RaceCar Definition

1 #pragma once
2 #include "Vector.h"
3 const int MaxPieces = 3;
4
5 struct MASS_PROPERTIES {
6  double xlength;
7  double ylength;
8  double mass;
```

```
 9  Vector designPosition;
10  Vector correctedPosition;
11  double localMomentOfInertia;
12  double momentOfInertiaCG;
13  double distanceFromCGSquared;
14  };
15
16  struct RACECAR {
17   MASS_PROPERTIES m[MaxPieces];
18   double totalMass;
19   Vector centerOfGravity;
20   double momentOfInertia;
21  };
22
23  void InitializeMassProperties (RACECAR& r);
24  void CalculateCG (RACECAR& r);
25  void CalculateMomentOfInertia (RACECAR& r)
```

RaceCar Implementation

```
 1  #include "RaceCar.h"
 2
 3  const double g = 32.174;
 4
 5  void InitializeMassProperties (RACECAR& r) {
 6   r.m[0].xlength = 16;
 7   r.m[0].ylength = 6;
 8   r.m[1].xlength = 3;
 9   r.m[1].ylength = 2;
10   r.m[2].xlength = 2;
11   r.m[2].ylength = 3;
12   r.m[0].mass = 4000 / g;
13   r.m[1].mass = 150 / g;
14   r.m[2].mass = 279.91 / g;
15   r.m[0].designPosition = Vector (r.m[0].xlength/2,
16                                   r.m[0].ylength/2, 0);
17   r.m[1].designPosition = Vector (10, 5, 0);
18   r.m[2].designPosition = Vector (2, 3, 0);
19  }
20
21  void CalculateCG (RACECAR& r) {
22   int i;
23   r.totalMass = 0;
24   for (i=0; i<MaxPieces; i++) {
25    r.totalMass += r.m[i].mass;
26   }
27   Vector moments;
28   for (i=0; i<MaxPieces; i++) {
29    moments += r.m[i].designPosition * r.m[i].mass;
```

```
30  }
31  r.centerOfGravity = moments / r.totalMass;
32  for (i=0; i<MaxPieces; i++) {
33   r.m[i].correctedPosition = r.m[i].designPosition
34                          - r.centerOfGravity;
35  }
36 }
37
38 void CalculateMomentOfInertia (RACECAR& r) {
39  int i;
40  double a, b, x, y;
41  r.momentOfInertia = 0;
42  for (i=0; i<MaxPieces; i++) {
43   a = r.m[i].xlength;
44   b = r.m[i].ylength;
45   r.m[i].localMomentOfInertia =
46                          r.m[i].mass / 12 * (a * a + b * b);
47   x = r.m[i].designPosition.x - r.centerOfGravity.x;
48   y = r.m[i].designPosition.y - r.centerOfGravity.y;
49   r.m[i].distanceFromCGSquared = x * x + y * y;
50   r.m[i].momentOfInertiaCG = r.m[i].localMomentOfInertia +
51       r.m[i].mass * r.m[i].distanceFromCGSquared;
52   r.momentOfInertia += r.m[i].momentOfInertiaCG;
53  }
54 }
```

Dealing with Forces

Newton's second law is
$$F = ma$$
where F is the force, m, the mass, and a the acceleration. However, the force is a vector quantity as is the acceleration. Further, the resultant force acting on an object is the sum of the individual forces. Hence, we have

Principle 6: The resultant force is the vector sum of each individual force acting on the object.
m **a** = sum of all **F**
or
a = sum of all **F** / m
Of course, this can be broken down into components along each of the three axes.

Principle 7: The linear momentum of an object is the mass time the velocity and is a vector.
Momentum = m **F**;

However, in 3D space, one must also consider the rotational motion of the object, which is also a vector.

Principle 8: The angular momentum of an object around its center of gravity is the force acting upon it at the distance vector from the center of gravity to the point of force application and must be perpendicular to that force direction. This is the cross product and is expressed
angular momentum cg = **r** x **F**

The total angular momentum of a complex object is the sum of the angular momentum of all pieces about the axis of rotation going through the center of gravity. Typically, one stores the angular velocity about the center of gravity, ω. Thus, the formula becomes
Total angular momentum of body = I ω, where I is the moment of inertia about the center of gravity.

Restated in terms of an angular acceleration, **α**, applied to the body,
total angular momentum = **I α**

Global Versus Local Coordinates

All of the equations shown thus far have been written in global coordinates, that is relative to (0, 0) of the simulation world. Now consider your race car is speeding down the track and is at some location (x, y) when another driver bumps your right front end slightly. This is a angular force being applied. In the real world, the bumped car is going to veer to the left in this case. To determine the impact of this bump, we must calculate the above angular force formulae, all of them!

Local coordinates are centered in the object. As such, once these properties are calculated, they will not change, unless the shape of the object is altered or you are factoring in fuel consumption effects. Thus, if you calculate these in local coordinates, they only need to be done once at initialization time, not at run time every time a new force is encountered.

We will see how this is done when we finally get to our rigid body simulator.

Tensors

In fact, our above inertia formulae are tensor quantities, not vectors. A tensor acts like a vector, with magnitude and direction, however, the magnitude may change with direction.

A common way to view a tensor is to compare a piece of paper and a piece of cloth. If you pull on the paper in either up-down or right-left, it has the same strength or ability to stretch in all directions. This is called isotropic, a change that is the same in all directions. However, when you stretch on a piece of cloth, the amount of stretch varies. Indeed, clothing cut on the bias, that is diagonal across the weave, tends to stretch considerably, while clothing cut along the woof and warp have a much smaller ability to stretch. This variability depending upon direction is called anisotropic.

Here, the moment of inertia is a tensor quantity because in 3D, a body may have very different reactions to an angular force being applied to it.

Take a boat for example. Assume that the Y axis is down the length of the boat and that the Z axis is vertical. Rotation about the Z axis, in other words turning, takes a good deal of force to turn the boat, ignoring its rudder. Likewise, rotation about the X axis, bow rising and falling, also takes a good deal of force to accomplish. However, rotation about the Y axis, side to side, is very easily done. In a canoe you can easily roll it over onto its side, but it is very hard to flip it end over end. This is the tensor in action, the magnitude of the moment of inertia varies depending upon the axis of rotation.

Principle 8: The total angular momentum in local coordinates is given by

total = $\mathbf{I}$ (dω / dt) + ω x ($\mathbf{I}\omega$)

Here, I the moment of inertia is constant throughout your simulation and can be calculated one time. ω is the angular velocity and (dω / dt) is its rate of change. Note it is the cross product, x.

Principle 9: In 2D space, the moment of inertia is a constant, a scalar quantity. In 3D space, it is a tensor and is a 3 x 3 matrix. It is a vector plus it can rotate along three axes.

Let's leave the tensor's impact until much later in our studies. Now, let's begin to put this into action, and that means linear and angular displacements, velocity, and acceleration. Given these, we can begin to do a number of different types of commonly needed game situations.

Kinematics: a Study of Motions

A rigid body consists of particles which remain at a fixed location with respect to all other particles comprising the body and have no relative linear or angular motions distinct from other particles of the body. The opposite of this is an object composed of particles. A plane, car, and a building are rigid bodies, while a fire cracker explosion is a particle system. A rigid body does not change its shape over time. With a rigid body, you must keep track of its orientation and dimensions and its linear and angular motions. With a particle, its dimensions are in effect a point, and thus you can ignore its dimensions and its angular velocity, but not its linear velocity.

With either of these two types, the body's position, velocity, and acceleration are key quantities with which to work. From elementary physics, we know that if we time how long an object takes to go from point s_1 to point s_2, we can calculate its velocity.

$V = (s_2 - s_1) / (t_2 - t_1)$

In many situations, the acceleration being applied to an object is constant over time, such as a ball falling to the ground from the top of a building. From basic physics we have the following formula. The symbol Δ means the change, delta, in the quantity. S is the distance, t is time, v is velocity, a is acceleration.

Game Programming Theory

Principle 10: In constant acceleration problems we have these relationships.

$a = (v_2 - v_1) / \Delta t$

$a = \frac{1}{2} (v_2^2 - v_1^2) / \Delta s$

$a = 2 (\Delta s - v_1 \Delta t) / (\Delta t^2)$

$\Delta s = \frac{1}{2} (v_2^2 - v_1^2) / a$

$\Delta s = \frac{1}{2} (v_1 + v_2) \Delta t$

$\Delta t = \frac{1}{2} \Delta s/(v_1 + v_2)$

$\Delta t = (\sqrt{v_1^2 + 2 a \Delta s} - v_1) / a$

$\Delta t = (v_2 - v_1) / a$

$v_2 = v_1 + a\Delta t$

$v_1 = \Delta s / \Delta t - \frac{1}{2} a \Delta t$

$v_1 = \sqrt{v_2^2 - 2 a \Delta s}$

Non-constant Acceleration: Drag Forces

In the real world, drag forces often operate on objects. If a bullet is fired and traverses a large distance, air friction will impact its flight. Shooting a pumpkin at a target will encounter drag forces due to its non-aero-dynamical shape. Drag forces are often proportional to the velocity squared.

Principle 11: Commonly, drag forces are cast into the following format.

$\mathbf{a} = - k \ \mathbf{v}^2$

where k is the object's drag coefficient. The negative sign indicates that the drag force is operating in the opposite direction from the object's velocity.

The current velocity of an object subject to a drag force is given by

$\mathbf{v_2} = \mathbf{v_1} / (1 + \mathbf{v_1} k t)$

and the distance traveled is

$\mathbf{s} = \ln (1 + \mathbf{v_1} k t) / k$

where ln is the natural logarithm.

74

Firing Guns, Rockets, and Related Projectiles in 2D Space

We can immediately put these equations to use in our game simulations. Assume that the body is fired along the X axis. Gravity works on the Y axis, or down. First, let's examine the equations to be solved ignoring air friction and air drag on the projectile. Figure 2.2 illustrates our situation.

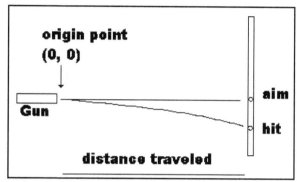

Figure 2.2 A Gun Shot

The origin point is at the end of the gun where the projectile is released. Since gravity operates only along the Y axis, its effect does not impact the equations of motion along the X axis. Letting V_m be the muzzle velocity, or the speed at which the bullet leaves the barrel, we have the following.

$a_x = 0$
$v_x = V_m$
$x = V_m\, t$

The Y axis components involve an acceleration due to gravity.

$a_y = -g$
$v_y = -g\, t$
$y = -\frac{1}{2} g\, t^2$

Given these equations, we can solve several different problems. One problem might be to plot the actual path of the projectile as a function of time. Another might be to calculate where the projectile will actually hit, as in the above figure. We know that distance equals velocity times time. So we can use the X axis set to find out how long it takes for the projectile to hit.

timeToHit = distanceTraveled / V_m

Given timeToHit, we plug that back into the y equation above to get

yhit = $-\frac{1}{2}$ g * timeToHit^2

For example, a 9mm pistol commonly has a muzzle velocity of about 1200 feet per second. A 30-06 Springfield rifle often has a muzzle velocity of about 2900 feet per second. A 22 caliber air gun has only about a 400 feet per second muzzle velocity. Let's say that the target is 500 feet distant.

What will be the drop distance from the aim point for each of these.

Drop Distance

9mm pistol	2.8 feet
30-06 rifle	0.5 feet
22 cal air	25.0 feet

If your game allows players to select different weapons, this drastic difference in results should be incorporated into the game, adding a level of skill in the use of various weapons.

What about adding in the effect of a cross wind upon the shot? Ah, the cross wind may blow the projectile to one side or the other. Now we are into 3D simulations.

Particle Motions in 3D Space

Let's begin by taking an example from my Complete WWII game. A battleship is softening up an invasion site by firing a long range artillery barrage at targets on shore. The parameters under the control of the firing crews are three. The elevation angle, e, can be varied from zero to forty-five degrees. The azimuth angle, a, can be varied between –90 degrees to + 90 degrees. Azimuth angle of zero degrees is perpendicular to the side of the ship, pointing toward the land, assuming that the ship is parallel to the shore line. Finally, the muzzle velocity can be varied by altering the number of powder bags placed in the barrel.

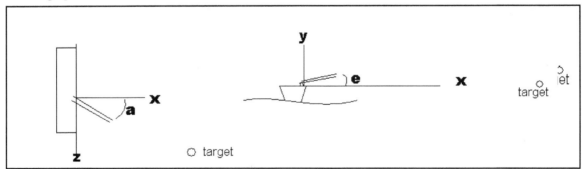

Figure 2.3 Battleship Firing Long Range

If we write the equations of motion as vectors, using the unit vectors **i**, **j**, **k**, we have the following, where **s** is the distance, **v** is the velocity, **a** is the acceleration, and **v**muzzle is the muzzle velocity as the shell leaves the barrel.

$\mathbf{s} = x\,\mathbf{i} + y\,\mathbf{j} + z\,\mathbf{k}$

$\mathbf{v} = d\mathbf{s}/dt = dx/dt\,\mathbf{i} + dy/dt\,\mathbf{j} + dz/dt\,\mathbf{k}$

$\mathbf{a} = d\mathbf{v}/dt$

Game Programming Theory

What are we given to solve the problem? We are given the azimuth, the elevation, and the direction of the muzzle velocity and its magnitude or speed. We are also given the length of the long barrel. Let us also assume for now that there is no drag component, no resistance to its flight and no cross winds. Thus, in the x direction, there is no acceleration and we can write the following.

$$\mathbf{v}_{muzzle} = v_{mx}\,\mathbf{i} + v_{my}\,\mathbf{j} + v_{mz}\,\mathbf{k}$$

We can use the vector direction cosines to find the three components, see chapter 1.

$$v_{mx} = v_m \cos \theta_x$$
$$v_{my} = v_m \cos \theta_y$$
$$v_{mz} = v_m \cos \theta_z$$

where v_m is the muzzle velocity's magnitude, dictated by the amount of powder used in the shot.

How do we calculate these three angles? Use the length of the barrel, L and the azimuth and elevation angles. The cosines rule gives us the following.

$$\cos \theta_x = l_x / L$$
$$\cos \theta_y = l_y / L$$
$$\cos \theta_z = l_z / L$$

We can find the three length values from the cannon and angles. The length of the cannon projected onto the xz plane is given by

$$lenxz = L \cos e$$

Thus,

$$l_x = L \cos(e) \cos(a)$$
$$l_y = L \cos(90 - e)$$
$$l_z = L \cos(e) \sin(a)$$

Now we can calculate the three angles and then the three components of the muzzle velocity.

Knowing the muzzle velocity vector, our equations of motion along the x axis become these as a function of time.

$$a_x = 0$$
$$v_x = v_{mx} = v_m \cos \theta_x$$
$$x = v_x\, t = (v_m \cos \theta_x)\, t$$

where x_{start} is l_x

The z axis components are similar.

$$a_z = 0$$
$$v_z = v_{mz} = v_m \cos \theta_z$$
$$z = v_z\, t = (v_m \cos \theta_z)\, t$$

where z_{start} is l_z

The y axis has an acceleration due to gravity.

$$a_y = -g$$
$$v_y = v_{my} + a\, t = (v_m \cos \theta_y) - g\, t$$

Game Programming Theory

The cannon's base is at some height above the water, plus the barrel extends upward some distance, depending upon the elevation. Hence, there is an initial y_0 position where the shell leaves the barrel's end beginning its flight. Let's let $y_{barrelbase}$ be the height of the bottom of the barrel above the origin point and $L \cos(90 - e)$ is the additional length of the barrel. So y_0 becomes

$$y_0 = y_{barrelbase} + L \cos(90 - e)$$

Now we can write the complete distance equation as a function of time along the y axis.

$$y = y_0 + v_{my} t + \tfrac{1}{2} a t^2$$
$$y = (y_{barrelbase} + L \cos(90 - e)) + (v_m \cos \theta_y) t - \tfrac{1}{2} g t^2$$

These equations form the basis for many game situations. Obviously, the firing of guns, rockets, and artillery pieces fit this scenario precisely. Yet, there are many other situations for which these equations apply. In baseball, the trajectory of the flying ball is governed by these equations. In fact, in any sport in which an object flies is a candidate for these equations of motion. In RPGs when a thief is attempting to make a jump or a vault, these equations govern his or her attempt. In any situation when an object misses its landing spot and begins to fall down, these equations govern the motion. In such cases, examine the final velocity when the object lands to assist in damage determination.

Rigid Body Motions in 3D Space

Our ultimate objective is to eventually be able to model a rigid body in 2D and 3D space. The formulas for displacement, s, velocity, v, and acceleration, a, in the previous section apply for a rigid body in 3D space as well, as long as they dictate the motion on the center of gravity or center of mass. Our efforts thus far are not wasted, we are getting closer to our goal.

However, with a rigid body another aspect must be considered, rotation about that center of mass or gravity. Thus, a second property must be monitored. We use the existing formulas to monitor the motion of the center of mass. Now we must also deal with equations to monitor the rotation about that center of mass. The parallel components are angular displacement, angular velocity, and angular acceleration.

The rotation can indeed be a complex situation, rotating in all three planes at the same time, such as a space craft rather out of control, rolling in all three planes. The three motions are called yaw, pitch, and roll. Attempting to simulate all three at the same time is rather complex, so for now, let's consider a simpler situation in which the rotation is confined to one of the three planes. Returning to our race car example, if it goes into a spin, the spin is confined to the xy plane. (Let's ignore the roll over and end over end crashes.) Figure 2.4 illustrates our car in a slight spin, confined to the xy plane.

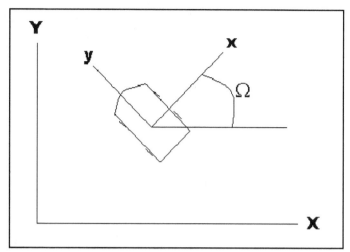

Figure 2.4 Local Axes and Euler's Angle

The upper case axes are the world coordinate scheme, while from the view point of the race car driver, the local axes are shown in lower case letters. Once more, we have the difference of viewpoint, local versus global coordinates. The angle omega is called the Euler angle and is the angle which the local coordinates are rotated from the global coordinate system. With pitch, roll, and yaw, three Euler angles are needed, one for each plane. As our car spins, the Euler angle will change and its rate is tied to the angular velocity of rotation, ω, about the center of the race car's gravity, while the angular velocity changes as a result of any angular acceleration, α.

It is vastly easier to calculate the rotational effects in local coordinates than global coordinates. Our basic three equations of motion become then, in local coordinates and Euler angle, and for a constant angular acceleration:

$\alpha = 0$

$\omega_2 = \omega_1 + \alpha\, t$

$\omega_2 * \omega_2 = \omega_1 * \omega_1 + 2\,\alpha\,(\Omega_2 - \Omega_1)$

$\Omega_2 = \Omega_1 + \omega\, t + \frac{1}{2}\,\alpha\, t^2$

Suppose that our race car while sliding (linear motion) and spinning (angular motion) touches a barrier wall. What will be the damage done? Suppose that its linear velocity is .5 miles an hour as it hits: barely a scratch on it. But suppose that at the same time it is spinning very rapidly as it hits? Now we have a serious instantaneous linear velocity addition coming from the rotational velocity as it hits! Another way of looking at this is a centrifugal force. Take a yo-yo and spin it around your head very fast. It has no linear velocity, only an angular one. Yet, if the yo-yo hits something, that angular velocity has an instantaneous impact or translation to the force of the hit on the object. That component is tangential to the circular orbit that the yo-yo is following as it circles your head.

Game Programming Theory

With our spinning car example, that point which hits the wall is at some distance, r, from the center of gravity and is following a circular path of rotation about the center of gravity of the car. The arc distance it travels, c, is given by

$$c = r \, \Omega$$

Note that the Euler angle is in radians, not degrees.

The velocity of that point is given by

$$v = r \, \omega$$

and is tangential to the arc at that point, or is perpendicular to the radius at that point.

The tangential acceleration is given by

$$\alpha_t = r \, a$$

where α_t is that tangential linear acceleration delivered at that spot. In other words, our race car delivers an acceleration of α_t at the point of impact with the wall. α_t is the centripetal acceleration and is always directed toward the axis of rotation.

A velocity is a vector, speed and direction. By changing speeds, you can obtain an acceleration. However, at a constant speed, you can continuously change direction to also produce an acceleration, as with the yo-yo.

The magnitude of the centripetal acceleration, αc is found from the tangential velocity.

$$\alpha_c = v^2 \, / \, r$$

Or

$$\alpha_c = r \, \omega^2$$

These are the scalar equations that work well when the angular motion is confined to a plane.

When you move into rotations involving two or three planes simultaneously, the vector forms must be used. These use the cross product.

$$\mathbf{v} = \mathbf{\omega} \times \mathbf{r}$$
$$\mathbf{\alpha_c} = \mathbf{\omega} \times (\mathbf{\omega} \times \mathbf{r})$$
$$\mathbf{\alpha_t} = \mathbf{\alpha} \times \mathbf{r}$$

The velocity of our car at the collision point is then a combination of linear and angular speeds.

$$\mathbf{v} = \mathbf{v_{cg}} + \mathbf{vt}$$

where $\mathbf{v_{cg}}$ is the velocity of the center of gravity and $\mathbf{v_t}$ is the tangential velocity at the impact point. Alternatively, we have

$$\mathbf{v} = \mathbf{v_{cg}} + (\mathbf{\omega} \times \mathbf{r})$$

Likewise the total acceleration is given by

$$\mathbf{a} = \mathbf{a_{cg}} + \mathbf{a_t} + \mathbf{a_c}$$

or

$$a = a_{cg} + (\omega \times (\omega \times r)) + (\alpha \times r)$$

We will begin to make use of these equations when we begin to combine all of the equations into a rigid body 2D simulator program.

Problems

Problem 2-1 Using a Sling in an RPG Game

This problem combines both linear and angular formulas to solve the problem. Suppose that you have a player who uses a simple sling as a weapon. The sling consists of a small leather strip attached to two three foot long strings. He places a one pound stone into the sling, swirls it in a circular pattern at his side until it is going one complete revolution per second. Then, he releases the stone. At the release point, the stone is four feet above the ground and begins its travels at an angle of forty-five degrees up from the ground. That is, the angle formed by the tangential velocity and the ground is forty-five degrees, guaranteeing the maximum traveling distance.

Use the angular rigid body equations above to calculate the muzzle velocity at the release point. Knowing the other facts, calculate how far the stone will travel using normal linear motion equations. Find the magnitude of the velocity at the point of impact, where y becomes 0.

Your computer program prompts the user to enter the weight of the stone, the number of revolutions per second, and the angle of release. Test your program with the values given above.

Be careful of your units.

Problem 2-2 The Battleship's Cannon

The battleship is undergoing training exercises and is lobbing 100 pound shells at stationary targets on the surface of the water quite some distance away. The length of its barrel is 16 feet and is located 30 feet above the water line.

Prompt the user to input the muzzle velocity, the elevation angle, and the azimuth angle. Then, calculate how far the shell travels (the magnitude of the distance traveled) and the point of impact (x, z) coordinates.

The program continues to prompt the user and show the results until the user enters some value that indicates that he or she wishes to terminate the program.

Chapter 3 Force and Kinetics

Armed with the basics of distance, velocity, and accelerations, we can now tackle forces. It is a force which makes an object move. A bat hitting a hardball, a foot kicking a soccer ball, exploding gases pushing a projectile, legs pushing off of the ground for a jump, a car hitting a wall, gravity pulling you down to the surface of the earth, all these are forces that are acting on an object.

Forces can be considered to fall into two categories: contact forces and field forces. The bat hitting the hardball is a contact force. The deliverer of the force makes direct physical contact with the object. With field forces, the force acts from a distance and might not be "visible" to the eye. Gravity is a major example of a field force, it acts on objects, yet we do not see it with our eyes. Electromagnetic attraction is another field force.

Newton's third law says that for every action there is an equal but opposite reaction. So for every force applied, there is an equal but opposite reacting force. Take a boat floating on a pond. Gravity is forcing the boat down into the water, but the water is forcing equally strong in the upwards direction, yielding a net balance, the boat is floating. Watch the next space shuttle launch to see another example. Exploding hot gasses force their way out of the bottom nozzle and the opposite force propels the shuttle upwards into the sky.

In this chapter, let's examine the very basics of forces that we will commonly encounter in writing games.

Gravity

General gravity is a force of attraction between two masses. The mass of the earth is pulling you towards the center of the earth while your body is pulling the earth toward the center of your mass. However, the magnitude of your body's mass compared to that of the earth's is completely negligible. The force is inversely proportional to the square of the distance between the two masses. When our space shuttles get sufficiently far from the earth's surface, the force of gravity lessens so significantly that a condition of "weightlessness" occurs.

The general gravity formula for any two objects is given by the following equation.
$$F = G\, m_1\, m_2 / r^2$$
This force is always directed along a line that connects the two masses. G is the universal gravity constant and is 6.673×10^{-11} N-m^2/kg^2 in the metric system or 3.436×10^{-8} ft^4/(lbs-s^4) in English units.

If on the surface of the earth, we use g (9.8 m/s^2 or 32.174 ft/s^2) which is valid only at sea level. If we plug the earth into the general gravity formula using as the second mass, m, at a height h from sea level, we have the following equation, where a is the acceleration.
$$ma = G\, M_e\, m / (R_e + h)^2$$
where the M_e, mass of the earth, is 5.98×10^{24} kg, and R_e, radius of earth, is 6.38×10^6 m.

If you are making a space ship game where ships fly about in outer space, use the first equation for the effects of gravity of near by stars and planets on your ship. If you are dealing with the earth at various heights above sea level, use this second equation. If you scenario is always on the earth's surface, just use the constant g force that we have been using for gravity.

The Effects of Friction

Friction arises from a surface interaction between two objects and always acts to resist motion. A frictional force is a contact force, always parallel or tangential to the surfaces in direct contact. The amount of the force is dependent upon the normal or perpendicular forces between the two contacting surfaces and is dependent upon the roughness of those two surfaces.

Frictional forces come in pairs: static frictional force and kinetic frictional force. Assume that we have a child's wooden block sitting on a board which is horizontal. The weight of the block supplies the normal or perpendicular force. Now using your finger, apply a tiny amount of force on the side of the block as if to push it along the board. As long as the block does not move, static friction force acts in the opposite direction from your finger's force, attempting to keep the block stationary, resisting your applied force.

Static frictional force is given by this equation.

$$\mathbf{F_{max}} = \mu_s \, \mathbf{N}$$

where $\mathbf{N}$ is the normal, perpendicular force between the two objects, the block's weight in this example, and μ_s is the experimentally determined coefficient of static friction. As long as the force that is applied is less than $\mathbf{F_{max}}$, the block will not move.

Once that maximum force is exceeded, then the block will move. However, at that point, the resistance to motion is usually very different and much less than that provided by static friction. This situation is called kinetic friction. It's equation is similar.

$$\mathbf{F_{max}} = \mu_k \, \mathbf{N}$$

where μ_k is the kinetic coefficient of kinetic friction, also empirically measured.

Here are some examples. You can see why we put oil in our cars and use Teflon bearings.

	μ_s	μ_k
Glass on glass	.94	.4
Wood on wood	.38	.2
Steel on steel	.78	.42
Oiled steel on steel	.1	.08
Rubber on pavement	.55	.4
Ice on ice	.1	.03
Teflon on Teflon	.04	.04

Fluid Dynamic Drag Forces

Fluid dynamic drag forces work like friction and tend to oppose the forward motion of an object immersed within the fluid. That fluid could be water or even air, in the case of flying an airplane. The forces result from the fluid flowing over the moving surfaces that are in contact with the fluid. The shape of the object, its speed, and the type of fluid determine the resultant drag. Additionally, pressure variations in the fluid create fluxuations in the drag. Complicating the picture even further, the object could be moving along the interface between two different fluids, such as a ship, part of which is in the water and part in the air.

Yes, in general, fluid drag forces are very complex to calculate. Let's begin with a very simple view to get ourselves familiar with the basics of how fluid drag forces impact our games. Let's use an idealized point of view of this viscous frictional component. There are two equations that apply, depending upon whether the object is slow or fast moving.

In the slow moving case, the fluid flow around the object is laminar, flow streamlines behind the moving object are undisturbed and parallel. If the object goes too fast, then the flow lines become turbulent, creating a chaotic wake behind the object, and the drag force is much greater. The two equations for viscous fluid drag force as a function of velocity are these.

$$F_v = -C_l v$$
$$F_v = -C_t v^2$$

where C_l is the laminar flow coefficient of drag and C_t is the turbulent flow coefficient of drag, both experimentally determined.

These are idealized equations and often do not match reality. Yet, in computer games, where a perfect match to reality is not always necessary, using these two equations can create a good deal of realism in your simulations. Further, in games, we can tweak these two coefficients to yield a good game balance, unlike an airplane designer who must actually fly the plane he or she is designing.

Pressure

Pressure is force applied per unit area, such as 14 pounds per square inch, psi. The resultant force is then dictated by the surface area in contact with that pressure.

$$F = P\,A$$

where A is the area and P the pressure.

Pressure always acts perpendicular or normal to the surface of the object to which that pressure is applied, yielding the direction component in our equations.

Buoyancy

Buoyancy is a force that is created when an object is immersed in a fluid, such as water, sea water, air, or a sea of ammonia of an outer planet. Normally, we think of buoyancy when dealing with objects floating on water. Yet, it is equally valid for balloons flying in the air.

Buoyancy is a function of the volume of the object and the density of the fluid in which it is immersed. It results from the difference in pressure between the fluid just above the object and the fluid just below the object. Pressure increases the deeper you go into the fluid, so that the pressure at the top of an object is less than the pressure at its bottom.

If we place a cube in a fluid, the buoyancy force is given by this.

$$F_b = \rho\,g\,s^3$$

where ρ is the fluid's density, g is gravity, and s is the length of a side of the cube. Its direction is vertical or straight upwards.

The pressures on the sides of the object are equal and cancel each other out, leaving only the difference between the top and bottom areas. To find an object's buoyancy force, simply calculate the volume of that object. As long as the object has a simple shape, such as a square, rectangle, sphere, cylinder, the calculation is simple. For more complex shapes, simply divide the object into a set of simpler shapes for which you can calculate the volume and add them up.

Springs and Dampers

Spring forces follow Hook's law. As a spring is compressed or extended, the force is applied equally to the objects connected to it on either end. This force is related to the at rest length, r, of the spring by this.

$$F_s = k_s \, (L - r)$$

where k is the spring constant and L is the stretched or compressed current length of the spring. Note that the force on one object would be F_s and the force on the other object would be $- F_s$.

A damper operates as a shock absorber on a car, dampening out some vibration or movement. Their force acts opposite of the object's velocity and is proportional to the relative velocity of the two connected objects and a damping constant.

$$F_d = k_d \, (v_1 - v_2)$$

In our race car example, springs and dampers are connected together. For example, the rear end of the car has a set of springs and a shock absorber on each side. In such cases where both are in operation together, we combine the two equations into a vector. The * means the dot product.

$$F_1 = - \{ k_s \, (L - r) + k_d \, [\, (v_1 - v_2) * \mathbf{L}] / L \} \; \mathbf{L} / L$$
$$F_2 = - F_1$$

where $\mathbf{L}$ is the length of the spring-damper while L is its magnitude.

Torque

Torque (sometimes called moment) is that quantity which causes rotational acceleration. Force causes linear acceleration. Torque is force times distance over which it acts. Hence, when applying a torque to an object, you must find the perpendicular or normal distance between the force source and the object's axis of rotation and multiply this by the force, yielding its magnitude.

Notice the difference in units. Force is pounds, newtons, and tons, while torque is foot-pounds, newton-meters, foot-tons.

Both force and torque are vector quantities. The force being applied which generates the torque is along the axis of rotation of the object, subject to the right hand rule for its direction. Curl your fingers around the axis of rotation and your thumb points in the direction of the torque. Use the symbol M for torque. Here, x is the cross product of two vectors.

M = r x F

To use these, let's write them in terms of their rectangular coordinates, using the unit vectors, i, j, and k.

$$\mathbf{r} = x\mathbf{i} + y\mathbf{j} + z\mathbf{k}$$
$$\mathbf{F} = F_x\mathbf{i} + F_y\mathbf{j} + F_z\mathbf{k}$$
$$\mathbf{M} = M_x\mathbf{i} + M_y\mathbf{j} + M_z\mathbf{k}$$

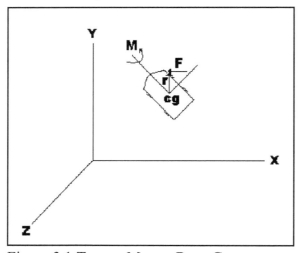

Figure 3.1 Torque M on a Race Car

First, one calculates the r distance, from the axis of rotation to the point of force application using local coordinates to find the distance r and then its two components in the xy plane. Second, given the force vector acting at that point, find the cross product to obtain the torque. In Figure 3.1, a force F is being applied at a distance r from the center of gravity. The resultant torque of a force applied in the xy plane to our race car will have only a z component, attempting to spin our race car in a circle.

If you have several forces that can contribute to the overall torque, calculate each one separately and then vector add them up.

Finally, a field force acts upon the entire body as a whole, and effects the center of mass or gravity and thus linear motion; no torque force is created. Contact forces at some point on the body and thus can generate a torque on the object.

Kinetics: Putting the Pieces Together

Now we are ready to put the pieces together into a whole package. We have then two critical equations that are sometimes called the equations of motion.

$$\mathbf{F} = m\,\mathbf{a}$$
$$\mathbf{M}cg = \mathbf{I}\,\boldsymbol{\alpha}$$

where **M**cg is the torque around the center of gravity, **I** the moment of inertia tensor and $\boldsymbol{\alpha}$ is the angular acceleration.

In game programming, we know or can estimate the forces acting upon an object. We need to find the resulting acceleration so that we can then find the velocity and distance traveled in a small period of time. We sum up all of the forces acting upon our object and then find the resultant acceleration. Knowing the small unit of time, we find the velocity and distance moved.

This means that the programmer must be able to identify and sum up all of the forces acting upon the object at a given moment in time.

The overall procedure to follow is this.

1. Calculate the object's mass properties, including its mass, center of mass, and moment of inertia.

2. Find and codify all forces and torques (moments) that are acting upon the object at this instant in time.

3. Vector sum all forces and torques.

4. Solve the two equations of motion for linear and angular accelerations.

5. Integrate with respect to our small unit of time to find the linear and angular velocities.

6. Integrate with respect to our small unit of time to find the linear and angular displacements.

7. Check for and handle any collisions.

8. Display or use in some manner the results.

The Destroyer Example

Let's take as an example one of the ships from my WWII game. The destroyer is leaving port and begins to apply maximum propeller thrust. What will be its position and speed as a function of time as it slowly gets up to speed?

The destroyer can be treated as a particle or a rigid body. Further, all action takes place in just two dimensions, where x is positive in the forward direction of motion, while positive y is vertical upwards. The origin will be the center of gravity of the destroyer, likely somewhere near the middle of the ship. The problem reduces to just 2D space.

Let's examine step 2, find and codify all forces and torques acting upon the destroyer. First, we have the thrust from the propellers generating a forward force towards the bow or positive x. Since it is in water, we have a fluid drag attempting to resist the forward motion of the ship, its direction is the opposite of the thrust, towards the stern or negative x direction.

But we also have buoyancy in operation as well. The weight of the ship is applying a downward force into the negative y direction, while the water or buoyancy is pushing the ship upwards in the positive y direction.

In the x direction, the sum of all the forces will be just the thrust minus the drag. We write the following, using T for thrust and D for drag forces.
$$T - D = m\,a$$
The thrust comes from the engines and will be a known quantity. The drag will be assumed to be of the form
$$D = -C\,v$$
where C is the drag coefficient and is opposite to the thrust. Our x axis equation reduces to the following.
$$T - C\,v = m\,a$$

Now we must integrate this and derive a formula for the speed, using $a = dv/dt$.
$$T - C\,v = m\,(\,dv\,/\,dt)\ \text{or}$$
$$dt = (m\,/\,(T - C\,v)\,)\,dv$$
Next, integrate dt from 0 to t and dv from v_1 to v_2.

Now here is where things get interesting, if that is the right choice of words. To do the integration requires substantial mathematical skills. The answer is
$$v_2 = T\,/\,C - e^{-(C/m)t}\,(T\,/\,C - v_1)$$
where v_1 is the initial speed, v_2 is the speed at another point in time t.

Game Programming Theory

From this equation, substitute for v_2 its equivalent, ds / dt, where s is the distance, and integrate that one. It yields

$$s_2 = s_1 + T/C \, t + (T/C - v_1) \, (m / C) \, e^{-(C/m)t} - (T/C - v_1) \, (m / C)$$

Now substitute back and get the acceleration equation in terms of these.
$a = (T - C \, v) / m$ or using our v, just
$$a = (T - C \, (T / C - e^{-(C/m)t} \, (T / C - v_1))) / m$$
With these three equations defined, we can now program our simulation.

Now can you see what I mean about math skills? If you are designing a game from scratch, you will need to take the force summations and do the substitutions and integrations. However, in practice, a game programmer is highly skilled in writing code, not in mathematics or physics or the life sciences. It is common practice to search through other published works, ebooks, magazines, the Internet, and various online forums to find such solutions that closely approximate your specific needs. Obviously, the more realistic your simulation must be, the more challenging the equations to be solved. Remember that often we can make simplifying assumptions to ease the complexity, without sacrificing game realism or playability. If every time the new position of an object must be calculated, the program requires ten seconds to compute its new location, no one will play the game, its altogether too slow.

What I suggest you do is begin to build up a library of reference materials which give key information needed for various scenarios, such as this one, a ship moving straight ahead. Then, when writing a new game, you have a collection of solutions from which to work. This is precisely what this course and book are about, building up a collection of mathematical models of various situations from which you can draw upon as needed later on when you begin to write your game.

The Complete Cannon 3D Space Example

The battleship firing a salvo inland in the last chapter ignored several key factors which must be included for grater realism. With any projectile, air drag will be a factor, likewise any wind will play a very significant role. If you are writing a sharpshooter game, both of these factors must be judged by your marksman because often the sharpshooter is firing from a very long range following the rule of one shot, one kill. If you are writing an RPG in which players may use a bow and arrow or a crossbow, again sir drag and wind must be factored in to accurately gauge their success at hitting the target.

Let's review the initial setup shown in the original figure, here 3.2.

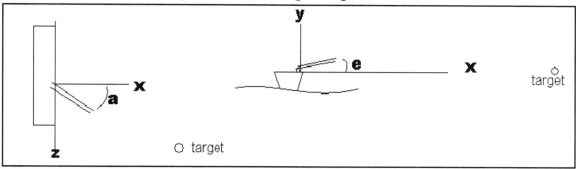

Figure 3.2 Battleship Firing at an Onshore Target

The angle of elevation e is given along with the azimuthal angle and the muzzle velocity. Now let's add in the other two key factors, air drag and wind speed. To deal with the air drag, the shape of the projectile is critical. Imagine the drag on a projectile shaped like a large box versus one shaped like a needle. For game simulations, it is usually sufficient to assume that the projectile is spherical in shape, which simplifies the situation. The drag force is given by

$$\mathbf{F_d} = -C_d \, \mathbf{v}$$

where Cd is the drag coefficient. The negative sign means that the drag force is in the opposite direction from the projectile's motion. At the high speeds of gun shots, it is more likely that the drag force is proportional to the velocity squared, but that makes the equations to be solved vastly more complicated.

Next, how do we handle the wind? If the wind is to move the projectile, then treat it similarly to that of an air drag.

$$\mathbf{F_w} = -C_w \, \mathbf{v_w}$$

Again the negative sign means that the wind will hinder the projectile if it is blowing opposite of the projectile's motion, but will aid it if it is blowing in the same direction. Recall that the y axis is vertical or upwards. So ignore any y axis components of the wind, unless you are shooting in a tornado. We have the components then as follows.

93

Game Programming Theory

$$\mathbf{F_w} = - C_w \, \mathbf{v_{wx}} \, \mathbf{i} - C_w \, \mathbf{v_{wz}} \, \mathbf{k}$$

Let γ be the wind direction angle and using the law of the cosines, we can get the following for the x and z planes.

$$F_{wx} = - Cw \, V_w \cos \gamma$$
$$F_{wz} = - Cw \, V_w \sin \gamma$$

Adding gravity in the y axis, we have
$$\mathbf{F_g} = - m \, g \, \mathbf{j}$$
where gravity pulls the projectile downward.

Next, you write out the equations of motion and then integrate each axis components to find v, s, and then a. The results are what we need to program the simulation. Here are the final equations.

$$v_{x2} = [\, e^{(-Cd/m)t} \, (C_w \, v_w \cos \gamma + C_d \, v_{x1}) - (C_w \, v_w \cos \gamma)] / C_d$$
$$s_{x2} = s_{x1} + m/C_d \, e^{(-Cd/m)t} \, [- (C_w \, v_w \cos \gamma) / C_d - v_{x1}] - [(C_w \, v_w \cos \gamma) / C_d] \, t$$
$$- m/C_d \, (- C_w \, v_w \cos \gamma / C_d - v_{x1})$$

$$v_{y2} = [\, e^{(-Cd/m)t} \, (C_d \, v_{y1} + m \, g) - m \, g \,] / C_d$$
$$s_{y2} = s_{y1} - (v_{y1} + m \, g / C_d) \, (m / C_d) \, e^{(-Cd/m)t} - m \, g \, t / C_d + m / C_d \, (v_{y1} + m \, g / C_d)$$

$$v_{z2} = [e^{(-Cd/m)t} \, (C_w \, v_w \sin \gamma + C_d \, v_{z1}) - C_w \, v_w \sin \gamma] / C_d$$
$$s_{z2} = s_{z1} + (m / C_d) \, e^{(-Cd/m)t} \, [- (C_w \, v_w \sin \gamma) / C_d - v_{z1}] - [(C_w \, v_w \sin \gamma) / C_d] \, t$$
$$- (m / C_d) \, [- (C_w \, v_w \sin \gamma) / C_d - v_{z1} \,]$$

The additional term, s_{z1}, represents the height at which the projectile leaves the barrel, and is the sum of the height of the gun above the ground plus the y axis projection of the barrel's length.

With equations this messy, programming efficiency raises its head. Notice that there are a lot of expressions that are repeated within the various formulas. For speed of execution, temporary variables should be setup to hold these expressions so that they only have to be calculated once.

We are given the two drag coefficients, C_d and C_w. The mass of the projectile is known. Let's assume that for the duration of the simulation, the wind's direction angle, γ, does not change during the flight and v_w is the magnitude of the wind's velocity or just wind speed and that it also does not change during the flight.

You might be wondering where the muzzle velocity, the elevation angle and the azimuth enter into the calculations. They are used to establish the initial velocity and direction vectors. Once the projectile has left the barrel, it is then subjected only to the forces of gravity, wind speed, and air drag, invariably landing somewhere. Thus, we still use the basic equations to calculate these two initial vectors as we did in the last chapter.

Game Programming Theory

To implement the these equations, one ought to put them into a reusable package, say an object oriented class called Gun. When one creates an instance of a Gun, you supply the basic parameters that do not change. Call the SetWindEffect() to install the wind's speed and direction. Call SetDragCoefficients() to store the two values, C_d and C_w. Next, one calls SetupShot() which install the current angles and other parameters for this specific shot. Then, one can call ComputeTrajectory() as many times as desired, passing in the amount of time that has passes since time zero of the firing. It returns the two final vectors for distance and velocity.

Here is the class definition, Gun.h; notice it uses our Vector class to reduce the number of variables and parameters.

```cpp
#pragma once
#include <cmath>
using namespace std;
#include "Vector.h"

const double g = 9.8;

/*********************************************************************/
/*                                                                   */
/* Gun: class to encapsulate the firing of a projectile that is      */
/*      subject to air drag and wind speed effects                   */
/*                                                                   */
/* x axis is toward the target                                       */
/* y axis is upwards                                                 */
/* z axis is right hand rule - curl hands from x to y axis,          */
/*         thumb points to +z                                        */
/*                                                                   */
/* uses metric system units                                          */
/*                                                                   */
/*********************************************************************/

class Gun {
protected:
  double baseHeight;       // barrel base height above sea level in meters
  double barrelLength;     // gun barrel's length in meters

  double Cw;               // coefficient of wind drag
  double Cd;               // coefficient of air drag

  double windDirection;    // wind direction in degrees
  double windSpeed;        // wind speed in meters per second

  double shellMass;        // shell mass in kilograms
  double elevationAngle;   // barrel's elevation above ground in degrees
  double azimuthAngle;     // barrel's azimuth angle in degrees
  double muzzleVelocity;   // shell velocity in meters per second

  Vector s1;               // initial location at end of barrel
```

95

```
Vector v1;                 // initial velocity at end of barrel

double cosw;               // cosine of wind direction
double sinw;               // sine of wind direction

public:
     Gun (double height, double length);
    ~Gun () {}
 void GetGunDimensions (double& height, double& length) const;

 void SetDragCoefficients (double air, double wind);
 void GetDragCoefficients (double& air, double& wind) const;

 void SetWindEffect (double speed, double direction);
 void GetWindEffect (double& speed, double& direction) const;

 void SetupShot (double mass, double elevation, double azimuth,
                 double muzVelocity);
 double GetShellMass () const;
 void GetShotParms (double& elevation, double& azimuth,
                 double& muzVelocity) const;

 void ComputeTrajectory (double time, Vector& s2, Vector& v2);
};
```

Here is the coding for the various functions, Gun.cpp. Notice how I calculate the values which are independent of the time in SetupShot(). This way, they do not have to be recalculated when the trajectory is computed. In ComputeTrajectory(), notice as well how I calculated one time the common terms used in the equations. This speeds up the amount of time the computer needs to do the calculations.

```
#include <iostream>
#include <iomanip>
using namespace std;

#include "Gun.h"

Gun::Gun (double height, double length) {
 // dimensions are in meters
 baseHeight = height;
 barrelLength = length;
}

void Gun::GetGunDimensions (double& height, double& length)const{
 height = baseHeight;
 length = barrelLength;
}
```

```
void Gun::SetDragCoefficients (double air, double wind) {
 Cw = wind;
 Cd = air;
}

void Gun::GetDragCoefficients (double& air, double& wind) const {
 air = Cd;
 wind = Cw;
}

void Gun::SetWindEffect (double speed, double direction) {
 windDirection = direction;
 windSpeed = speed;
}

void Gun::GetWindEffect (double& speed, double& direction)const {
 speed = windSpeed;
 direction = windDirection;
}

void Gun::SetupShot (double mass, double elevation,
                     double azimuth, double muzVelocity) {
 shellMass = mass;              // in kilograms
 elevationAngle = elevation;    // in degrees
 azimuthAngle = azimuth;        // in degrees
 muzzleVelocity = muzVelocity;  // in meters per second

 // one time only, calculate initial conditions at the end of the
 // barrel where the shell becomes a projectile
 double eRadians = DegreesToRadians (elevationAngle);
 double aRadians = DegreesToRadians (azimuthAngle);
 double e90Radians = DegreesToRadians (90. - elevationAngle);

 // compute the law of cosines to find the 3 angles
 double lx = barrelLength * cos (eRadians) * cos (aRadians);
 double ly = barrelLength * cos (e90Radians);
 double lz = barrelLength * cos (eRadians) * sin (aRadians);
 double cosx = lx / barrelLength;
 double cosy = ly / barrelLength;
 double cosz = lz / barrelLength;

 // compute initial x, y, z coordinates of projectile
 s1.x = lx;
 s1.y = baseHeight + ly;
 s1.z = lz;
```

```
// compute the initial velocity of shell as it leaves barrel
    v1.x = muzzleVelocity * cosx;
    v1.y = muzzleVelocity * cosy;
    v1.z = muzzleVelocity * cosz;

 // save wind direction cosine and sin values
 cosw = cos (DegreesToRadians (windDirection));
 sinw = sin (DegreesToRadians (windDirection));
}

double Gun::GetShellMass () const {
 return shellMass;
}

void Gun::GetShotParms (double& elevation, double& azimuth,
                        double& muzVelocity) const {
 elevation = elevationAngle;
 azimuth = azimuthAngle;
 muzVelocity = muzzleVelocity;
}

void Gun::ComputeTrajectory (double time, Vector& s2, Vector& v2)
{
 // compute common terms in the equations one time
 double e = exp (-Cd / shellMass * time);
 double CwVwCosW = Cw * windSpeed * cosw;
 double CwVwSinW = Cw * windSpeed * sinw;

 // compute x values
 v2.x = (e * (CwVwCosW + Cd * v1.x) - CwVwCosW) / Cd;
 s2.x = s1.x + shellMass / Cd * e * (-CwVwCosW / Cd - v1.x)
   - CwVwCosW / Cd * time - shellMass / Cd *
  (-CwVwCosW / Cd - v1.x);

 // compute y values
 v2.y = (e * (Cd * v1.y + shellMass * g) - shellMass * g) / Cd;
 s2.y = s1.y - (v1.y + shellMass * g / Cd) * shellMass / Cd * e
    - shellMass * g * time / Cd + shellMass / Cd *
   (v1.y + shellMass * g / Cd);

 // compute z values
 v2.z = (e * (CwVwSinW + Cd * v1.z) - CwVwSinW) / Cd;
 s2.z = s1.z + shellMass / Cd * e * (-CwVwSinW / Cd - v1.z)
        - CwVwSinW / Cd * time - shellMass / Cd *
        (-CwVwSinW / Cd - v1.z);
}
```

Motions of Rigid Bodies

When we move from a particle such as the shell into a rigid body such as a race car, we must add in angular motion into the equations. Our equations of motion then consist of a set for linear motion and a set for angular motion. Normally, we track the center of mass using the linear motion equations and track the body's rotation in terms of local coordinates and relative angular velocity and acceleration.

The two fundamental equations are these, where the vectors are shown in bold face.

$\mathbf{F} = m\,\mathbf{a}$

$\mathbf{M}_{cg} = \mathbf{I}\,\alpha$

For 2D space, we must sum the forces on the x and y axes and sum the angular forces.

$\text{Sum}\,(F_x) = m\,a_x$

$\text{Sum}\,(F_y) = m\,a_y$

$\text{Sum}\,(M_{cg}) = I\,\alpha$

Since the linear motion is in the xy plane, the angular acceleration is about the z axis. Hence, we only need to calculate the moment of inertia about the z axis. However, you will need to keep track of exactly where each force is applied to the rigid body.

Let's work out a simple example to illustrate these points. If a force is applied to the top of our race car, how easy is it to tip our race car over onto its side? For race car, you can substitute a tractor trailer rig, a tank, a boat, and so on.

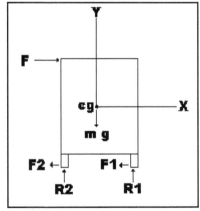

Figure 3.3 Tipping Over a Car

Assume the car has a height h and a width w. A force F is applied at the top. Friction at the two tires, R_1 and R_2, exert forces in the opposite direction from F. If the car was on a sheet of ice, most likely the car will just slide across the ice. If the force is small enough, the car merely leans slightly. For the sake of this example, let's put the center of gravity very high, at h/2, as it might be for a heavily loaded semi truck. Gravity exerts a downward force on the center of gravity as shown. At the exact point where tipping over begins, the force at R_2 is 0 and the acceleration is 0. As it rolls, the acceleration quickly increases, however.

Now write out the sums of all the forces acting on the car at the instant the roll over begins. Don't forget that there are four tires.

Sum $(F_x) = F$

Sum $(F_y) = 2\,R_1 + 2\,R_2 - mg = 0$, at the tipping point

Sum $(M_{cg}) = F\,(h/2) + 2\,R_2\,(w/2) - 2\,R_1\,(w/2) + 2\,F_1\,(h/2) + 2\,F_2\,(h/2) = I\,\alpha = 0$, at the tipping point. However, at the tipping point, R_2 becomes zero as the tire lifts off of the ground. Thus,

$2\,R_1 - mg = 0$

$R_1 = mg\,/\,2$

Rewriting the third equation,

$F\,(h/2) - 2\,(mg\,/\,2)\,(w/2) + 2\,F_1\,(h/2) = 0$

$F = m\,g\,w\,/\,h - 2\,F_1$

So the tipping force is proportional to the width divided by the height of the race car. F_1 is the force of friction, hence we need this term to be as large as possible, hence, we use wide tires with a lot of surface area to increase the friction. We keep the center of gravity as low as possible and keep the width large compared to the height.

Problems

Problem 3-1 Realistic Drag Coefficients

Search the Internet using Google for realistic drag coefficients. Use these search values: "air drag coefficient" and "wind drag coefficient." Find a pair of values that would be realistic for the sample program Gun in this chapter.

Using the Gun class given in this chapter, write a program to empirically answer these questions.

1. Assuming a shell weight of 500 pounds and an elevation angle of 45 degrees, azimuth of 0, what is the needed muzzle velocity to shoot a shell 10 miles in no wind? (Watch out for the unit conversions.)

2. Using the muzzle velocity found in 1 above, assume a tail wind of 50 miles per hour. Now how far can the shell travel before it hits the ground?

3. Assuming the muzzle velocity found in 1 above, assume a 50 mph cross wind. When the shell lands, how far to the left or right does it land?

Chapter 4 A Rigid Body 2D Simulator

Armed with all of the concepts thus far, we can now write our first 2D rigid body simulator. Because of all the variables needed to describe both linear and angular motions, an object oriented (OOP) class is the ideal programming element. However, the course assumption is that you are just beginning to be introduced to object oriented programming. With this restriction in mind, I will lump everything into one class, FlyingBoat. (Footnote: In reality, much of the basic coding of the 2D simulator could be reused for any number of different bodies. Normally, I would program the rigid body simulator as a base class and derive the objects from the base class, using the principles of inheritance.)

Setting Up the Rigid Body Class

What are we going to simulate? We need something that is fairly simple so that the mechanisms behind the rigid body simulator can be easily viewed. In later chapters, more challenging objects will be presented.

For this simulation, let's use an imaginary air ship. In *The Incredible Adventures of Jack Flanders*, the main character flew about the world in a floating pirate ship. Made from wicker and filled with gas balloons, the pirate ship looked like a galleon from earth, but flew in the air. I admit the concept has intrigued me since I first heard/read the book. Let's assume that it gets its power from a main jet which pushes out air to the stern. (Don't ask where the air comes from; spoils the imagination.) In order to steer the boat, a pair of bow jets can provide a push to the starboard or port sides. These steering jets are located up front, near the bow of the ship.

The first action is to gather the basic boat specifications.
Length: 200 feet
Width: 100 feet
Height: 50 feet (only needed to obtain an estimate of the projected area for air resistance)
Projected Area of boat (estimated): 1000 sq. feet
Center of Gravity: width/2, length/2
Weight: 2000 pounds (unloaded)
Mass: 62.16 slugs (weight / 32.174)
Center of Drag Location: width/2, 3 feet aft or behind the center of gravity
Note: by having the drag center offset from the center of gravity, the craft offers some resistance to the steering jet's actions, making the pirate ship more easily controlled.

Game Programming Theory

To figure the mass moment of inertia, all rotation is about the z axis. Rather than making an attempt to figure out this complex shape, let's assume that it is close to a floating rectangular solid. Thus, its Izz value is 1/12 * m * (length * length + width * width).

Mass Moment Inertia: 259,000 slugs-ft-s^2
Jet Pusher: at stern and width/2
Side Steering Jets: 5 feet from front and at each side edge of the boat
Main Jet Push Maximum: 3000 lbs
Steering Jets Max: 300 lbs
Top Speed: 50 feet per second (34 mph)

The linear drag coefficient is set to .35, which is an arbitrary guess at what the drag might be on this imaginary pirate ship. Because of the large cross section for turning, I set the angular drag coefficient rather large, tending to resist turning substantially, 200000.

The local coordinate system has its origin point at the center of gravity, which is the middle of the pirate ship. Positive x is in the forward direction of motion, positive y is to the starboard side, while positive z is directly upwards.

The first action is to define the class FlyingBoat and code the constants and member variables to hold the needed parameters that define the flying pirate galleon. Here is the data portion of the file FlyingBoat.h. The #pragma once directive tells the compiler to include this file only one time in the entire compilation. Notice that I also include our Vector class definition because many of our members will be vector quantities.

```
#pragma once
#include "Vector.h"

const double MaxJetPush = 3000.;
const double JetPushIncrement = .01 * MaxJetPush;
const double SteeringJetPush = 300.;
const double LinearDragCoefficient = .35;
const double AngularDragCoefficient = 200000.;
const double RHO = 0.0023769; // sea level air desity in slugs/ft^3

/**************************************************************/
/*                                                          */
/* Class: FlyingBoat                                        */
/*                                                          */
/**************************************************************/

class FlyingBoat {
public:
 double width;        // dimensions of flying boat
 double length;
 double height;
 double totalMass;    // total mass of flying boat in slugs
```

```
double inertia;         // mass moment of inertia of flying boat in local
                        // coordinates

double projectedArea;    // area over which drag operates
Vector position;         // position in earth coordinates
Vector velocity;         // velocity in earth coordinates
Vector velocityLocal;    // velocity in local coordinates
Vector angularVelocity;  // angular velocity in local coordinates

double orientation;   // orientation angle because +Y is downward

Vector totalForce;    // total force on flying boat
Vector totalMoment;   // total moment (torque) on flying boat
                      // about z-axis

double jetPushForce;      // magnitude of the jets' force
Vector portPushForce;     // port jet's current force
Vector starboardPushForce; // starboard jet's current force

Vector positionCenterDragToCenterGravity;
Vector positionCenterPushToCenterGravity;
Vector positionPortJetToCenterGravity;
Vector positionStarboardJetToCenterGravity;

Vector otherAppliedForces;         // currently none
Vector otherAppliedForcesPosition; // currently none
public:
enum JetsOn { None, Port, Starboard };
```

I also took the liberty to add a public class enumerated data type JetsOn. This enum will allow us to specify which steering jet to turn on to rotate the ship. Within class member functions, we can use Port and Starboard as data values. However, outside the FlyingBoat class, we must also use the class qualifier: FlyingBoat::Port. This is identical to coding ios::fixed, for example, where ios:: is the class qualifier for the public enumerated data type values.

Next, we need to identify what basic FlyingBoat functions are going to be needed and add them to the class definition.

```
    FlyingBoat ();
    ~FlyingBoat () {}
void Initialize ();
void SetStartingValues (Vector pos, Vector vel);
void SetJets (JetsOn which);
void AdjustMainJet (bool upwards);
```

The constructor function's purpose is to initialize all of the member variables to their starting values so that as soon as an instance of the FlyingBoat is created, it is in a stable state. I added the function Initialize() to take care of these details. This way, if one wishes to start the simulation over a second time, Initialize() can be called as well to reset every variable back to their initial state.

However, the initial location and speed will is subject to change. Hence, I added a special function SetStartingValues() so that the position and speed can be set later on, once we know where we want the ship to be located. At some point, the steering jets will need to be activated to turn the ship. SetJets() is passes which steering jet is to be activated and it will turn on the appropriate jet or even turn them both off, if a straight line path is now desired. AdjustMainJet() is called to increase the overall ship's speed or reduce it.

Finally, two functions are needed to perform the very basic rigid body in two dimensions simulation. We'll examine these two functions shortly.

```
void CalculateLoads ();
void IntegrateEuler (double deltaTime);
```

Next, we must implement these simple functions in the FlyingBoat.cpp file. The first include is to handle the windows programming situation. This example will be using a window application to show the movement in a continuous environment.

```
#include "StdAfx.h"
#include "FlyingBoat.h"

FlyingBoat::FlyingBoat () {
 width = 100;
 length = 200;
 height = 50;
 totalMass = 62.16;
 inertia = 259000.;
 projectedArea = 1000;
 orientation = 0;
 jetPushForce = 0;          // magnitude of the jets' force
 positionCenterDragToCenterGravity = Vector (-3, 0, 0);
                                     // 3' behind C of G
 positionCenterPushToCenterGravity = Vector (-length/2, 0, 0);
                                     // 100' behind C G
 positionPortJetToCenterGravity = Vector (length/2 - 5, width/2, 0);
 positionStarboardJetToCenterGravity = Vector (length/2-5,-width/2,0);
 Initialize ();
}

void FlyingBoat::Initialize () {
 position = velocity = velocityLocal = angularVelocity =
         totalForce = Vector (0,0,0);
 totalMoment = portPushForce = starboardPushForce = Vector (0,0,0);
}

void FlyingBoat::SetStartingValues (Vector pos, Vector vel) {
```

```
Initialize ();
position = pos;
velocity = vel;
vel.Normalize ();
double angle = acos (vel.x) * 180 / PI;
if (vel.x > 0 && vel.y < 0) angle -= 90;
if (vel.x < 0 && vel.y > 0) angle += 90;
orientation = angle;
}


void FlyingBoat::SetJets (JetsOn which) {
 if (which == None) {
  portPushForce = starboardPushForce = Vector (0, 0, 0);
 }
 else if (which == Port) {
  portPushForce = Vector (0, -SteeringJetPush, 0);
  starboardPushForce = Vector (0, 0, 0);
 }
 else {
  portPushForce = Vector (0, 0, 0);
  starboardPushForce = Vector (0, SteeringJetPush, 0);
 }
}

void FlyingBoat::AdjustMainJet (bool upwards) {
 if (upwards) {
  jetPushForce += JetPushIncrement;
 }
 else {
  jetPushForce -= JetPushIncrement;
 }
}
```

These functions are quite simple, simply assigning the needed starting values to the member variables or setting the correct side turning jets on or off.

Integration of Equations of Motion

The basic situation is that we have some equation of motion that can be simplified to the following.
        F = m dv/dt
We need to be able to calculate the position of our rigid body at some interval of time beyond its initial position and speed.

        Thus, rearranging we have
        dv = F/m dt
That is, an infinitesimally small change in time results in an F/m change in the velocity. This is a tiny change in velocity that occurs as a result of the forces acting on the body during the tiny interval of time. It can be written this way.
        delta v = F/m delta t
Thus, the new velocity is v original plus delta v, for sufficiently tiny delta t's.

        Knowing the new velocity, we can get the new position this way.
        s new = s original + delta time * (the new velocity just found)

        In performing this action, remember that the interval of time must be very small. The larger the change in time is, the larger the errors in the approximation. If the change in time is as large as one second, the results are likely to be considerably wrong, delta time must be very small. Theoretically, if you made delta time exceedingly small, the error would be very, very small indeed. However, if you need the new position of the body determined and shown on the screen every second and made delta time be say .000001 seconds, the time required to do all of these calculations would slow the action down to that of a snail, completely unusable. Making delta time of the order of .01 works much better, since the extensive calculations must be done only a hundred times before you display the results on the screen.

        There are a number of different methods by which this integration can be performed. The fancier methods yield greater accuracy, but take more calculation time. It is always a trade-off of accuracy versus speed of calculation. The simplest of these methods is called Euler's Method, which we will examine first.

Euler's Method

Assume that we have a function v (t), where v is the velocity and t is the time. Taylor's theorem allows you to express the value of the function at some other point in time by knowing about the function and its derivatives. Specifically, the Taylor's expansion for v(t) at a small interval of time later is given by the following.

$$v (t + \Delta t) = v(t) + \Delta t\, v'(t) + \Delta t^2/2!\, v''(t) + \Delta t^3/3!\, v'''(t) + \ldots$$

Here v'(t) is the derivative of velocity, v"(t) is the second derivative of velocity, and so on. Euler's method uses only the first derivative of velocity. However, we know what that is, it is the acceleration, $F = m\,a$, or $a = F/m$. The sum of all of the omitted terms of the expansion yields the truncation error.

Thus, Euler's method yields

$$v (t + \Delta t) = v(t) + \Delta t\, v'(t)$$

or substituting our values

$$v_{new} = v_0 + \Delta t\, F/m$$

Assuming that we know the total forces acting during this small time interval and the magnitude of that tiny time interval and the mass of our rigid body, we can calculate the acceleration, F/m. Multiplying that by the delta time and adding in the initial velocity before this tiny increment in time, we have the new velocity. The new position is then the original position plus the delta time times the new velocity.

While this is a very simple method, it has problems with stability. That is, sometimes, if the delta time is too large, the error becomes very large and diverges from the exact mathematical solution. Frequently, by making the interval, delta time, even smaller, the divergence can be eliminated, of course, this requires more computational time for each new shown position on the screen.

Implementing Euler's Method

To implement this method, we must have an accurate tabulation of the total vector force acting on our rigid body, including both linear and angular components. The angular components often arise from the use of the steering jets, while the linear component comes from the main jet thruster in the stern of the pirate ship.

This means that before we can to the actual Euler's calculations, we must recalculate the various forces acting on the ship. This is encapsulated into the CalculateEulerLoads() function.

```
void FlyingBoat::CalculateEulerLoads () {
 Vector sumForces;    // stores the sum of forces
 Vector sumMoments;   // stores the sum of moments
 Vector thrust;       // thrust or push vectors

 // reset the force and moment acting on the pirate ship
 totalForce = totalMoment = Vector (0, 0, 0);

 // calc the thrust vector, which acts through the ship's CG
 thrust = Vector (1, 0, 0);
 thrust *= jetPushForce;

 // calculate forces and moments in local coords
 Vector localVelocity;
 double localSpeed;
 Vector drag;
 Vector result;
 Vector temp;

 // calculate the aerodynamic drag force by getting local velocity
 // which includes the velocity from linear motion of the ship and
 // from the velocity at each element due to the rotation of the ship
 temp = angularVelocity ^ positionCenterDragToCenterGravity;
 localVelocity = velocityLocal + temp;
 localSpeed = localVelocity.Magnitude(); // local air speed

 // Find the direction that drag acts - opposite direction from vel
 if (localSpeed > EPS) {
  localVelocity.Normalize();
  drag = - localVelocity;

  // Find the resultant force on the element and add it to the
  // running total of resultant forces
  double t = .5 * RHO * localSpeed * localSpeed * projectedArea;
  // drag from sides of ship
  result = drag * LinearDragCoefficient * t;
  sumForces += result;
```

```
  // Find the moment about the CG of this element's force and add it
  // to the running total of these moments
  sumMoments += positionCenterDragToCenterGravity ^ result;
}

// Find any port & starboard jet push forces and add to sum of forces
// Find the moment about the CG of this element's force & add to
// running total
sumForces += portPushForce;
sumMoments += positionPortJetToCenterGravity ^ portPushForce;
sumForces += starboardPushForce;
sumMoments += positionStarboardJetToCenterGravity ^
             starboardPushForce;

// Add in any other additional forces that have been applied
// to the ship, such as collisions
sumForces += otherAppliedForces;
sumMoments += otherAppliedForcesPosition ^ otherAppliedForces;

// Find the rotational drag component, if any
if (angularVelocity.Magnitude() > EPS) {
  double t = 0.5 * RHO * angularVelocity.z * angularVelocity.z *
            projectedArea * AngularDragCoefficient;
  Vector tv;
  tv.z = angularVelocity.z > 0.0 ? - t : t;
  sumMoments += tv;
}

// Finally, add in the main propulsion jet thrust - note that there
// is no angular momentum component, since the main jet acts in line
// through the center of gravity
sumForces += thrust;

// Convert forces from model space to earth space
totalForce = GlobalToLocalCoords_2D (orientation, sumForces);
totalMoment += sumMoments;
}
```

Now with the total force calculated, and mass being constant, we can proceed to perform Euler's method to find the new velocity and speed. Note that the small time interval, delta time, is passed to the function. Note also that the total forces acting must be determined as a first action, so CalculateEulerLoads() is called.

```
void FlyingBoat::IntegrateEuler (double deltaTime) {
  Vector a;
  Vector dv;
  Vector ds;
  double aa;
  double dav;
  double dr;
```

```
CalculateEulerLoads (); // find the current forces and moments

// integrate linear equation of motion
a = totalForce / totalMass;

dv = a * deltaTime;
velocity += dv;

ds = velocity * deltaTime;
position += ds;

// integrate angular equation of motion:
aa = totalMoment.z / inertia;

dav = aa * deltaTime;
angularVelocity.z += dav;

dr = RadiansToDegrees (angularVelocity.z * deltaTime);
orientation += dr;

velocityLocal = GlobalToLocalCoords_2D (-orientation, velocity);
}
```

Pgm04a Illustrates Euler's Method

I utilized the basic chase and intercept methods from Chapter 2. Pgm04a is once more a Windows application. Once more, you are not responsible for the Windows application coding. When the user selects the menu item Actions — Basic Chase, the DoSimulation() function is called. There are two FlyingBoat objects, a and d, a for attacker, and d for defender.

The simulation begins by re-initializing and setting up the two pirate ships and showing them on the screen. The critical time interval is set to .01 seconds. Every 100 frames, the ships are shown on the screen, that is once every second. The simulation runs for 130 seconds total before stopping. If a ship should move off-screen, the coordinate that is out of range is adjusted to bring it back into view once more, a rather crude approach. We are concerned with only the instructions highlighted in boldface.

```
void CMainFrame::DoSimulation () {
 a.Initialize ();
 d.Initialize ();
 a.SetStartingValues (Vector (200, 200, 0), Vector (-20, 20, 0));
 d.SetStartingValues (Vector (400, 400, 0), Vector (15, -15, 0));
 {
  CClientDC dc (this);
  RenderFlyingBoat (dc, a, AttackerColor);
  RenderFlyingBoat (dc, d, DefenderColor);
 }
 double deltaTime = .01;
 int    frameCount = 0;

 long count = 0;
 Vector predicted;
 while (count < 130) {
  UpdateMove (d, deltaTime);

  if (which == BasicChase)
   DoBasicChase (a, d);
  else if (which == Interception)
   predicted = DoIntercept (a, d);

  UpdateMove (a, deltaTime);

  if (frameCount >= 100) {
   CClientDC dc (this);
   dc.Rectangle (0, 0, size.cx, size.cy);
   RenderFlyingBoat (dc, a, AttackerColor);
   RenderFlyingBoat (dc, d, DefenderColor);
   dc.Ellipse ((int) predicted.x - 3, (int) predicted.y - 3,
               (int) predicted.x + 3, (int) predicted.y + 3);
   frameCount = 0;
```

```
   Sleep (100);
   count++;
  }
  frameCount++;
  HandleGoingOffScreen (a);
  HandleGoingOffScreen (d);
 }
}

void CMainFrame::HandleGoingOffScreen (FlyingBoat& p) {
 if (p.position.x > size.cx)
  p.position.x = 0;
 else if (p.position.x < 0)
  p.position.x = size.cx;
 if (p.position.y > size.cy)
  p.position.y = 0;
 else if (p.position.y < 0)
  p.position.y = size.cy;
}
```

The coding to deal with the actual movement of the ships has been placed into a separate pair of files, a header that provides only the normal function prototypes and a cpp file which implements them, Simulation.h and Simulation.cpp.

UpdateMove() just calls the IntegrateEuler() function for this FlyingBoat object.

```
#include "Simulation.h"

void UpdateMove (FlyingBoat& b, double deltaTime) {
 b.IntegrateEuler (deltaTime);
}

void DoBasicChase (FlyingBoat& a, FlyingBoat& d) {
 Vector lineOfSight = d.position - a.position;
 Vector local = GlobalToLocalCoords_2D (-a.orientation, lineOfSight);
 local.Normalize ();
 FlyingBoat::JetsOn which = FlyingBoat::None;
 if (local.y < EPS)
  a.SetJets (FlyingBoat::Port);
 else if (local.y > EPS)
  a.SetJets (FlyingBoat::Starboard);
 else
  a.SetJets (FlyingBoat::None);
}

Vector DoIntercept (FlyingBoat& a, FlyingBoat& d) {
 Vector vClosing = d.velocity - a.velocity;
 Vector dClosing = d.position - a.position;
```

```
double tClosing = dClosing.Magnitude() / vClosing.Magnitude();
Vector predicted = d.position + d.velocity * tClosing;
Vector lineOfSight = predicted - a.position;
Vector local = GlobalToLocalCoords_2D (-a.orientation, lineOfSight);
local.Normalize ();
if (local.y < EPS)
  a.SetJets (FlyingBoat::Port);
else if (local.y > EPS)
  a.SetJets (FlyingBoat::Starboard);
else
  a.SetJets (FlyingBoat::None);
  return predicted;
}
```

Notice that once the new line of sight has been found, the ship must be turned towards the desired location. This is now accomplished by turning on one of the steering jet pushers. The CalculateLoads() function then adds this angular component into the total forces acting upon the pirate ship. Figure 4.1 shows a screen shot of the action.

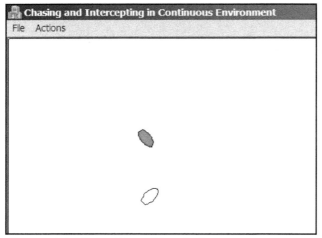

Figure 4.1 FlyingBoat Simulation

Improvements in the Integration Method

Obviously, to have a more accurate solution, one can just include one or more additional terms of the Taylor series. However, finding the mathematical expression that describes v(t) as given by the following, can be difficult.

$$+ \Delta t^2/2! \ v''(t) + \Delta t^3/3! \ v'''(t) + \ldots$$

That is, we need the second and third derivative functions of the velocity! This can be a very difficult challenge to even work out mathematically! However, we can replace the v''(t) term with another Taylor series expansion for that! Similarly, for additional terms.

The Improved Euler Solution adds in one more term, the v''(t) term. In your math courses, you will learn how to do just this. From a programming point of view, we only need the resultant equations, expressed in our motion terms.

$v_{new} = v_0 + \frac{1}{2} (k_1 + k_2)$
where
$k_1 = \Delta t \ F_0/m$ and F_0 is the total force at the start of the time interval as before
$k_2 = \Delta t \ F_1/m$ and F_1 is the total force acting at $t_0 + \Delta t$
F_1 = forces acting at F_0 + that acting at k1 or Δt

Calculating the F_1 component requires redetermining the velocity and re-calculating the entire loads on the ship using the new velocity component and then one can calculate k_2 and the real ending velocity new. Thus, we must make a copy of our entire ship instance as the first step. Then, go ahead and calculate both the angular and linear accelerations, since they are likely to be very different values. Using those, compute two values of k_1, say $k_{1linear}$ and $k_{1angular}$. Now, alter the copied version of the object by adding in the new $k_{1linear}$ and $k_{1angular}$ velocities to its velocity and angularVelocity members. On the copy, we now CalculateImprovedLoads() and then find $k_{2linear}$ and $k_{2angular}$. At last, we can calculate the new pair of vectors by adding in the new linear and angular velocities from these two terms.

Note that the improved method is going to calculate the angular components in the integration process and not in the calculate loads function as it was done with the basic Euler method. Thus, the CalculateImprovedLoads() function no longer has the following coding in it.

```
// remove these lines to get the CalculateImprovedLoads function
// Find the rotational drag component, if any
if (angularVelocity.Magnitude() > EPS) {
  double t = 0.5 * RHO * angularVelocity.z * angularVelocity.z *
            projectedArea * AngularDragCoefficient;
  Vector tv;
  tv.z = angularVelocity.z > 0.0 ? - t : t;
  sumMoments += tv;
}
```

Game Programming Theory

Here is the IntegrateImprovedEuler() function. First, make a copy of the original settings for use in computing the second set. Notice that we are now calculating the angular velocity here instead of in the calculate load function.

```
void FlyingBoat::IntegrateImprovedEuler (double deltaTime) {
// make a copy of the original object for k2
FlyingBoat copy (*this);
Vector k1, k2;
double k1a, k2a;
Vector a;
Vector dv;
Vector ds;
double dr;
double aAngular;

CalculateImprovedLoads (); // find the current forces and moments

// integrate linear equation of motion for k1, k1a
a = totalForce / totalMass;
k1 = a * deltaTime;
aAngular = totalMoment.z / totalMass;
k1a = aAngular * deltaTime;

// now work on the copy to find k2, k2a
copy.velocity += k1;
copy.angularVelocity.z += k1a;
copy.CalculateImprovedLoads ();

a = Vector (0,0,0);
a = copy.totalForce / copy.totalMass;
k2 = a * deltaTime;
aAngular = copy.totalMoment.z / copy.inertia;
k2a =  aAngular * deltaTime;

// calculate the final resultant velocity, angular velocity,
// and position
velocity += .5 * (k1 + k2);
angularVelocity.z += .5 * (k1a + k2a);
position += velocity * deltaTime;

// correct the orientation angle
dr = RadiansToDegrees (angularVelocity.z * deltaTime);
orientation += dr;
// adjust the velocity vector back to local coords
velocityLocal = GlobalToLocalCoords_2D (-orientation, velocity);
}
```

Game Programming Theory

Next, I took Pgm04a and added a second attacking pirate ship, shown in green instead of red. When the simulation runs, the red attacking ship uses the Euler Method for the integration while the green ship uses the Improved Euler Method. Both attacking ships are shown. Further, both attackers are located at the exact same initial location, one over the top of the other. Each attacker ship is handled similarly during the simulation run. If there is any difference in the results between the two methods, you will see two ships appearing instead of one. The only difference in the client coding is

```
UpdateMove (a, deltaTime);
UpdateImprovedMove (a2, deltaTime);
```

The first attacker, a, uses the Euler method, while the second, a2, uses the improved Euler method. Figure 4.2 shows a screen shot showing the differences in the results between these two methods.

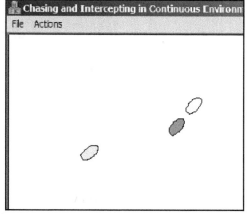

Figure 4.2 Improved Euler (green)
with Euler (red)

117

Rigid Body 2D Simulators

To create a rigid body 2D simulator, four key elements are required.

First is the model, which is your object to be simulated, here the pirate ship. Again, collect the specifications of the object so that they can be programmed.

Second is the method by which you integrate the equations of motion. The Euler method is very fast in terms of calculation speed. The Improved Euler method is slower but more accurate. There are other methods available which require even more computing power but which yield greater accuracy.

Third is the method or methods to allow and handle user controlling information. In these examples, there is no method for the user to control either ship, primarily because in a Windows programming environment, such is closely tied to the Windows platform and the presumed student programming background is only basic C++ programming. Windows programming is an entire course in and of itself.

Fourth is the method used to render the results on the screen. In a real Windows game, the rendering is done using the graphical user interface and utilizing DirectX. Often the ships would be small, artistically done, bitmap images, not the crude pencil drawings I am using here. Again, such programming greatly exceeds the level of programming required for this course.

This course covers the first two steps of your simulation. In the advanced courses, for example DirectX Programming, we will add in the remaining two key steps.

Programming Problems

Chapter 5 Flocking and Potential Function-Based Movement

Often in games, the computer must control a group of units, such as a flock of birds flying, a herd of grazing animals, a swarm of insects, a squadron of fighter planes. In nature, these groups tend to operate somewhat together. Observe a swarm of birds flying south for the winter. They travel in a loose formation. Each individual unit is moving independently of the others, yet in the same general direction. This behavior is called flocking, a loosely coordinated group movement. Flocking adds realism to game simulations.

Craig Reynolds defined the basic algorithms for this in his 1987 SIGGRAPH paper "Flocks, Herds, and Schools: A Distributed Behavioral Model." He coined the word "boids" to refer to his simulated flocks, which closely resemble schools of fish or flocks of birds. Go out and observe some flocks. Notice that sometimes the flock has a leader; when the leader moves, so do all of the others, yet they all move in roughly the same direction.

Potential functions can provide an alternative to the chasing and evading methods of the first chapter. Those required a good deal of checking logic to implement. With a potential function, the complexity of control logic is replaced by one simple equation that calculates the force between the two units and controls the resultant movement, chasing or avoiding.

Flocking

I invite you to go out and watch some flocks or recall some you have seen. At one moment, all of the flock is moving more or less in one direction. Then the tip changes direction and the rest of the swarm follows suit rather like a wave motion which propagates throughout the flock. The basic model devised by Craig Reynolds assumes that there is no leader in the flock, the flock operates as if it has a group mind controlling its motion. Given this situation, his model to predict the behavior is governed by three simple rules.

1. Cohesion: each unit steers towards the average position of its neighbors

2. Alignment: each unit steers so as to align itself with the average heading of its neighbors

3. Separation: each unit steers to avoid hitting its neighbors

Thus, each unit must be able to steer, be aware of its local surroundings, be aware of where the group is heading. Once more, let's not get heavily involved in the rigid two dimensional body physics of the units. Save that until later. Instead, I apply a steering force similar to the last chapter.

These same principles apply to a tile-based game as well. Use the line of sight methods heading toward a specific point expressed as tile coordinates (row, col).

What do we mean by a unit being aware of its local surroundings? Each unit has a forward field of view that extends some radius r outward from its point of view and encompasses an angular degree field of view as shown in Figure 5-1.

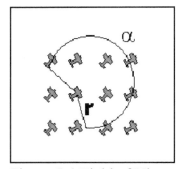

Figure 5-1 Field of View

This field of view angle can be large or small. The larger it is, the more neighbors it can see. If the angle is very small, it can only see the one in front of it and the flocking action is more like a straight line parade than a flock. Both have their uses. If a squadron of biplanes is being simulated, as in the figure above, then a wide field of view is best. If, however, you are simulating a platoon of soldiers marching to their combat zone, then a very narrow field of view is desired so that they march more or less in a single line, following their point man.

The next consideration applies to the three rules. When implementing these three rules, each rule provides some input into the final result. One rule should not be allowed to dominate over the other two. For example, if we make the separation rule, avoiding other units, to be paramount, the overall effect will be for the flock to disperse. If we make the cohesion rule so strong that it totally dominates the simulation, then the units will be so condensed that they will not be able to avoid other units or objects, collisions will result.

How are these rules combined into a whole package?

There is no hard and fast formula that completely handles the integration of the three rules. However, if you allow the steering of a unit to be a combination from all three rules, your simulation stands a good chance of being realistic. Still, you will need to do some fine tuning by trial and error to make the best looking action in the game.

When the units are far apart, the separation rule (avoidance of collisions) ought to supply very little to the overall solution, while the cohesion rule adds the largest component to the result. When the units are very close together, then the separation rule has dominance over cohesion, since they are so close together that following others can hardly be avoided. Thus, the avoidance or separation rule should be formulated based upon distance, the inverse of the distance. That way, when they are close, a larger factor is applied, but when units are farther apart, the inverse of the distance then adds in a much smaller factor. Similarly with alignment. If the unit's current alignment is way off from the group, make a larger steering correction; if the unit's alignment is close to the average, make only a small change.

Of course, the field of view ahead becomes a critical factor. If a unit has a very small forward field of view, few neighbors can be seen, only the few directly in front of it are visible. Overall, this tends to force the group of units into a line formation. If a unit has a wide field of view, it's likely that a lot of neighbors are visible, yielding a group move, more or less.

Those units who find themselves at the "head of the pack" become "leaders" of those who are located behind them. That is, those at the head with no units in front of them act as leaders for those who are following behind them. This can add a some realism to a herd animal pack, the group follows the ones in the lead, whether they are going in the "right direction" or not. On the other hand, the direction the leaders are going might be subject to other requirements indicating a higher intelligence. For example, when in the lead, a unit might have orders to intercept the enemy units, if possible. These "interceptor leaders" can fly a direct intercept course while the flock behind it ought to follow them. The sample program will utilize both leaders and interceptors. If these do not make sense in your game, omit the relevant coding.

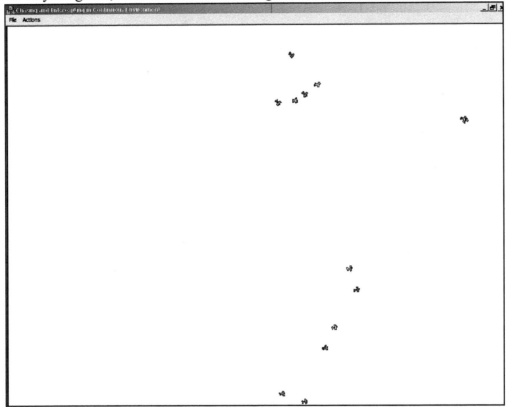

Figure 5.2 Flocking Flying Boats

In Figure 5.2, the defender is shown in yellow. Interceptors are always green. Basic flocking units are red, except when they become promoted to leaders, in which case they are blue.

Implementing the Flocking Algorithm in a Continuous Environment (Pgm05a)

Let's use my Flying Boat example from the last chapter. Instead of drawing the ugly looking boats, let's draw them looking like small biplanes, looking at them from the topside downward. The class has a few alterations. I added an enumerated identifier called Who which identifies an instance as being the Defender or the Attacker. Flocking applies to the attacker boats.

```
/******************************************************************/
/*                                                                */
/* Class: FlyingBoat                                              */
```

```
/*                                                                       */
/************************************************************************/

enum Who { Attacker, Defender };

class FlyingBoat {
public:
 Who      who;              // Attacker or Defender
 bool     isInterceptor;
 bool     isLeader;
```

Additionally, the pair of bools specify whether or not this flying boat is a leader or an interceptor. The flocking calculations will be specifying a variable amount of steering jet push force, depending on the situation. Hence, I needed to provide a second version of the SetJets() function.

```
void SetJets (JetsOn which, double amount);
```

Otherwise, our FlyingBoat class is pretty much the same. Below are the minor changes to add these new member data.

```
FlyingBoat::FlyingBoat () {
 width = 100;
...
 Initialize ();
 isInterceptor = isLeader = false;
}

void FlyingBoat::SetWho (Who w) {
 who = w;
}

void FlyingBoat::Initialize () {
...
 isInterceptor = isLeader = false;
}

void FlyingBoat::SetStartingValues (Vector pos, Vector vel,
                                    bool interceptor, bool leader) {
 Initialize ();
 position = pos;
 velocity = vel;
 vel.Normalize ();
 double angle = acos (vel.x) * 180 / PI;
 if (vel.x > 0 && vel.y < 0) angle -= 90;
 if (vel.x < 0 && vel.y > 0) angle += 90;
 orientation = angle;
 isLeader = leader;
 isInterceptor = interceptor;
```

```
}

void FlyingBoat::SetJets (JetsOn which, double amount) {
 portPushForce = starboardPushForce = Vector (0, 0, 0);
 if (amount > SteeringJetPush) {
  amount = SteeringJetPush;
 }
 else if (amount < EPS) {
  amount = 0;
 }
 if (which == Port) {
  portPushForce = Vector (0, -amount, 0);
 }
 else if (which == Starboard) {
  starboardPushForce = Vector (0, amount, 0);
 }
}
```

The Windows CMainFrame class adds the new instances.

```
FlyingBoat defender;
FlyingBoat flock[FLOCKSIZE];
FlockViewAngle angle;
```

The implementation function is called when the user selects the menu item DoSimulation. It begins by initializing the defender and the array of attackers in the flock array, displaying them at their starting locations on the screen.

```
void CMainFrame::DoSimulation () {
 int i;
 {
  CClientDC dc (this);
  defender.SetStartingValues (Vector (800, 600, 0), Vector (15,-15,0),
                                      false, false);
  RenderFlyingBoat (dc, defender, DefenderColor);
  int row = -1;
  for (i=0; i<FLOCKSIZE; i++) {
   int j = i % 4;
   if (j == 0) row++;
   int y = 700 + 30*row;
   flock[i].SetStartingValues (Vector (100 + 30*j, y, 0),
                                Vector (20, 20, 0),
                  i>FLOCKSIZE/2, (y == 700 ? true : false));
   RenderFlyingBoat (dc, flock[i], AttackerColor);
  }
 }

 int    frameCount = 0;
 double deltaTime = .01;
```

Game Programming Theory

The main simulation loop first moves the defender and then handles the entire flock, one flying boat at a time, calling DoFlocking() followed by UpdateMove(). All of the actual work is done in DoFlocking().

```
long count = 0;
while (count < 230) {
 UpdateMove (defender, deltaTime);
 HandleGoingOffScreen (defender);

 for (i=0; i<FLOCKSIZE; i++) {
  DoFlocking (flock, i, angle, defender, FLOCKSIZE);
  UpdateMove (flock[i], deltaTime);
  HandleGoingOffScreen (flock[i]);
 }

 if (frameCount >= 100) {
  CClientDC dc (this);
  dc.Rectangle (0, 0, size.cx, size.cy);
  RenderFlyingBoat (dc, defender, DefenderColor);
  for (i=0; i<FLOCKSIZE; i++) {
   RenderFlyingBoat (dc, flock[i], AttackerColor);
  }
  frameCount = 0;
  count++;
 }
 frameCount++;
 }
}
```

The Simulation.h file contains the function prototypes and the enumerated type FlockViewAngle, which allows us to choose the field of view for all of the attacker units.

```
#pragma once
#include "FlyingBoat.h"

enum FlockViewAngle { NotUsed, WideView, MediumView, NarrowView };

void UpdateMove (FlyingBoat& b, double deltaTime);
void DoFlocking (FlyingBoat flock[], int id, FlockViewAngle view,
                 const FlyingBoat& defender, int flockSize);
```

The function DoFlocking() is given the array of flying boats, the id of the current boat to do, the view angle enum, the array size, and a reference to the defender boat. The function defines a number of constants, including the arbitrarily chosen angles that correspond to the three possible views. The angles are in degrees. Since in any simulation, one will have to adjust the three rules so that one does not dominate over the others, tweaking factors are defined here as well.

```
void DoFlocking (FlyingBoat flock[], int id, FlockViewAngle view,
                 const FlyingBoat& defender, int flockSize) {
 // adjustable field of views
```

```
const int WideViewRadius = 200;
const int MediumViewRadius = 50;
const int NarrowViewRadius = 30;

// adjustable angle factors 1 => 45 degrees
const int AngleFactorFrontView = 1; // 1 = 45 degrees
const int AngleFactorBackView = 1;  // 1 = 45 degrees

// adjustable flocking parameters
const double TweakSeparationFactor = .551;
const double TweakCohesionFactor = 10.;
const double TweakAlignmentFactor = 86.;
const double TweakChaseFactor = 100.;
const double TweakInterceptFactor = 100;
const double TweakSteeringForce = 1;

const double PI = acos (-1.);

// temp variables to avoid looking these values up repeatedly
double boatLength = flock[id].length;
double boatMiddle = boatLength / 2;

int  numberNeighbors = 0;
// holds the number of visible neighbors to this one

Vector avgPosition;   // initially 0,0,0
Vector avgVelocity;   // initially 0,0,0
Vector steeringForce; // initially 0,0,0
Vector distanceFrom, u, v, distanceLocal;

// work variables
double m;
int    numberInFront = 0;
bool   inView;
int    RadiusFactor;
int    j;

// determine if flocking is needed or not
bool mustDoFlock = view == NotUsed ? false : true;

// set the current view angle based on type of view
double viewType = view == WideView ? WideViewRadius :
        (view == MediumView ? MediumViewRadius : NarrowViewRadius);

// id specifies the current boat for which we need to determine
// the correct action to take
// for each boat in the flock not this one, calculate its situation with
// respect to this boat and then set up this boat's action/reaction to the
// whole flock
```

Game Programming Theory

The first action is to loop through the flock array and compute the number of other boats that are in front of this one. Next, find out if the current flock boat is in view by this one, and if so, accumulate the velocity and position vectors so that an average can be later calculated. However, the separation rule must be applied to each individual boat in the flock. The other two rules are applied using the average velocity and position of the flock.

```
for (j=0; j<flockSize; j++) {
  if (id == j) continue; // do not do this one
  inView = false;          // assume current one is not in view as yet
  // find the global and local distance current boat is from this one
  distanceFrom = flock[j].position - flock[id].position;
  distanceLocal = GlobalToLocalCoords_2D (-flock[id].orientation,
                                          distanceFrom);
  // now determine if the current one is in front of this one
  if (distanceLocal.x > 0 &&
      fabs (distanceLocal.y) <
            fabs (distanceLocal.x) * AngleFactorFrontView &&
      distanceFrom.Magnitude() <= boatLength * NarrowViewRadius) {
    numberInFront++;
  }
}
```

Remember in this simulation, the boats sail forward along the +x axis, not the y axis. Let's look at the wide field of view first, shown in Figure 2.3.

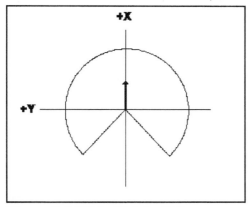

Figure 2.3 Wide Field of View

A boat is in view if the local x distance is positive, that is ahead of us. However, it may also be visible if it's local x distance is less than ours, appearing in either of our two flank side views. By taking the absolute value of the x and y values, we reduce our checking to just one side, not two. If the other boat's y value is greater than the x distance time AngleFactorBackView, which has been set to 1.0, then it is visible. A value of 1.0 for this angle factor yields a 45 degree area of coverage. If the angle factor is less than 1.0, then the area will be closer to the -x axis, giving an even greater peripheral viewing area. If greater than 1.0, it is closer to the y axis, giving an even larger blind spot to our rear. Again, the amount of side viewing area is a programmer tweakable quantity.

```
  // now determine whether or not the current boat is in view of this
```

```
//  one, based on the viewing angle and location, setting both the
//  bool inview and the RadiusFactor
if (view == WideView) {
 inView = distanceLocal.x > 0 ||
          (distanceLocal.x < 0 && fabs (distanceLocal.y) >
             fabs (distanceLocal.x) * AngleFactorBackView);
 RadiusFactor = WideViewRadius;
}
```

For the medium view, the local distance along the x axis must be positive, there is no side viewing allowed.

```
else if (view ==MediumView) {
 inView = distanceLocal.x > 0;
 RadiusFactor = MediumViewRadius;
}
```

For the narrow view, we limit the viewing angle even more. Not only does the local distance between us have to be positive, but also it has to reside in the narrow forward cone of view, this time dictated by AngleFactorFrontView, which is set to 1.0. A value of 1.0 means 45 degrees to either side of straight ahead. If the angle factor is greater than 1.0, then the field of view is enlarged, getting closer to the y axis. If the angle factor is less than 1.0, the forward field of view is even more restricted than 90 degrees total.

```
else if (view == NarrowView) {
 inView = distanceLocal.x > 0 &&
          fabs (distanceLocal.y) < fabs (distanceLocal.x) *
                                    AngleFactorFrontView;
 RadiusFactor = NarrowViewRadius;
}
```

Now, if the current one is in view of this one and both are either interceptors or both are not interceptors, add the current one into the sums of velocity and position, incrementing the number of neighbors seen by this one.

```
if(inView && (flock[id].isInterceptor == flock[j].isInterceptor)) {
 if (distanceFrom.Magnitude() <= boatLength * RadiusFactor) {
  avgPosition += flock[j].position;
  avgVelocity += flock[j].velocity;
  numberNeighbors++;
 }
}
```

At last, we can apply the separation rule between the current one in the flock and this one. If they are close, the steering force to be applied is larger; if they are distant, the steering force is smaller because of the division by separation distance.

```
if (inView) {
 if(distanceFrom.Magnitude() <= boatLength * 2) {
```

```
    m = distanceLocal.y > 0 ? -TweakSeparationFactor :
        (distanceLocal.y < 0 ? TweakSeparationFactor : 0);
    steeringForce.y += m * TweakSteeringForce /
                          distanceFrom.Magnitude();
    }
  }
}
```

Here the loop has ended. We have processed all boats and applied the separation rule. Now we can calculate the averages and apply the cohesion and alignment rules, but only if we are dealing with a flocking action and if there is at least one neighbor.

```
if (mustDoFlock && numberNeighbors > 0) {
```

To apply the cohesion rule, we must find the average position of all neighbors and the deviation of this one from that average.

```
    avgPosition /= numberNeighbors; // find avg position of neighbors
    v = flock[id].velocity;         // normalize this one's velocity
    v.Normalize();
    u = avgPosition - flock[id].position;
    u.Normalize();
    if (fabs (v * u) < 1.0) { // acos needs a value between -1 and +1
     // convert u into local coords. if y < 0, neighbor is to our left
     Vector w = GlobalToLocalCoords_2D (-flock[id].orientation, u);
     m = w.y < 0 ? -TweakCohesionFactor :
                 (w.y > 0 ? TweakCohesionFactor : 0);
     steeringForce.y += m * TweakSteeringForce * acos (v * u) / PI;
    }
```

To apply the alignment rule, we must find the average velocity of the flock and compare it to this one's velocity.

```
    avgVelocity /= numberNeighbors; // get avg velocity
    u = avgVelocity;                // and normalize it
    u.Normalize();
    v = flock[id].velocity;         // normalize this one's velocity
    v.Normalize();
    if (fabs (v * u) < 1.) { // acos needs a value between -1 and +1
     Vector w = GlobalToLocalCoords_2D (-flock[id].orientation, u);
     m = w.y < 0 ? -TweakAlignmentFactor :
                 (w.y > 0 ? TweakAlignmentFactor : 0);
     steeringForce.y += m * TweakSteeringForce * acos (v * u) / PI;
    }
}
```

At this point, simple flocking is complete. However, if the units are combatants, as in this case, the units might be chasing, intercepting, or perhaps evading. Ideally one would have some way of telling whether or not the flock is to chase the enemy unit(s) or evade or ignore the other units. Here I hard coded such a bool to true so that we can see how to add in these effects.

```
bool chase = true;
```

To deal with a chase or intercept situation in a flock, first determine if this unit is a leader or not. If no other flocking units are in front of this one, it is promoted to a leader.

```
if (chase) {
flock[id].isLeader = numberInFront == 0 ? true : false;
```

Further, if this one is a leader or if we are not flocking, then that boat can either chase or intercept. Here, the isInterceptor bool differentiates between these two possibilities to illustrate how it is programmed.

```
if (flock[id].isLeader || !mustDoFlock) {
 if(!flock[id].isInterceptor) {
 // here, go chase the defender
 u = defender.position;
 Vector d = u - flock[id].position;
 Vector w = GlobalToLocalCoords_2D (-flock[id].orientation, d);
 m = w.y< 0 ? -TweakChaseFactor : (w.y > 0 ? TweakChaseFactor : 0);
 steeringForce.y += m * TweakSteeringForce;
 }
 else {
 // here, do an intercept of the defender
 Vector s1, s2, s12;
 double tClose;
 // find the closing velocity
 Vector Vr12 = defender.velocity - flock[id].velocity;
 s12 = defender.position - flock[id].position; // range to close
 tClose = s12.Magnitude() / Vr12.Magnitude();   // time to close
 s1 = defender.position + defender.velocity * tClose;
 Vector Target = s1;
 s2 = s1 - flock[id].position;
 Vector w = GlobalToLocalCoords_2D (-flock[id].orientation, s2);
 m = w.y < 0 ? -TweakInterceptFactor :
                     (w.y > 0 ? TweakInterceptFactor : 0);
 steeringForce.y += m * TweakSteeringForce;
 }
 }
}
```

At this point, the game engine would also need to check for and avoid collisions with other non-flying boats, such as land obstacles, shoals, rock out-croppings and such. Thus far, we have not yet discussed collisions and their detection and impact. Hence, I will do nothing about collisions here.

At this point, all of the possible forces have been accumulated for this current boat. The last step is to apply the requested amount of push thrust to the boat as its steering force.

```
double amount = steeringForce.Magnitude ();
if (amount > EPS) {
 if (steeringForce.y > EPS) {
 flock[id].SetJets (FlyingBoat::Starboard, amount);
```

```
    }
   else {
     flock[id].SetJets (FlyingBoat::Port, amount);
    }
  }
  else {
    flock[id].SetJets (FlyingBoat::None);
  }
}
```

With the forces applied now known, UpdateMove() calls IntegrateEuler() to calculate the new velocity and position of this boat. Look back again at Figure 5.2 which shows the ending positions of the ships after the simulation finished. Play around with Pgm05a, adjusting the various parameters significantly and see the results. Become familiar with how these three rules are applied and interact and how you can adjust them.

Alternate Method for Movement: Potential Function-Based Movement

In molecular physics, the Lenard-Jones potential function is used to describe the interatomic molecular potential energy between molecules. It is used to describe how a chunk of matter stays together, such as a block of iron, a pencil, your keyboard, your mouse. Molecules of an object tend to stay sufficiently close so that the overall effect is the object appears solid, even though the individual atoms and molecules are in motion. They are constrained from getting too close to one another and yet also restrained from getting too far apart from each other, yielding a "solid." This potential energy function is used to describe such behavior. The equation for the potential energy is this.

$$U = -\frac{A}{r^n} + \frac{B}{r^m}$$

U is the potential energy, r is the distance between the two molecules, A and B are forces of attraction and repulsion, n and m are powers chosen to fit the function to the molecules in question.

What is the behavior of this function? We can view the positive term as a repulsion force tending to keep two objects apart, while the negative term is an attraction force tending to make the two objects come together or a cohesion factor. At large distances, r, neither term exerts any real force on the two objects. As the distance decreases, depending upon our choice for m and n, the attraction force can be stronger, but as they get too close, the repulsion force can dominate. It's all in our choice of n and m values. If we let n be 2 and m be 3, then the repulsion force dies down more swiftly than the attraction force. That is, when the distance between the two objects is too small, the repulsion force dominates, but quickly subsides as the distance is increased at which point attraction dominates. Yet as the distance increases further, neither plays any significant role in the forces acting between the two objects.

Ah, this sounds awfully parallel to flocking's cohesion and separation rules, as well as chasing and evading rules! In fact, this is precisely correct. We can replace our basic chase algorithm with a potential function and accomplish similar results. We must just choose n, m, A, and B to create a good behavior in our simulations.

In Pgm05b, I reworked the previous Pgm04a with the flying boats to utilize a potential based function for the basic chase algorithm. Since the amount of steering force applied will be a variable amount, I added the alternative SetJets() function which takes the amount to be applied as well as which pusher, port or starboard.

The only other changed coding is that for the DoBasicChase() function. Here, I inserted the potential function, using arbitrary values for the four parameters.

```
void DoBasicChase (FlyingBoat& a, FlyingBoat& d) {
 Vector lineOfSight = d.position - a.position;
 Vector v = lineOfSight;
 v.Normalize ();
 double A = 2000;
 double B = 4000;
 double n = 2;
 double m = 3;
 double r = lineOfSight.Magnitude () / a.length;
 double U = - A / pow (r, n) + B / pow (r, m);

 Vector local = GlobalToLocalCoords_2D (-a.orientation, U * v);
 double amount = local.Magnitude ();
 if (local.y < EPS)
  a.SetJets (FlyingBoat::Port, amount);
 else if (local.y > EPS)
  a.SetJets (FlyingBoat::Starboard, amount);
 else
  a.SetJets (FlyingBoat::None, 0.);
}
```

Run the sample program and notice that once more we have a nice looking chase, proving that the potential based function does indeed work well in these situations. This potential function can then be used for both chasing and evading scenarios. It can also be used to handle avoiding obstacles that may be in an object's path. Even more interestingly it can be used to create a swarm of objects, such as bees or wasps, which generally swarm and hover about as a collective unit.

However, there is a side effect, significant time is required to do the calculation, primarily because of the two calls to the power function. If there are a lot of objects on which this potential function calculation must be performed, execution game speed may suffer. Hence, in such cases, one should insert a test of the actual separation distances. If the distance is too large for the potential function to exert any significant force, skip doing the time consuming calculation.

Programming Problems

Problem 5-1 Buffalo on the Move

Create a tile-based simulation of a herd of twelve buffalos and one hunter, using the Screen class provided. The hunter's initial location is at row 0, column 0, or the upper left corner of the screen. Create a herd of buffalo which begin located somewhere in the lower right quadrant of the screen.

Buffalo properties include its position vector and its speed vector along with a bool for isLeader and hasDetectedHunter, both initially false. Buffalo's speed can be zero, one or two tiles per turn, discrete values. Always round to the nearest integer amount after calculations are done.

A buffalo can detect the hunter when the distance vector magnitude is 10 tiles or less. Once detected, the leader attempts to get out of the way of the hunter, by turning and accelerating at once to a maximum speed magnitude of two tiles per turn, subject to the separation rule.

The separation rule is that no two buffalo can occupy the same tile location (row and column). All buffalos in the herd will follow the leader at all times, maintaining a tight cohesion and alignment, subject to their maximum speeds allowed. Should a buffalo move off the screen, use a method similar to the one that I have used in the boat simulation to find it a new location that is on the screen.

The four arrow keys control the movement of the hunter, whose maximum movement is also two tiles per turn. The hunter's objective is to move across the screen (not moving off screen at any time) and get to the bottom right corner of the screen. If a buffalo should occupy the same space as the hunter, the game is over and the hunter loses. If the hunter reaches the bottom corner, the hunter wins and the game simulation is over.

Note that the acceleration of a buffalo can be 0, 1 or 2 tiles (absolute value). Thus, you can use greatly simplified motion equations in the simulation. There is no angular motion component, just a linear acceleration vector.

Chapter 6 Pathfinding Algorithms

Pathfinding means to locate and follow a path from where an object is located to some known destination location. This is one of the most commonly needed algorithms in many games. Further, the number of considerations surrounding finding the path can be enormous and no single method works in every scenario. Let's examine some of these scenarios.

Are there any obstacles present? Are they stationary or moving? Is the destination location stationary or moving? Are there any terrain complications, such as a swamp, mountains, hills, roads, and forests? Can the object move equally well across all such terrain features or is there a bonus for certain terrain? For example, vehicles move better along roads than across country and better across country than in mountainous terrain. Boats must be constrained to water paths. Is the shortest path the one that is desired or is the path that takes the least time what is needed? Perhaps, the object is just meandering about exploring the land. The list of possibilities can be very lengthy.

We have already discussed two methods for path finding. In chapter one, the most basic of all methods incremented or decremented the object's position vector each turn, based on whether its x and y locations were greater than or less than the destination's coordinates. This yielded a non-optimum looking path in many situations; both x and y coordinates were decremented or incremented until one arrived at the destination's coordinate and then the remaining travel was either horizontal or vertical until the destination was reached, a highly non-optimum path.

We also saw that the Bresenham algorithm corrected this deficiency, computing a straight line path to the destination point. In many situations, this algorithm is all that we need. However, the moment that obstacles are present or terrain considerations arise, both of these simple solutions fail.

Dealing with Obstacles

Several possible answers to obstacles in the way of pathfinding are available. One simple approach when a barrier to travel is encountered is to move in a random direction this turn. Hopefully, the next turn a better situation will arise. For example, a large boulder lies between Frodo and a goblin, such that the goblin cannot see Frodo. Have the goblin move in some randomly chosen direction, but obviously not into the boulder, this turn. Next turn, the goblin may well be able to see Frodo and continue on its straight line path to intercept him. This works well if there are few obstacles present. The pseudocode for random move is

> if destination is visible then
>> move toward destination
> else
>> move in a random direction, but not into the obstacle

However, when the obstacle is large or are numerous, this does not work at all well because way too many moves may be required before the destination becomes visible, if at all. Instead, in such situations, we need to trace a path around the obstacle.

Tracing a Path Around Obstacles

Let's begin with what we know: the location of the object and the location of the destination point. Given these two points, we can use the Bresenham line of sight to calculate a straight line path to the desired location. The object then begins to walk that path. However, when it encounters an object at one of the locations into which it needed to move while following the calculated path, the object must stop and navigate around the barrier.

How do we navigate around the barrier? We know the direction that the object would have been moving had the obstacle not been encountered. In a tile based game, the eight possibilities are shown in Figure 6-1.

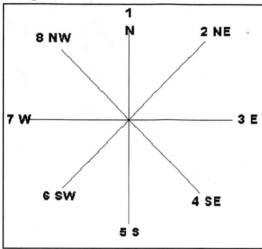

Figure 6-1 Compass Rose

Knowing the intended direction, we can then make some intelligent choices. For example, assume that the intended path was due north, direction 1 in Figure 6-1, and that there is an obstacle at that location. We should try direction 8 or 2 next. Should those also encounter an obstacle, try 7 or 3. Failing those, then try 6 or 4. As a last resort, try 5, backing up. If the original direction was due south, direction 5, then we should try 4 or 6 next and so on.

Eight constant arrays of can hold the possible choices, given an original direction that was blocked. All we need to do is determine which choice of the eight is the original direction and copy that constant array into our working array of possible tries. Methodically, we can then iterate through this array of direction possibilities, trying the most beneficial ones first, backing up, last.

Once we have moved the object to a new location by moving along the barrier, we can then check and see if the object has now rejoined at last the original path it was following. If so, the tracing is finished, just continue to follow the original path. Pgm06a illustrates this algorithm, showing the path the goblin takes to reach Frodo, moving around the intervening forest trees. See Figure 6-2.

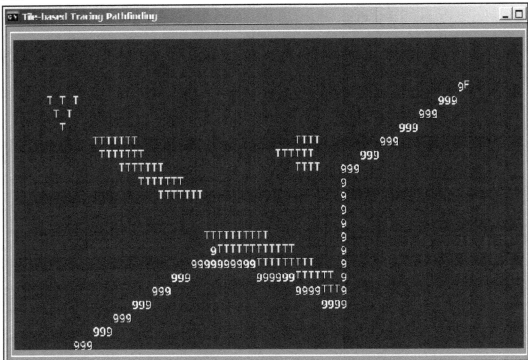

Figure 6-2 Simple Tracing Around Obstacle

Notice one non-optimum aspect: once clear of the forest, the goblin moves due north until it finds the original path it ought to be following. A much better algorithm would be to have the goblin, once clear of the forest, strike out on a new straight line path to Frodo. This is shown in Figure 6-3, the output from the second half of Pgm06a. Here, when the original path to Frodo is obstructed, once a possible move is made, a new path is constructed. If the next step on that path is obstructed, again another possible bypass move is made and a new path from there is calculated. The net result is that once finally clear of the forest, the goblin strikes out on a straight line path to Frodo, a much more realistic scenario indeed. The drawback is the overhead of repeated calculations of new possible paths each time.

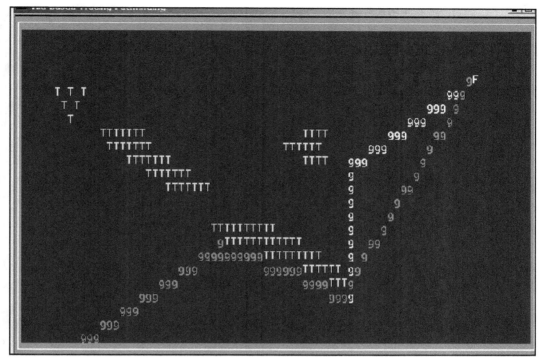

Figure 6.3 Tracing Around Obstacle with Improved Algorithm

Let's see how each method can be implemented. The starting point is the playing field, which I stored in a file, field.txt. The border 'T' letters will not be shown, I used them for a visual reference. The other 'T' represent trees of the dense obstructions.

```
TTTTTTTTTTTTTTTTTTTTTTTTTTTTTTTTTTTTTTTTTTTTTTTTTTTTTTTTTTTTTTTTTTTTTTTTTTTTTTTTTTTTTT
T                                                                                    T
T                                                                                    T
T                                                                                    T
T                                                                                    T
T        T  T  T                                                                      T
T         T  T                                                                        T
T          T                                                                          T
T              TTTTTTT                              TTTT                              T
T              TTTTTTT                              TTTTTT                            T
T               TTTTTTT                             TTTT                              T
T                TTTTTTT                                                              T
T                 TTTTTTT                                                             T
T                                                                                     T
T                                                                                     T
T                             TTTTTTTTT                                               T
T                             TTTTTTTTTTTT                                            T
T                              TTTTTTTTTT                                             T
T                                  TTTTTT                                             T
T                                     TTT                                             T
T                                                                                     T
T                                                                                     T
T                                                                                     T
T                                                                                     T
TTTTTTTTTTTTTTTTTTTTTTTTTTTTTTTTTTTTTTTTTTTTTTTTTTTTTTTTTTTTTTTTTTTTTTTTTTTTTTTTTTTTTT
```

139

Game Programming Theory

After the usual includes and const ints that define the screen dimensions and hence array sizes, I also included some const ints for the arrow keys, though they are not yet needed. Next, I defined a structure to encapsulate a position location in the two-dimensional tiled space, Point. However, a structure can have member functions just as a class. For coding convenience, I coded two Point constructor functions, one that takes no parameters and one that takes an x, y pair of values. Also, the algorithms will need to compare two points to see if they are the same. The easiest way to handle this is to provide two operator functions, == and !=. These work similar to the operator overloaded functions of a class.

```cpp
#include <iostream>
#include <fstream>
#include <iomanip>
using namespace std;
#include "Screen.h"

const int MaxRows = 24;
const int MaxCols = 80;
const int MaxPathElements = 200;
const int NotOnPath = -1;

const int UpArrow = 72; // the special key codes for the arrow keys
const int DownArrow = 80;
const int LeftArrow = 75;
const int RightArrow = 77;

// Point encapsulates a tile based game location on the screen
// two constructor functions are provided for convenience
// additionally, two comparison operator functions allow easy testing
// of a pair of points - by having the two operator function
// prototypes imbedded within the structure definition, they then
// apply to the Point object, similar to classes
struct Point {
 int x;
 int y;
 Point () { x = y = 0; }
 Point (int xx, int yy) { x=xx; y=yy; }
 bool operator!= (const Point& p) const { return x!=p.x || y!=p.y; }
 bool operator== (const Point& p) const { return x==p.x && y==p.y; }
};

void LoadField (char field[][MaxCols+1], Screen::Color fieldColor[][MaxCols]);
void ShowField (Screen& s, char field[][MaxCols+1],
                Screen::Color fieldColor[][MaxCols]);
void Bresenham (Point pathX[], int max, Point& mover, const Point& target);
void DoTraceMethod1 (Screen& s, Point goblin, const Point& frodo,
                char field[][MaxCols+1],
                Screen::Color fieldColor[][MaxCols]);
bool IsValidPath (char field[][MaxCols+1], const Point& p);
Point TracePath (char field[][MaxCols+1], const Point& g,  const int tries[]);
void ObtainTravelDirection (const Point& g, const Point& p, int tries[]);
```

```
int  BackOnPath (const Point& g, const Point path[], int iStart);
void DoTraceMethod2 (Screen& s, Point goblin, const Point& frodo,
                char field[][MaxCols+1],
                Screen::Color fieldColor[][MaxCols]);
```

The main() function sets up the screen object as usual. Next, it calls LoadField() followed by ShowField(). Frodo and the goblin are just instances of a Point structure in this example, no other properties are needed, only their respective locations. Both are shown at their starting locations. The demonstration calls DoTraceMethod1() and, after pressing any key, calls DoTraceMethod2().

```
int main () {
  cin.sync_with_stdio (); // if you want to use cin
  Screen s (Screen::Blue, Screen::BrightYellow);

  s.SetTitle ("Tile-based Tracing Pathfinding");
  s.DrawBox (0, 0, 24, 79, Screen::Gray, Screen::BrightYellow);

  char          field[MaxRows][MaxCols+1];      // the playing field
  Screen::Color fieldColor[MaxRows][MaxCols];//colors of obstacles

  // load and show the entire field
  LoadField (field, fieldColor);
  ShowField (s, field, fieldColor);

  // set up and show the fixed Frodo character
  Point frodo (70, 4);
  s.GoToXY (frodo.x, frodo.y);
  s << 'F';

  // setup and show the initial position of the goblin
  Point goblin (10, 23);
  s.GoToXY (goblin.x, goblin.y);
  s << 'g';
  s.GoToXY (0, 25);

  // Method 1: follow original path to destination, moving around
  // any obstacles, once clear, move directly back to the original
  // path and then resume the original course
  DoTraceMethod1 (s, goblin, frodo, field, fieldColor);
  s.GoToXY (frodo.x, frodo.y);
  s << 'F';
  s.GoToXY (0, 25);
  s.GetAnyKey ();

  // Method 2: follow original path to destination, when an
  // obstacle is encountered, find a reasonable next move,
  // recalculate a new direct path to destination and try to
```

141

```
// follow that repeat when any new obstacle appears
DoTraceMethod2 (s, goblin, frodo, field, fieldColor);
s.GoToXY (frodo.x, frodo.y);
s << 'F';
s.GoToXY (0, 25);
s.GetAnyKey ();

  return 0;
}

// Load the playing field with Trees that block movement and line of
sight
void    LoadField    (char    field[][MaxCols+1],Screen::Color
fieldColor[][MaxCols]) {
 ifstream infile ("field.txt");
 if (!infile) {
  cerr << "Error: cannot open file field.txt\n";
  exit (1);
 }

 // each string is 80 characters long, plus 1 for the null terminator
 // to make inputting of the strings easy
 int row, col;
 for (row=0; row<MaxRows; row++) {
  infile.get (field[row], MaxCols+1);
  char c;
  infile.get (c); // input the CR+LF codes marking the end of the line
 }

 // report any errors on input and abort
 if (!infile) {
  infile.close ();
  cerr << "Error: cannot input all rows and columns of the field\n";
  exit (2);
 }
 infile.close ();

 // now insert the proper colors into the fieldColor array where the
 // obstacles are located
 for (row=0; row<MaxRows; row++) {
  for (col=0; col<MaxCols; col++) {
   if (field[row][col] != ' ')
    fieldColor[row][col] = Screen::BrightGreen;
   else
    fieldColor[row][col] = Screen::BrightYellow;
  }
 }
}
```

```
// ShowField: displays all rows and columns ignoring the borders
// which have already been drawn. If you do not want to waste these
// locations, then display all 80 columns on all rows
void ShowField (Screen& s, char field[][MaxCols+1],
                Screen::Color fieldColor[][MaxCols]){
 for (int row=1; row<MaxRows; row++) {
  for (int col=1; col<MaxCols-1; col++) {
   s.GoToXY (col, row);
   s.OutputUCharWith (field[row][col], row, col, Screen::Blue,
                      fieldColor[row][col]);
  }
 }
}
```

I revised the Bresenham() function to accept more streamlined parameters, an array of Point structures for the path, and a pair of Point references for the mover and the target locations. This makes parameter passing easier. None of the basic coding has changed in any other way.

```
/******************************************************************/
/*                                                                */
/* Bresenham: calculates the straight line path to a target in    */
/*            a tile based game                                   */
/*   Revison to utilize a Point structure                         */
/*   path is the answer array of up to max elements which is      */
/*   filled with successive moves for the mover to reach the end  */
/*   target position where mover specifies the initial            */
/*   location of the moving element                               */
/*                                                                */
/******************************************************************/

void Bresenham (Point path[], int max, Point& mover, const Point& target)
{
 // nextX and nextY hold the orc's next position
 int nextX = mover.x;
 int nextY = mover.y;

 // deltaX and deltaY hold the difference between the locations
 int deltaX = target.x - mover.x;
 int deltaY = target.y - mover.y;

 // stepX and stepY hold how much to inc or dec each time
 int stepX = deltaX < 0 ? -1 : 1;
 int stepY = deltaY < 0 ? -1 : 1;

 // clear out the answer arrays, using invalid screen coord: -1
 for (int i=0; i<max; i++) {
  path[i] = Point (-1, -1);
 }

 // install the starting location in the answer arrays
```

```
path[0] = mover;

// double the total difference between locations
// and take the absolute value to remove negative signs
deltaX = abs (deltaX * 2);
deltaY = abs (deltaY * 2);

// set the current step to 1, [0] holds the original location
int currentStep = 1;
int fraction;

// two cases: is the x length greater than the y length?
if (deltaX > deltaY) {
 // x > y, so constantly move x but control when to move y
 // fraction controls times to move in y
 fraction = deltaY * 2 - deltaX;

 // now fill in all steps the orc must take to reach player
 while (nextX != target.x && currentStep < max) {
  if (fraction >= 0) { // fraction is still > 0, must move in y
   nextY += stepY;      // add another y step to total y move
   fraction -= deltaX; // remove one column amount
  }
  // here, we have moved enough in y to justify moving in x
  nextX += stepX;
  // now add in another y move for next iteration
  fraction += deltaY;
  // store this move in the answer array
  path[currentStep].x = nextX;
  path[currentStep++].y = nextY;
 }
}

// here, y is greater than the x length
else {
 // fraction controls times to move in x for each y move
 fraction = deltaX * 2 - deltaY;
 // fill in all steps the orc takes to get to the player
 while (nextY != target.y && currentStep < max) {
  if (fraction >= 0) { // fraction > 0, so must move in x
   nextX += stepX;      // add another x to total move
   fraction -= deltaY; // remove one row amount
  }
  // here we have moved enough in x to justify moving in y
  nextY += stepY;
  // add in the x move to fraction for next iteration
  fraction += deltaX;
  // store this move in the answer array
  path[currentStep].x = nextX;
  path[currentStep++].y = nextY;
```

144

```
    }
  }
}
```

Now for the actual algorithms. DoTraceMethod1() first calculates the line of sight path from the mover to the target, saving it in the array of Point structures called path. iPath stores the index of where we are at in this array, move by move. The array tries contains the directions to try to move toward when an obstacle is encountered. It is based upon the direction of movement that would have occurred, had the obstacle not been encountered. Obviously, going backwards is the worst choice, while veering slightly to the left or right would be the best choices to try first. When an obstacle is encountered, notice that the coding works its way around the object until it can move directly back onto the original line of sight path, before continuing on to the destination.

```
// DoTraceMethod1: Finds a path to destination and follows it until
// obstacle is found. Traces a reasonable way around it and then
// moves directly back to the original path and continues following
// the original path
void DoTraceMethod1 (Screen& s, Point goblin, const Point& frodo,
                     char field[][MaxCols+1],
                     Screen::Color fieldColor[][MaxCols]) {
  Point path[MaxPathElements];
  // construct one time the path to the destination point
  Bresenham (path, MaxPathElements, goblin, frodo);

  int iPath = 0;  // keeps track of the last used element of the path
  int tries[8];   // holds the original direction of travel when the
                  // obstacle was encountered so that reasonable way
                  // around the obstacle can be found
  Point g = goblin;
  Point proposed = path[iPath]; // the proposed next move

  // continue until we arrive at the destination point
  while (g != frodo) {
   // two possibilities: the next step is a valid location to use
   if (IsValidPath (field, proposed)) {
    iPath++;            // increment to get the next one to try
    // make this valid move by showing the goblin
    s.OutputUCharWith ('g', proposed.y, proposed.x, Screen::Blue,
                       Screen::BrightYellow);
    g = proposed;       // and place the goblin at this good location
    proposed = path[iPath]; // get the next possible location to try
   }

   // the next step hits an obstacle, so trace around it
   else {
    // first, find our direction of travel so we can make intelligent
    // attempts to move around the barrier - tries is filled with the
    // directions to try to get around the barrier
    ObtainTravelDirection (g, proposed, tries);
```

```
// make all moves necessary to get around the barrier
while (true) {
  // find the next location to which to move
  proposed = TracePath (field, g, tries);
  // show the goblin at the new location
  s.OutputUCharWith ('g', proposed.y, proposed.x, Screen::Blue,
                     Screen::BrightYellow);
  g = proposed; // and place goblin at this new location
  // find out if we are now back onto the original path
  // BackOnPath returns the index of the path array where we can now
  // continue on the original way or NotOnPath if we are not yet
  // back to the original path
  int x = BackOnPath (g, path, iPath);
  if (x != NotOnPath) { // here we have finally found the original
                        // path again
    iPath = x;          // so adjust the index into the path array
    break;              // and leave the trace around obatacle loop
  }
}
      }
    }
  }
}
```

The function BackOnPath() examines the original line of sight path we were following, beginning at that point where we had to leave it because of the obstacle. If our current location coincides with a location somewhere on the remaining path, it returns the index of that location. However, if the current location is not yet anywhere on the original path, it returns NotOnPath which is a -1.

```
int BackOnPath (const Point& g, const Point path[], int iStart) {
  for (int i=iStart; i<MaxPathElements; i++) {
    if (path[i] == Point (-1, -1)) return NotOnPath;
    if (path[i] == g) return i;
  }
  return NotOnPath;
}
```

The function IsValidPath() returns true if the proposed location is a valid one, that is, no restricting terrain. It returns false if there is some form of restriction.

```
bool IsValidPath (char field[] [MaxCols+1], const Point& p) {
  return field[p.y] [p.x] == ' ';
}
```

The function ObtainTravelDirection() fills up the tries array with a logical set of possible directions in which to try to move so as to get around an obstacle. The memcpy function copies a block of memory, independent of what it might contain. It is highly optimized for speed and is a very fast way to copy an array of values. If we were going north, for example, then the most logical directions to try first would be NE and NW; if those fail, try E and W, and so on.

```
void ObtainTravelDirection (const Point& g, const Point& p,
                             int tries[]) {
 int differenceX = p.x - g.x;
 int differenceY = p.y - g.y;
 const int tryN[8]  = {8, 2, 7, 3, 6, 4, 5, 1};
 const int tryNE[8] = {1, 3, 8, 4, 7, 5, 6, 2};
 const int tryE[8]  = {2, 4, 1, 5, 8, 6, 7, 3};
 const int trySE[8] = {3, 5, 2, 6, 1, 7, 8, 4};
 const int tryS[8]  = {4, 6, 3, 7, 2, 8, 1, 5};
 const int trySW[8] = {5, 7, 4, 8, 3, 1, 2, 6};
 const int tryW[8]  = {6, 8, 5, 1, 4, 2, 3, 7};
 const int tryNW[8] = {7, 1, 6, 2, 5, 3, 4, 8};
 if (differenceY < 0 && differenceX == 0)
  memcpy_s (tries, sizeof(tryN), tryN, sizeof (tryN));
 else if (differenceY < 0 && differenceX > 0)
  memcpy_s (tries, sizeof(tryN), tryNE, sizeof (tryNE));
 else if (differenceY == 0 && differenceX > 0)
  memcpy_s (tries, sizeof(tryN), tryE, sizeof (tryE));
 else if (differenceY > 0 && differenceX > 0)
  memcpy_s (tries, sizeof(tryN), trySE, sizeof (trySE));
 else if (differenceY > 0 && differenceX == 0)
  memcpy_s (tries, sizeof(tryN), tryS, sizeof (tryS));
 else if (differenceY > 0 && differenceX < 0)
  memcpy_s (tries, sizeof(tryN), trySW, sizeof (trySW));
 else if (differenceY == 0 && differenceX < 0)
  memcpy_s (tries, sizeof(tryN), tryW, sizeof (tryW));
 else if (differenceY > 0 && differenceX < 0)
  memcpy_s (tries, sizeof(tryN), tryNW, sizeof (tryNW));
 else {
  cerr << "Error in TracePath - cannot find a direction to go\n";
  exit (3);
 }
}
```

The function TracePath() uses this array of tries directions to find a location in which to move that is allowed. It goes through each element in turn, checking to see if the object can move into this location. As soon as an acceptable move is found, it returns that location to the caller.

```
Point TracePath (char field[][MaxCols+1], const Point& g, const int
tries[]) {
 Point t;
 for (int i=0; i<8; i++) {
  t = g;
  if (tries[i] == 1) {
   t.y--;
  }
```

```
else if (tries[i] == 2) {
  t.y--;
  t.x++;
}
else if (tries[i] == 3) {
  t.x++;
}
else if (tries[i] == 4) {
  t.x++;
  t.y++;
}
else if (tries[i] == 5) {
  t.y++;
}
else if (tries[i] == 6) {
  t.x--;
  t.y++;
}
else if (tries[i] == 7) {
  t.x--;
}
else if (tries[i] == 8) {
  t.x--;
  t.y--;
}
else  {
  cerr << "Error in TracePath - cannot find a direction\n";
  exit (3);
}
if (field[t.y][t.x] == ' ')
  return t; // found a location to which to move
}
cerr << "Error in TracePath - cannot find a direction to go\n";
exit (3);
}
```

As you can see from glancing at Figures 6-2 and 6-3, this can yield a non-optimum recovery once the obstruction has been circumvented. The function DoTraceMethod2(), while using more computer power, produces a much more acceptable result. It finds a path to destination and follows it until an obstacle is found. It traces a reasonable way around it one move at a time, recalculating a new direct path to the destination after each move. Just as soon as it is free from the obstacle, it continues on the new current direct path to the destination.

```
void DoTraceMethod2 (Screen& s, Point goblin, const Point& frodo,
                               char field[][MaxCols+1], Screen::Color
fieldColor[][MaxCols]) {
```

```
Point path[MaxPathElements];
Bresenham (path, MaxPathElements, goblin, frodo);
int iPath = 0;
int tries[8]; // holds the original direction to keep on trying to go
Point g = goblin;
Point proposed = path[iPath];
while (g != frodo) {
  if (IsValidPath (field, proposed)) {
    iPath++;
    s.OutputUCharWith ('g', proposed.y, proposed.x, Screen::Blue,
                        Screen::BrightRed);
    g = proposed;
    proposed = path[iPath];
  }
  else { // obstacle found, trace around it
    ObtainTravelDirection (g, proposed, tries);
    proposed = TracePath (field, g, tries);
    s.OutputUCharWith ('g', proposed.y, proposed.x, Screen::Blue,
                        Screen::BrightRed);
    g = proposed;
    // now construct a new direct path to the destination
    Bresenham (path, MaxPathElements, g, frodo);
    iPath = 0;
  }
 }
}
```

Picking Up and Following a Trail and Following a Road

Your party of characters has been taking a short cut across a wide valley, which, unbeknown to your party, is home to a troll. He comes back from cutting some firewood and sniffs at the trail your party has left. "Um, food!" he exclaims and begins to follow after the party. At this time, your party is miles away down the valley, very out of sight of the troll. So how can he find the trail and how can he follow it? Here is another scenario quite commonly encountered.

The common solution parallels Hansel and Gretel, the passing of a party leaves invisible breadcrumbs for the troll to follow. That is, an array stores each location to which the party moves. The number of elements in the array determine how long that trail becomes. If the array size is large, a long path can be stored, simulating the leaving of a well-defined trail. If the size is small, only the last few locations are stored, leaving a ill-defined trail or perhaps one of short duration. When the array is full, write over the oldest entry. That the players are leaving such trails should not and will not be known to them as a rule. Their opponents, then, can be alert for trails and can be programmed to detect a trail and then follow it, as desired.

Game Programming Theory

In Pgm06b, Frodo moves first for fifteen turns, leaving a bread crumb trail. Then, the goblin appears, entering from an edge. The goblin finds the trail and follows it catching up to Frodo. In a game situation, time also plays a role in several ways. First, after a period of time has elapsed, perhaps all traces of the bread crumbs disappear. Rate of movement between the two parties is a factor as well. Here, the goblin and Frodo are going to move at the same rate. If, however, a goblin moved twice as fast as Frodo, then the game engine must make two moves for every one of Frodo's moves. Weather can play a factor, heavy rains can wash out a trail left by the party. A trail over rocky ground is harder to follow than one left on soft, grassy plains, but let's ignore all of these factors and see how the bread crumb trail can be implemented.

Another action NPCs must sometimes do is follow a road or follow along some terrain feature, such as a path that is marked on the map. In this program, if the goblin encounters the road before it finds the trail, it will begin following the road. However, the goblin subsequently finds the trail, it abandons the road in favor of fresh meat.

Much of the coding from the previous example can be reused. First, examine the replacement field.txt file which now has a road marked on it, using the 'R' character.

```
TTTTTTTTTTTTTTTTTTTTTTTTTTTTTTTTTTTTTTTTTTTTTTTTTTTTTTTTTTTTTTTTTTTTTTTTTTTTTTTTT
T                                                                      RR   T
T                                                                      RR   T
T                                                                      RR    T
T                                                                     RR     T
T      T T T                                                         RR      T
T       T T                                                         RR       T
T        T                                                         RR        T
T           TTTTTT                        TTTT                    RR          T
T           TTTTTT                       TTTTT                  RR            T
T            TTTTTTT                      TTTT                 RR             T
T             TTTTTTT                         RRRRRRRRRRRRRRRR               T
T              TTTTTTT      RRRRRRRRRRRRRRRRRRRRRRRRRRRRRRRR                 T
T                RRRRRRRRRRRRRRRRRRRRRRRRRRRRRRRR                           T
T                RRRRRRRRRR                                                 T
T          RRR        TTTTTTTTT                                             T
T         RRRR       TTTTTTTTTTTT                                           T
T        RRR           TTTTTTTTTT                                           T
T        RRR              TTTTTTTTT                                         T
T       RRR                  TTTTT                                          T
T      RRR                     TTT                                          T
T      RRR                                                                  T
T     RR                                                                    T
T     RR                                                                    T
T     RR                                                                    T
TTTTTTTTTTTTTTTTTTTTTTTTTTTTTTTTTTTTTTTTTTTTTTTTTTTTTTTTTTTTTTTTTTTTTTTTTTTTTTTTTT
```

Much of the coding is exactly the same. However, to handle properly movement, I added an enum for the direction of travel and an array size for the maximum number of bread crumbs to leave behind for the trail. Also shown are the new prototypes for the additional functions.   The main() function first allows frodo to move fifteen times and then the goblin appears and takes up to thirty moves, stopping sooner if it finds frodo.

```
#include <iostream>
```

```
...
const int MaxTrail = 15;
...
enum TravelDirection {North = 1, NorthEast, East, SouthEast, South,
                      SouthWest, West, NorthWest};
...

void InitializeTrail (Point trail[]);
void AddToTrail (Point trail[], const Point& frodo);
void MoveCharacter (Screen& s, Point& frodo, Point trail[],
                    char field[][MaxCols+1]);
void MoveGoblin (Screen& s, Point& goblin,
                 TravelDirection& goblinDirection,
                 Point trail[], char field[][MaxCols+1]);
bool FoundTheTrail (const Point& goblin, Point& proposed,
                    Point trail[]);
bool FoundTheRoad (const Point& g, Point& proposed,
                   char field[][MaxCols+1]);
bool CanGoThisDirection (const Point& g, Point& proposed,
                         TravelDirection dir,
                         char field[][MaxCols+1]);
bool FollowTheRoad (const Point& g, Point& proposed,
                    TravelDirection& dir, char field[][MaxCols+1]);
void ApplyDirectionWeighting (int analyze[], TravelDirection dir);

int main () {
...
...
 // set up and show the fixed Frodo character
 Point frodo (70, 4);
 s.GoToXY (frodo.x, frodo.y);
 s << 'F';

 Point trail[MaxTrail];
 InitializeTrail (trail);
 AddToTrail (trail, frodo);
 MoveCharacter (s, frodo, trail, field);

 // setup and show the initial position of the goblin
 Point goblin (78, 4);
 s.GoToXY (goblin.x, goblin.y);
 s << 'g';
 TravelDirection goblinDirection = West;
 int count = 30;
 while (count > 0 && goblin != frodo) {
  MoveGoblin (s, goblin, goblinDirection, trail, field);
  count--;
 }
...
```

Game Programming Theory

```
 return 0;
}
```

LoadField has a slight change to properly display the road.

```
void LoadField (char field[][MaxCols+1],
                Screen::Color fieldColor[][MaxCols]) {
...
 // now insert the proper colors into the fieldColor array where the
 // obstacles are located
 for (row=0; row<MaxRows; row++) {
  for (col=0; col<MaxCols; col++) {
   if (field[row][col] == 'T')
    fieldColor[row][col] = Screen::BrightGreen;
   else if (field[row][col] == 'R')
    fieldColor[row][col] = Screen::Yellow;
   else
    fieldColor[row][col] = Screen::BrightYellow;
  }
 }
}
...
```

```
// InitializeTrail: sets all points to invalid point
void InitializeTrail (Point trail[]) {
 for (int i=0; i<MaxTrail; i++) {
  trail[i] = Point (-1, -1);
 }
}
```

AddToTrail() adds this new point to the trail at element 0, after moving all points down one element. Why? When another searches the trail array, they will begin with element 0. Hence, we want the most recent location to be at that location. The search of the trail then yields the most recent, closest location.

```
void AddToTrail (Point trail[], const Point& frodo) {
 for (int i=MaxTrail-1; i>0; i--) {
  trail[i] = trail[i-1];
 }
 trail[0] = frodo;
}
```

MoveCharacter() moves the character fifteen moves and stops. The arrow keys control movement. However, frodo is not allowed to move into the forest. This function illustrates how to deal with detection of the special keys, such as the arrow keys, using the GetSpecialKey() function.

```
void MoveCharacter (Screen& s, Point& frodo, Point trail[],
                    char field[][MaxCols+1]) {
 unsigned char skey, key;
```

152

```
int i=0;
Point proposed;
while (i<15) {
  key = s.GetSpecialKey (skey);
  proposed = frodo;
  switch (skey) {
   case UpArrow:
    proposed.y--;
    break;
   case DownArrow:
    proposed.y++;
    break;
   case LeftArrow:
    proposed.x--;
    break;
   case RightArrow:
    proposed.x++;
    break;
  }
  if (IsValidPath (field, proposed)) {
   frodo = proposed;
   i++;
   s.GoToXY (frodo.x, frodo.y);
   s << 'F';
   AddToTrail (trail, frodo);
  }
 }
}
```

The MoveGoblin() function illustrates several key features. First, it shows how to pick up and then follow a trail of bread crumbs. Secondly, it shows how you can have an NPC follow along a road or a path marked on a map. Specifically, the goblin's first action is to see if it has picked up a trail; if so, follow it. If no trail is found, then it checks to see if it has found a road and is not yet on it. If a road is found, the goblin alters direction to follow on down the road. If it is on a road, the goblin continues on the road. This can be tricky when the road is more than one tile wide. How can it determine which way to move? The compass rose of directions aid this decision making process. If the goblin is not on a road and has not found a road nor a trail, it then attempts to continue in the same direction it has been traveling. Of course, it could encounter an obstacle at that location. If an obstacle is found, the goblin uses the same approach as before to navigate around that barrier.

```
void MoveGoblin (Screen& s, Point& goblin, TravelDirection& direction,
                 Point trail[], char field[][MaxCols+1]) {
 Point proposed = goblin;
 if (FoundTheTrail (goblin, proposed, trail)) {
  goblin = proposed;
 }
 else if (field[goblin.y][goblin.x] == 'R' &&
          FollowTheRoad (goblin, proposed, direction, field)) {
  goblin = proposed;
```

```
}
else if (FoundTheRoad (goblin, proposed, field)) {
 goblin = proposed;
}
else if (CanGoThisDirection (goblin, proposed, direction, field)) {
 goblin = proposed;
}
else {
 int tries[8];
 ObtainTravelDirection (goblin, proposed, tries);
 goblin = TracePath (field, goblin, tries);
}
s.GoToXY (goblin.x, goblin.y);
s << 'g';
}
```

FoundTheTrail() loops through the trail array of points beginning with element 0 of the trail. For each trail point, it checks all eight compass directions to see if there is a bread crumb there, indicating the trail. As soon as it finds a match, the proposed variable is filled with this new location and the function returns true, a trail has been found. If no trail is found, the function returns false.

```
bool FoundTheTrail (const Point& g, Point& proposed, Point trail[]) {
 for (int i=0; i<MaxTrail; i++) {
  if (Point (g.x+1, g.y) == trail[i]) {
   proposed = trail[i];
   return true;
  }
  else if (Point (g.x-1, g.y) == trail[i]) {
   proposed = trail[i];
   return true;
  }
  else if (Point (g.x, g.y+1) == trail[i]) {
   proposed = trail[i];
   return true;
  }
  else if (Point (g.x, g.y-1) == trail[i]) {
   proposed = trail[i];
   return true;
  }
  else if (Point (g.x+1, g.y+1) == trail[i]) {
   proposed = trail[i];
   return true;
  }
  else if (Point (g.x+1, g.y-1) == trail[i]) {
   proposed = trail[i];
   return true;
  }
  else if (Point (g.x-1, g.y+1) == trail[i]) {
   proposed = trail[i];
   return true;
```

```
  }
  else if (Point (g.x-1, g.y-1) == trail[i]) {
   proposed = trail[i];
   return true;
  }
 }
 return false;
}
```

The FoundTheRoad() function operates in a similar manner. It compares the terrain in the eight compass directions from the current goblin location to see if a road is there. Again, if it finds a road, the 'R' character, the proposed point is set to the location of that road tile and returns true. However, if the road is not found, false is returned.

```
bool FoundTheRoad (const Point& g, Point& proposed,
                      char field[] [MaxCols+1]) {
 if (field[g.y][g.x+1] == 'R') {
  proposed = Point (g.x+1, g.y);
  return true;
 }
 else if (field[g.y][g.x-1] == 'R') {
  proposed = Point (g.x-1, g.y);
  return true;
 }
 else if (field[g.y+1][g.x] == 'R') {
  proposed = Point (g.x, g.y+1);
  return true;
 }
 else if (field[g.y-1][g.x] == 'R') {
  proposed = Point (g.x, g.y-1);
  return true;
 }
 else if (field[g.y+1][g.x+1] == 'R') {
  proposed = Point (g.x+1, g.y+1);
  return true;
 }
 else if (field[g.y+1][g.x-1] == 'R') {
  proposed = Point (g.x-1, g.y+1);
  return true;
 }
 else if (field[g.y-1][g.x+1] == 'R') {
  proposed = Point (g.x+1, g.y-1);
  return true;
 }
 else if (field[g.y-1][g.x-1] == 'R') {
  proposed = Point (g.x-1, g.y-1);
  return true;
 }
 return false;
}
```

Game Programming Theory

The CanGoThisDirection() function uses the current direction of travel to determine if it can continue in that direction. First, it adjusts the proposed next point according to the direction of travel. However, this may take it off of the screen. If off screen, the goblin is force back onto the screen. Finally, the field is checked for obstacles. If none are found, true is returned. If a barrier exists, false is returned and the goblin must find some other location to which to move.

```
bool CanGoThisDirection (const Point& g, Point& proposed, TravelDirection dir,
                         char field[][MaxCols+1]) {
  proposed = g;
  switch (dir) {
   case North:
    proposed.y--; break;
   case South:
    proposed.y++; break;
   case East:
    proposed.x++; break;
   case West:
    proposed.x--; break;
   case NorthEast:
    proposed.y--;
    proposed.x++; break;
   case NorthWest:
    proposed.y--;
    proposed.x--; break;
   case SouthEast:
    proposed.y++;
    proposed.x++; break;
   case SouthWest:
    proposed.y++;
    proposed.x--; break;
  }

  if (proposed.x < 1)
   proposed.x = MaxCols - 2;
  else if (proposed.x > MaxCols - 2)
   proposed.x = 1;
  if (proposed.y < 1)
   proposed.y = 23;
  else if (proposed.y > 23)
   proposed.y = 1;

  if (field[proposed.y][proposed.x] != 'T')
   return true;
  return false;
}
```

Game Programming Theory

The FollowTheRoad() function is the most interesting function in the program, adding a good deal of AI to NPC movement. The situation: the goblin is on the road and has been traveling in some compass direction. The desired outcome is for the goblin to continue following on down the road and in the proper direction. You cannot just check the eight nearest field neighbors for the presence of a road, 'R', that is doomed to failure. Suppose we have the road layout given above. It begins this way with the goblin first encountering the road as indicated.

```
        RR<- goblin enters here
     RR
  RR
```

A simple search of near field locations will wind up with the goblin going perpetually back and forth between two tiles as shown! I know, I tried it with this program.

```
        gg<- goblin enters here
     RR
  RR
```

I'm afraid following a road or designated path is more complex than this. We must assign weights to each of the eight possible directions of travel, with continuing in the same direction having the largest weight and reversing course having the least weight. In other words, if you are walking down a wide road, the most desirable move is to continue on in the same direction. Slightly less desirable is to make a slight turn to the right or left. Even less desirable are sharp turns either way. Most undesirable is to be forced to turn around and reverse course.

The process begins with constructing a compass rose array of possibilities. Note, that the array size is nine, not eight. This way, we can use the compass rose enum values directly, ignoring element 0 entirely. Into this compass rose array, we place one of two values. A 0 indicates no road is present in this location. A 10 indicates the presence of another road tile. 10 is an arbitrary number chosen because it is different from 0 and because weighting will be increasing or decreasing that value and it must not become 0, indicating no road.

Once the array is filled, ApplyDirectionWeighting() is called to alter the road values based upon the current direction of travel. Once the direction has been applied, the largest value in the array is then found. Specifically, we need the index of that largest number, because it will become the compass rose direction of travel, a number 1 through 8, hopefully. Of course, there is always the possibility that the road ends. Thus, if the index is 1 through 8, then that becomes the new direction of travel and the proposed new location is created, based upon this direction of travel. However, if the road ends, the function returns false.

```
bool FollowTheRoad (const Point& g, Point& proposed,
                    TravelDirection& dir,
                    char field[][MaxCols+1]) {
 int analyze[9] = {0}; // not using element 0 - others correspond to
                       // compass directions
 // insert 10 if this one is a road, 0 if not
 analyze[1] = field[g.y-1][g.x] == 'R' ? 10 : 0;
 analyze[2] = field[g.y-1][g.x+1] == 'R' ? 10 : 0;
```

```
analyze[3] = field[g.y][g.x+1] == 'R' ? 10 : 0;
analyze[4] = field[g.y+1][g.x+1] == 'R' ? 10 : 0;
analyze[5] = field[g.y+1][g.x] == 'R' ? 10 : 0;
analyze[6] = field[g.y+1][g.x-1] == 'R' ? 10 : 0;
analyze[7] = field[g.y][g.x-1] == 'R' ? 10 : 0;
analyze[8] = field[g.y-1][g.x-1] == 'R' ? 10 : 0;

// weight the possibilities - continuing the original direction
// having the bigger weight and reversing direction a much lesser wt.
ApplyDirectionWeighting (analyze, dir);

// find the best direction to go
int max = 0;
int imax = 0;
for (int i=1; i<9; i++) {
 if (analyze[i] > max) {
  max = analyze[i];
  imax = i;
 }
}

// apply choice - if any
proposed = g;
if (imax > 0 && imax < 9) {
 // reset the direction of travel
 dir = (TravelDirection) imax;
 // alter proposed to go that direction
 switch (imax) {
  case North:
   proposed.y--;
   break;
  case NorthEast:
   proposed.y--;
   proposed.x++;
   break;
  case East:
   proposed.x++;
   break;
  case SouthEast:
   proposed.y++;
   proposed.x--;
   break;
  case South:
   proposed.y++;
   break;
  case SouthWest:
   proposed.y++;
   proposed.x--;
   break;
  case West:
```

```
    proposed.x--;
    break;
  case NorthWest:
    proposed.y--;
    proposed.x--;
    break;
  }
  return true;
}
return false; // failed, out of road??
}
```

The ApplyDirectionWeighting() function weights each direction of travel. If continuing in the same direction, +2 is added. If reversing direction, -1 is added. A slight change to the left or right adds +1, while a hard left or right is left unchanged.

```
void ApplyDirectionWeighting (int analyze[], TravelDirection dir) {
 switch (dir) {
  case North:
   analyze[North] += 2;
   analyze[NorthEast]++;
   analyze[NorthWest]++;
   analyze[South]--;
   break;
  case NorthEast:
   analyze[NorthEast] += 2;
   analyze[East]++;
   analyze[North]++;
   analyze[SouthWest]--;
   break;
  case East:
   analyze[East] += 2;
   analyze[NorthEast]++;
   analyze[SouthEast]++;
   analyze[West]--;
   break;
  case SouthEast:
   analyze[SouthEast] += 2;
   analyze[East]++;
   analyze[South]++;
   analyze[NorthWest]--;
   break;
  case South:
   analyze[South] += 2;
   analyze[SouthEast]++;
   analyze[SouthWest]++;
   analyze[North]--;
   break;
  case SouthWest:
   analyze[SouthWest] += 2;
```

```
analyze[South]++;
analyze[West]++;
analyze[NorthEast]--;
break;
case West:
analyze[West]  += 2;
analyze[NorthWest]++;
analyze[SouthWest]++;
analyze[East]--;
break;
case NorthWest:
analyze[NorthWest]  += 2;
analyze[North]++;
analyze[West]++;
analyze[SouthEast]--;
break;
}
}
```

Note, in all these functions, notice how easy it is to deal with these directions because of the convenient enumerated values, such as NorthEast. By using compass rose directions, the programmer can easily envision what actions are occurring. This is a major benefit to using enums, making the coding more readable and less error prone. Always use enums when possible.

Node Navigation

As you can see, navigation or pathfinding can be time-consuming as well as utilizing lots of CPU calculation power. If the game has lots of NPCs with which to deal, this can overload overall response significantly. Further, we have been looking at a single screen only. What if the game world consists of many such screens connected together? How can an NPC navigate from one end of the world to the other?

The answer lies in a carefully constructed table of navigation nodes, where each node strategically placed so that every node is in full view (unobstructed line of sight) of at least one other navigation node. Figure 6-4 illustrates this concept.

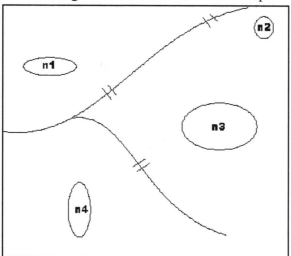

Figure 6-4 Navigation Nodes

In Figure 6-4, four nodes are defined. Each node might represent a village, for example. The long curved lines represents rivers, presenting a barrier to overland travel. Three bridges are also indicated. Perhaps this game world spans four screen's worth of image. How can an NPC navigate from the village at n1 to the village at n4, which is on a completely different screen view? Further, assume that there is are roads that connect these villages, from n1 to n2 and n3, from n2 to n1 and n3, from n3 to n1, n2, and n4. The ideal solution for the NPC who is in village n1 who needs to get to village n4 would be to travel to n3 and then on to n4.

One time only during the game design phase, the ideal series of individual movement steps to get from any given node to the next can be computed and stored. Here, we would store the explicit steps as n1n2, n1n3, n2n3, and n3n4, perhaps stored in a file for easy retrieval when needed.

The navigation table is a two-dimensional array of the possibilities, showing the connections between the nodes. The elements of the diagonal are empty and not used.

The Navigation Table

		Ending Node			
		n1	n2	n3	n4
Starting Node	n1	x	n1n2	n1n3	n1n3
	n2	n1n2	x	n2n3	n2n3
	n3	n1n3	n2n3	x	n3n4
	n4	n3n4	n3n4	n3n4	x

Let's say that we desire to go from village n4 to village n1. Find n4 in the starting node row. Read across the table to find the destination node, n1. In that element, we find the navigation rules to get from n4 to n3. Once at n3, we use the table again, looking up the starting row as n3. Reading across the table, we find the n1 column and discover the next path we must follow is n1n3. Viola, any NPC can then easily follow the predetermined travel routes from one location to another. Navigation Nodes are very useful when dealing with a large game field. It is also useful for onscreen navigation as well, perhaps from rooms to rooms. Further, since all of the detailed movement steps have been created before the game is started and stored perhaps in files, no computer time is needed to do all of the extensive calculations, greatly speeding up the game play.

The A* Pathfinding Algorithm

In fact, the whole arena of optimum pathfinding is considered closed by most game programmers. The A* algorithm represents an optimum method for finding the shortest path from point A to point B, particularly in a tile-based game. It is likely the most used method for finding paths in games. It is guaranteed to find the best path between two points. It can even take the cost of entering specific terrain tiles into account. For example, many games offer a road bonus, often twice as fast as going cross-country, and so on. The A* handled any number of terrain features and their relative costs for movement.

Unfortunately, this algorithm requires rather complex logic and the use of some data structures, namely a linked list of items. The list consists of nodes which are linked forward and backward to the next and previous nodes in the list. Each node also contains the user's data that the node represents. To keep track of the list of nodes, a pointer to the first node, a pointer to the last node, a pointer to the current node under consideration, and a count of the number of nodes in the list are stored. Figure 6-5 shows what the linked list data structure looks like.

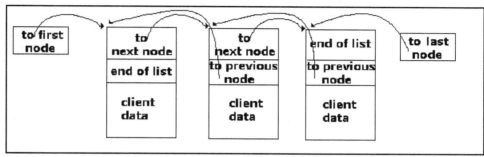

Figure 6-5 A Double Linked List

The logic of the A* algorithm appears rather simple at first glance, though how it works will take a bit of study. Here is the fundamental A* algorithm. It utilizes an open and a closed list.

add the starting node to the open list
while the open list is not empty {
    current node is the lowest cost node from the open list
    if this current node is the ending location, the path is complete, break
    move this node to the closed list
    for each adjacent tile location to the current location {
        if it is not in the open list, or not in the closed list, or
            not an obstacle, or not out of the boundary of the search
        then calculate its cost and add it to the open list
    }
}
if the list is empty, there is no solution
else starting with the ending location, follow the parent nodes back to the starting node,
    which is the best path

Before we examine the implementation of this algorithm, let's see what an ideal answer for our client code might be. In a tile-based game, ideally, the result would be an array of Point structures, the first of which is the starting location and the last being the ending point. Given this, we can easily plot the path on screen.

Next, since the game world could be large, the algorithm ought to be able to handle a particular subset of the game space. Hence, we ought to be able to specify the minimum and maximum values the x, y coordinates can have for the path finding.

The terrain map ought to be available to the A* algorithm, so that it can automatically detect any obstacles as well as all of the other terrain features. Finally, it ought to be just a single function call that generates the optimum path for us.

Game Programming Theory

Pgm06c uses our previous field map to find the fastest route for the goblin to travel to get to Frodo. Here is the main function. Notice that there is very little client coding required. The LoadField() and ShowField() functions are the same as before. The key lines are highlighted in boldface.

```
include <iostream>
#include <fstream>
#include <iomanip>
using namespace std;

#include "Screen.h"
#include "Point.h"
#include "AStar.h"

void LoadField (char field[][MaxCols+1],
                Screen::Color fieldColor[][MaxCols]);
void ShowField (Screen& s, char field[][MaxCols+1],
                Screen::Color fieldColor[][MaxCols]);

int main () {
  cin.sync_with_stdio (); // if you want to use cin
  Screen s (Screen::Blue, Screen::BrightYellow);

  s.SetTitle ("Tile-based Tracing Pathfinding");
  s.DrawBox (0, 0, 24, 79, Screen::Gray, Screen::BrightYellow);

  char           field[MaxRows][MaxCols+1];      // the playing field
  Screen::Color fieldColor[MaxRows][MaxCols];   // colors of obstacles

  // load and show the entire field
  LoadField (field, fieldColor);
  ShowField (s, field, fieldColor);

  // set up and show the fixed Frodo character
  Point frodo (61,5);
  s.GoToXY (frodo.x, frodo.y);
  s << 'F';

  // setup and show the initial position of the goblin
  Point goblin (1, 1);
  s.GoToXY (goblin.x, goblin.y);
  s << 'g';

  // find the A* fastest path for the goblin to take
  Point* path;
  int     count;
  AStar a (goblin, frodo, field, 1, 1, 78, 23, path, count);

  // now show that found path
```

164

```
for (int i=0; i<count; i++) {
  s.GoToXY (path[i].x, path[i].y);
  s << 'g';
}
delete [] path;

// reshow Frodo
s.GoToXY (frodo.x, frodo.y);
s << 'F';

s.GoToXY (0, 25);
s.GetAnyKey ();

return 0;
}
```

Figure 6-6 shows the resultant output and path that the goblin can take. Because of the road bonus, this is the fastest route.

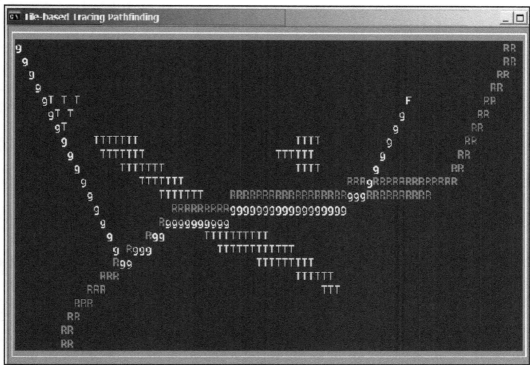

Figure 6-6 The Fastest Path for the Goblin to Follow to Get to Frodo

The A* algorithm requires the use of two data structures, which you should soon be studying in your programming classes, the double linked list and the growable array. Here, I have borrowed those two classes from the Data Structures course, exactly as-is. These two container classes, as they are sometimes called, store void pointers to the nodes. The alternative is to use the parallel structures from the Standard Template Library, STL. My usage of these two classes here are strictly normal client coding.

The beginning point is to define what our node structures will contain. Here is the start of the AStar.h file.

```
#pragma once
#include "Point.h"
#include "DoubleLinkedList.h"
#include "Array.h"


/***************************************************************/
/*                                                             */
/* A* Pathfinding Algorithm for a Tile-based Game              */
/*     with terrain costs factored into the solution           */
/*                                                             */
/*   returns an array of Points and the number of points in it */
/*   caller must delete [] array;                              */
/*                                                             */
/***************************************************************/


enum Type {Unused, Open, Closed};

// Node: contains the data about a specific tile
struct Node {
 Type   type;       // which list it is on, open or closed
 Point  loc;        // the location of this tile
 Node*  ptrparent;  // the parent node of this tile
 int    cost;       // total cost to enter this tile
 int    level;      // level cost to enter this tile
 int    heuristic;  // heuristic cost to enter this tile
 int    tCost;      // terrain cost to enter this tile
```

The Node structure contains a Type enum value indicating whether this node is in the open or closed list. The member loc contains the Point location of this tile. The member ptrparent contains the memory address of the parent node of this tile.

The member cost contains the total cost involved in moving into this tile location. The total cost is composed of three parts. First, the basic cost, or level, is the count of how many tiles this one is from the starting tile. The very first tile has a cost of 0. The eight surrounding tiles have a level cost of 1, and so on. Since we are storing a pointer to the parent of this tile, this tile's basic level cost is one more than its parent's basic level cost.

Second is the heuristic cost to enter this tile. Here, we ignore all potential obstacles and all unviewed as yet tiles, and just calculate potentially how far from the destination tile this one is.

Game Programming Theory

Simply subtract the ending x location from this tile's x location and similarly for the y coordinates. However, take the absolute value of these two numbers, since they could be negative. The heuristic cost is the larger of the two numbers, representing potentially how far away the ending location actually is from this tile.

Third, the cost to enter this terrain is determined, based on what terrain element is in this tile. In this example, I am giving a double movement road bonus for travel on roads. Thus, a clear terrain tile will cost 2 to move into it, while a road tile will cost only 1 to move into it.

The total cost is the sum of these three parts. Since there are so many members of the Node structure, I took the liberty of adding two constructor functions to alleviate having to make numerous assignments to fill an instance up.

```
// two Node structure constructor functions to avoid doing
// lots of assignment statements
Node (Type t = Unused, const Point& l = Point (0, 0),
      Node* ptrp = 0,
      int c = 0, int lev = 0, int h = 0, int tc = 0) {
  loc = l;
  type = t;
  ptrparent = ptrp;
  cost = c;
  level = lev;
  heuristic = h;
  tCost = tc;
}

Node (const Node& n) {
  type = n.type;
  loc = n.loc;
  ptrparent = n.ptrparent;
  cost = n.cost;
  level = n.level;
  heuristic = n.heuristic;
  tCost = n.tCost;
}
};
```

With the Node structure defined, next comes the definition of the AStar class. I used a class so that I did not have to pass many parameters to the additional functions of the class.

```
class AStar {
protected:
 DoubleLinkedList list;
 // a double linked list data structure storing void*
 Array answer;
```

167

```
// a growable array of void* data structure

    Point start;              // the starting tile location
    Point end;                // the ending tile location
    int minX;                 // smallest X coordinate allowed
    int minY;                 // smallest Y coordinate allowed
    int maxX;                 // largest X coordinate allowed
    int maxY;                 // largest Y coordinate allowed

public:
  // returns answer and count to caller
    AStar (const Point& s, const Point& e, char f[][MaxCols+1],
           int minx, int miny, int maxx, int maxy, Point* &answer,
           int& count);
```

Notice that the constructor is the only function callable by client code. It is passed the starting and ending points, the playing field, the range of allowed x, y coordinates. It is also passed a reference to what will become the client's array of Point structures, holding the answer. This function will eventually allocate that array and fill up the count reference with the number of elements in the array. It is the client's responsibility to delete this array when it is finished using the found path.

```
    ~AStar ();

protected:
    Node*  FindLowestCostNode ();
    void   RemoveFromOpen (const Node* ptrcurrent);
    void   CheckNode (const Node* ptrcurrent,
                      char field[][MaxCols+1], int x, int y);
    bool   IsInList (const Point& p);
    Point* BuildAnswerList (Node* ptrend, const Point& s,
                            int& count);
};
```

The remaining functions of the class are for internal use only and are protected from client coding invocation. Now, let's examine the implementation in AStar.cpp.

```
#include "AStar.h"

// the entire operation is performed from within the constructor
AStar::AStar (const Point& s, const Point& e,
              char field[][MaxCols+1],
              int minx, int miny, int maxx, int maxy,
              Point* &answer, int& count) {
    start = s;
    end = e;
    minX = minx;
    minY = miny;
```

```
maxX = maxx;
maxY = maxy;

// add the starting tile to the open list
Node* ptrcurrent = new Node (Open, s);
list.AddAtHead (ptrcurrent);

// main loop ends when there are no more items in list or
// we've reached the ending location

while (list.GetSize () != 0) {
 // finds the next lowest cost node in the open list
 ptrcurrent = FindLowestCostNode ();
 if (ptrcurrent->loc == end) break;
 // stop - at the ending point

 ptrcurrent->type = Closed;          // mark this one as closed

 // attempt to add to open list all of this one's neighbors
 CheckNode (ptrcurrent, field, ptrcurrent->loc.x+1,
          ptrcurrent->loc.y+1);
  CheckNode (ptrcurrent, field, ptrcurrent->loc.x+1,
          ptrcurrent->loc.y);
  CheckNode (ptrcurrent, field, ptrcurrent->loc.x+1,
          ptrcurrent->loc.y-1);
  CheckNode (ptrcurrent, field, ptrcurrent->loc.x,
          ptrcurrent->loc.y+1);
  CheckNode (ptrcurrent, field, ptrcurrent->loc.x,
          ptrcurrent->loc.y-1);
  CheckNode (ptrcurrent, field, ptrcurrent->loc.x-1,
          ptrcurrent->loc.y+1);
  CheckNode (ptrcurrent, field, ptrcurrent->loc.x-1,
          ptrcurrent->loc.y);
  CheckNode (ptrcurrent, field, ptrcurrent->loc.x-1,
          ptrcurrent->loc.y-1);
}
if (list.GetSize () == 0) { // no solution found
 answer = 0;
 count = 0;
}
else { // build the answer solution
 answer = BuildAnswerList (ptrcurrent, s, count);
}
}
```

Game Programming Theory

Notice that the coding in the constructor follows exactly the pseudocoding given earlier. Now, let's examine the details, beginning with how we find the lowest cost next node to try.

```
// finds the lowest cost node in the open list, if any
Node* AStar::FindLowestCostNode () {
 list.ResetToHead ();
```

ResetToHead() sets the current pointer back to the start of the list so that we can step our way through the list, node by node, beginning with the first one. However, we must first skip over all closed nodes to find the very first open node.

```
// skip over any beginning nodes that are not open
Node* ptrn = (Node*) list.GetCurrentNode ();
if (ptrn == 0) return 0;
while (ptrn && ptrn->type != Open) {
 list.Next ();
 ptrn = (Node*) list.GetCurrentNode ();
}
if (ptrn == 0) return 0; // no open nodes left, so return
```

If there are no more open nodes, then we are done, return a NULL pointer that the caller can check. Armed with the first open node in the list, save that cost as the currently lowest cost and vitally important, save its address or pointer so that we can later return the address of the lowest cost node.

```
// now find the lowest cost node in the open list
int minCost = ptrn->cost;
Node* ptrlow = ptrn;
list.Next ();
while (ptrn = (Node*) list.GetCurrentNode ()) {
 if (ptrn->type == Open && ptrn->cost < minCost) {
  // this one has a lower cost, so choose it temporarily
  ptrlow = ptrn;
  minCost = ptrn->cost;
 }
 list.Next ();
}
 return ptrlow; // here, this one is the lowest cost node
}
```

Most of the hard work is done in CheckNode(). First, eliminate from further consideration any tile which is out of bounds. Second, eliminate any tile which contains an obstacle, the forest in our case. Third, eliminate any tile that we have already examined, one that is already in the open or closed list. In order to determine this, I call the IsInList() function, which returns true if the tile with this location is already in our linked list.

```
// CheckNode: if this location is allowed and not in the open or
// closed list, calculate its cost and add to the open list
void AStar::CheckNode (const Node* ptrcurrent,
                       char field[] [MaxCols+1],
                       int x, int y) {
  // make sure this location is allowed, if not, return
  if (x < minX || x > maxX || y < minY || y > maxY) return;
  // if this location is an obstacle, return
  if (field[y][x] == 'T') return;
  // if this location is already in the open or closed list, skip
  // construct a point from this tile's coordinates
  Point t (x, y);
  if (IsInList (t)) return;
```

If we get to this point, it is a valid tile that we have not yet checked. Now we must calculate the total cost to enter this tile. The heuristic cost is the larger of the two differences in coordinate locations, ignoring the sign.

```
  // here, it must be added to the open list,find its total cost
  // first, find its heuristic cost - from here to the end point
  int dx = labs (end.x - t.x);
  int dy = labs (end.y - t.y);
  int h = dx > dy ? dx : dy;
```

Calculate the cost to enter this tile, based upon terrain costs. Here, clear terrain costs 2 to enter, while a road tile costs only 1. The level cost is one more than its parent tile. Allocate a new Node and add it to the tail end of the linked list.

```
  char c = field[t.y] [t.x];
  int tcost = c == 'R' ? 1 : 2;

  // calculate its level cost, one greater than parent location
  int lev = ptrcurrent->level + 1;

  // sum the costs involved with this tile
  int totalCost = lev + h + tcost;

  // add this new location to the open list
  Node* ptrn = new Node (Open, t, (Node*) ptrcurrent, totalCost,
                         lev, h, tcost);
  list.AddAtTail (ptrn);
}
```

The IsInList() fuction returns true if this tile or point is already in the open or closed list. To find out, simply iterate through the entire list and compare this Point to each one in the list. If we find a match, then check if its type is Open or Closed. If so, return true, else return false. If we do not find this point at all, return false.

```
bool AStar::IsInList (const Point& p) {
 list.ResetToHead ();
 Node* ptrn;
 while (ptrn = (Node*) list.GetCurrentNode ()) {
  if (ptrn->loc == p) {
   if (ptrn->type == Open || ptrn->type == Closed)
    return true;
   else
    return false;
  }
  list.Next ();
 }
 return false;
}
```

Since the container class is dynamically allocating memory and we are as well, the AStar destructor must iterate through the list and delete all Nodes that we have allocated. The compiler will call the linked list class destructor to delete the list nodes themselves.

```
AStar::~AStar () {
 list.ResetToHead ();
 Node* ptrn;
 while (ptrn = (Node*) list.GetCurrentNode ()) {
  delete ptrn;
  list.Next ();
 }
}
```

The last function, BuildAnswerList(), is going to build us our path in a format that we can easily use in our client programs. It begins by constructing another linked list which contains only the nodes of the path that it found to be the best solution, from start to end. Now, we can determine just how many Point structures will be needed in the answer array. Thus, we can now allocate an array of Point structures to hold them. Vitally important, note that the function will be returning the memory address of this new array, while storing in the reference variable count, the number of elements in the array.

```
Point* AStar::BuildAnswerList (Node* ptrend, const Point& s,
                               int& count) {
 // beginning with the ending location,
 // move back through parents to get to
 // the start, adding these to the answer linked list
 Node* ptrnew = new Node (*ptrend);
 DoubleLinkedList answer;
 answer.AddAtTail (ptrnew);
 Node* ptrparent = ptrend->ptrparent;
 while (ptrparent) {
```

```
ptrnew = new Node (*ptrparent);
answer.AddAtTail (ptrnew);
ptrparent = ptrparent->ptrparent;
}
// now allocate and fill an array of Point structures to hold
// the found path
answer.ResetToHead ();
count = answer.GetSize ();
Point* a = new Point [count];
for (int i=0; i<count; i++) {
ptrnew = (Node*) answer.GetCurrentNode ();
a[i] = ptrnew->loc;
answer.Next ();
delete ptrnew;
}
return a;
}
```

If you have not yet studied the linked list data structure, when you do cover it in your programming class, return to this example and review how it is used here. If you are puzzled about how this algorithm works, consult the many books and Internet websites that illustrate the method, step by step, complete with numerous pictures.

For a tile-based game, this is all we need from A*. However, how about a continuous environment which has no tiles? The A* can still be used there if one can somehow overlay the continuous environment with a two dimensional grid of nodes, each one representing a section of space.

A* can be put to use in a completely different scenario, often called influence mapping. Instead of storing terrain effects, store what the characters do. For example, let's say you have a party of adventurers moving through a dungeon setting. Whenever they encounter an opponent, the first action the party takes is to launch a fireball spell, attempting to wound or weaken as many opponents as they can on the first strike. This action is then noted in the two dimensional array of the field, that is, upon encountering opponents, fireball them. Armed with this, later on, when other opponents are discovered, the A* solution can detect this as the likely first reaction on the player's part and the opponents can then position themselves vastly differently, such as spaced widely apart and at widely varying distances from the entrance to their chamber, effectively nullifying the "always fireball them" attitude. This gives the opponents some intelligence, learning from the player's actions!

Programming Problems

Problem 6-1 The Chase

Use the field.txt file and the functions to load and show the field as given in the example program, Pgm06c. Locate five wolves at various locations in the upper left corner of the field. Locate Red Riding Hood on the first road tile in the upper right corner.

Red Riding Hood's motion is controlled by the arrow keys. The objective, to exit the screen somewhere at the bottom. If so, Red Riding Hood wins. If a goblin arrives at Red Riding Hood's tile, Red Riding Hood loses the game. The game goes in turns, with Red Riding Hood moving first.

Note that the road bonus is in effect for both sides. Whenever Red Riding Hood moves along a road tile, move two road tiles for each arrow key choice. Similarly for the wolves, should they encounter the road.

After each Red Riding Hood move, the wolves should follow the best possible path to intercept Red Riding Hood. Use whatever algorithm you wish from this chapter. Show each wolf in a different color. Do not "erase" their previous positions as either side moves, as in my examples. This way you can follow their paths.

Chapter 7 Scripting and Finite State Machines

Scripting means inputting data from a file into the game engine in order to create an effect upon the game operation in some manner. Scripts can be used to initialize various parameters, such as NPC attributes. They can control what actions the computer controlled opponent will take under specific circumstances. Scripts can control verbal interaction between the player and the opponents. Scripts can even be used for event handling, such as a character triggering a poison gas trap while attempting to unlock a treasure chest.

A Scripting Ini-like File

Many basic parameters that define the opponent can be inputted via a script as opposed to being hard coded within the program. However, hard coding makes game changes inflexible, requiring a rebuild of the program when altered. It is wise to store such data external to the program so that they can be tweaked and changed during the development phase without requiring program changes. Sometimes a database can be used to store all the basic properties, as I have done in my WWII game. Other times, a simple script works admirably.

For example, suppose that your NPC properties consist of strength, dexterity, constitution, and health points. The script file could be any one of these.
```
Strength = 18
Dexterity=16
CONSTITUTION = 17
health=10
```
or
```
18 16 17 10
```
or
```
Section: Fighter
Strength=18
Dexterity=16
Constitution=17
Health=10
```

In the first example, one must watch out for case and for one or more blanks. The second case is simple by exceedingly error prone, since one does not know for what the numbers apply. I do not recommend this second way. The third way is rather similar to Window's ini files, in that many different sections can be present in one file and each section may have numerous key values. When you write Strength=18, this is called a key word parameter and provides a good idea what it represents. The section line is a positional parameter, no = sign is present.

A game may have a very sophisticated scripting engine or a simple one, depending upon the needs and size of the game. Further, the scripting file very likely contains ASCII text and thus is readable by savvy players. If such is your worry, simply encrypt the file. One simple way would be to always subtract 32 from every byte being stored, rendering it unreadable, except with a hex editor. In this chapter, we will ignore encryption, as that would be added last, once everything else has been debugged.

Let's see how the Window's ini style scripting can be effectively implemented. What we desire is a single, common interface by which scripted data can be loaded at runtime as needed by the program. If you have one hundred NPCs scattered throughout the game, it makes no sense to load and store all of their properties when the game starts. Rather, load only those which are needed and only when they are needed. In fact, there is nothing wrong with writing updated data back out to the scripting file for later use!

If we write a generic scripting read function, what would it need to do its job? The function would need the filename, unless there is only one scripting file, the section to load, and the keyword(s) to locate and retrieve. It should be capable of handling all of the basic data types. Here is the Script.h file.

```
#pragma once
#include <iostream>
#include <fstream>
#include <iomanip>
#include <string.h>
#include <strstream>
using namespace std;

// Script: encapsulates I/O to a text ini-like file

class Script {
protected:
 char filename[_MAX_PATH];
 ifstream infile;
 ofstream outfile;
 long position;

public:
     Script (const char* file, bool& ok);
   ~Script ();
 bool FindSection (const char* section);
 bool GetKeyWord (const char* key, int& value);
 bool GetKeyWord (const char* key, long& value);
```

```
bool GetKeyWord (const char* key,  short& value);
bool GetKeyWord (const char* key,  char& value);
bool GetKeyWord (const char* key,  float& value);
bool GetKeyWord (const char* key,  double& value);
bool GetKeyWord (const char* key,  bool& value);
bool GetKeyWord (const char* key,  char* value,
                 unsigned int maxLength);

bool PutSection (const char* section);
void PutKeyWord (const char* key,  int value);
void PutKeyWord (const char* key,  long value);
void PutKeyWord (const char* key,  short value);
void PutKeyWord (const char* key,  char value);
void PutKeyWord (const char* key,  float value);
void PutKeyWord (const char* key,  double value);
void PutKeyWord (const char* key,  bool value);
void PutKeyWord (const char* key,  char* value);
bool PutEnd ();
};
```

The constructor saves the filename and then attempts to open it for input. When FindSection() is called, if it finds the section, the DOS file offset to the first keyword of this section is stored. All of the Getxxx functions then reset the DOS file offset pointer back to the start of this section and then begin looking for the keyword line. This way, the order of keyword lookup does not have to match the actual text file.

```
#include "Script.h"
#include <io.h>
#include <errno.h>

// Script: opens the input file
Script::Script (const char* file, bool& ok) {
 strcpy_s (filename, sizeof (filename), file);
 infile.open (filename);
 ok = infile.good ();
}

// ~Script: closes all opened files
Script::~Script () {
 infile.close ();
 outfile.close ();
}

// FindSection: finds this section in the file, saving the
//              file offset to the beginning of the section
bool Script::FindSection (const char* section) {
```

```
char line[80];
while (infile.getline (line, sizeof(line))) {
  if (_strnicmp (line, "Section: ", 9) == 0) {
   if (_stricmp (&line[9], section) == 0) {
    position = infile.tellg ();
    return true;
   }
  }
 }
 return false;
}
```

The _strnicmp() function is used to compare case insensitively the beginning characters of the line string to the "Section: " string. However, we cannot compare the entire line string, because it also has the name of this section after that value. Hence, we control the length to compare, stopping after the nine characters. If we have found a line that begins with the section identifier, next compare case insensitively the remainder of the line with the value provided by the user. If this one it the right one, use the tellg() function to retrieve the DOS file offset to this point and save it in position.

All of the Get functions will first reset the DOS file offset pointer back to this spot. Remember the DOS file offset pointer is the current position in the input file where the next extraction will occur. Again, _strnicmp() is used to find the keyword. When the correct line is found that contains this keyword, an input string stream is created wrapped around the remainder of the line after the = sign. This way, we can extract the desired values with good error control over the results.

```
// Gets and int
bool Script::GetKeyWord (const char* key, int& value) {
  infile.seekg (position, ios::beg);
  char line[80];
  while (infile.getline (line, sizeof(line))) {
   if (_strnicmp (line, key, strlen(key)) == 0) {
    istrstream is (line+strlen(key));
    is >> value;
    if (!is) {
     value = 0;
     return false;
    }
    return true;
   }
  }
  return false;
}

// Gets a long
bool Script::GetKeyWord (const char* key, long& value) {
  infile.seekg (position, ios::beg);
```

```
char line[80];
while (infile.getline (line, sizeof(line))) {
 if (_strnicmp (line, key, strlen(key)) == 0) {
  istrstream is (line+strlen(key));
  is >> value;
  if (!is) {
   value = 0;
   return false;
  }
  return true;
 }
}
return false;
}


// Gets a short
bool Script::GetKeyWord (const char* key, short& value) {
 infile.seekg (position, ios::beg);
 char line[80];
 while (infile.getline (line, sizeof(line))) {
  if (_strnicmp (line, key, strlen(key)) == 0) {
   istrstream is (line+strlen(key));
   is >> value;
   if (!is) {
    value = 0;
    return false;
   }
   return true;
  }
 }
 return false;
}

// Gets a char letter
bool Script::GetKeyWord (const char* key, char& value) {
 infile.seekg (position, ios::beg);
 char line[80];
 while (infile.getline (line, sizeof(line))) {
  if (_strnicmp (line, key, strlen(key)) == 0) {
   istrstream is (line+strlen(key));
   is >> value;
   if (!is) {
    value = 0;
    return false;
   }
   return true;
```

```
   }
 }
 return false;
}

// Gets a float
bool Script::GetKeyWord (const char* key, float& value) {
 infile.seekg (position, ios::beg);
 char line[80];
 while (infile.getline (line, sizeof(line))) {
  if (_strnicmp (line, key, strlen(key)) == 0) {
   istrstream is (line+strlen(key));
   is >> value;
   if (!is) {
    value = 0;
    return false;
   }
   return true;
  }
 }
 return false;
}

// Gets a double
bool Script::GetKeyWord (const char* key, double& value) {
 infile.seekg (position, ios::beg);
 char line[80];
 while (infile.getline (line, sizeof(line))) {
  if (_strnicmp (line, key, strlen(key)) == 0) {
   istrstream is (line+strlen(key));
   is >> value;
   if (!is) {
    value = 0;
    return false;
   }
   return true;
  }
 }
 return false;
}

// Gets a bool
bool Script::GetKeyWord (const char* key, bool& value) {
 infile.seekg (position, ios::beg);
 char line[80];
 char type[10];
```

```
while (infile.getline (line, sizeof(line))) {
  if (_strnicmp (line, key, strlen(key)) == 0) {
   istrstream is (line+strlen(key));
   is.get (type, sizeof(type));
   if (!is) {
    value = false;
    return false;
   }
   if (_stricmp (type, "true") == 0)
    value = true;
   else if (_stricmp (type, "false") == 0)
    value = false;
   else
    return false;
   return true;
  }
 }
 return false;
}

// Gets a character string
bool Script::GetKeyWord (const char* key, char* value, unsigned int
maxLength) {
 infile.seekg (position, ios::beg);
 char line[80];
 while (infile.getline (line, sizeof(line))) {
  if (_strnicmp (line, key, strlen(key)) == 0) {
   istrstream is (line+strlen(key));
   is.get (value, maxLength);
   if (!is) {
    value[0] = 0;
    return false;
   }
   return true;
  }
 }
 return false;
}
```

The PutSection() function is more complex. We wish to replace a section of the text file or perhaps add a new section. Thus, we must copy the entire contents of the existing file to a new temporary file, omitting all lines within the section to be replaced, assuming it is present. The function's outer loop inputs successive lines and if these lines are not part of the section to be rewritten, it writes them out to the new file. However, if the beginning of the section to be rewritten is found, all lines in that section are read in, but ignored.

```
bool Script::PutSection (const char* section) {
 outfile.open ("temp.txt");
 if (!outfile) return false;
 char line[80];
 while (infile.getline (line, sizeof(line))) {
  if (_strnicmp (line, "Section: ", 9) == 0 &&
      _stricmp (&line[9], section) == 0) {
   while (infile.getline (line, sizeof(line))) {
    if (_strnicmp (line, "Section: ", 9) == 0) {
     outfile << line << endl;
     break;
    }
   }
  }
  else
   outfile << line << endl;
 }
 infile.close ();
 outfile << "Section: " << section << endl;
 return true;
}

// Writes an int
void Script::PutKeyWord (const char* key, int value) {
 outfile << key << value << endl;
}

// Writes a long
void Script::PutKeyWord (const char* key, long value) {
 outfile << key << value << endl;
}

// Writes a short
void Script::PutKeyWord (const char* key, short value) {
 outfile << key << value << endl;
}

// Writes a single character letter
void Script::PutKeyWord (const char* key, char value) {
 outfile << key << value << endl;
}

// Writes a float
void Script::PutKeyWord (const char* key, float value) {
 outfile << key << value << endl;
}
```

```
// Writes a double
void Script::PutKeyWord (const char* key, double value) {
 outfile << key << value << endl;
}

// Writes a bool
void Script::PutKeyWord (const char* key, bool value) {
 outfile << key << (value ? "true" : "false") << endl;
}

// Writes a character string
void Script::PutKeyWord (const char* key, char* value) {
 outfile << key << value << endl;
}
```

The PutEnd() function handles the remaining details. Since all data have been rewritten, the output file is closed. Next, the original input file which is to be replaced with this new one is deleted. If that was successful, the new temporary file is renamed to be the same as the original file.

```
bool Script::PutEnd () {
 outfile.close ();
 if (remove (filename) == -1) {
  cerr << "Error: could not delete file: " << filename << endl;
  return false;
 }
 if (rename ("temp.txt", filename) != 0) {
  cerr << "Error: could not rename file temp.txt to " << filename
       << endl;
  return false;
 }
 infile.open (filename);
 return true;
}
```

The remove() function, defined in <io.h>, is passed the filename to be deleted. It is sent to the recycle bin. It returns 0 if all is okay and a -1 if it fails to delete the file. The rename() function is passed the old name followed by the new filename. It returns a non-zero value if it fails, 0 if it succeeds.

With these I/O primitives in hand, we can now write any number of classes that can store data in these ini-like text files. I chose to illustrate the method by a beginning outline of an NPC class. The NPCs are identified by a number which can easily be converted to and from a string. The game can keep track of NPCs by arrays of ints. The actual data that defines an NPC is stored in an ini-like file. Six attributes, strength, intelligence, and so on, are stored conveniently in an array of ints. However, for display purposes and for storage in the ini file, the character string identifier must be shown, such as "Strength." By having a parallel array of constant character strings, this can easily be accomplished. Each property of the class must have a string keyword for the ini-like file. An = sign can be appended to each of the AttrName strings to create the keyword strings.

NPC.h

```
#pragma once
#include <iostream>
#include <iomanip>
using namespace std;

const int MaxName = 21;
const int MaxAttributes = 6;
const int MaxAttrLen = 13;

const char AttrName[MaxAttributes][MaxAttrLen] = {
            "Strength", "Intelligence", "Wisdom",
            "Dexterity", "Constitution", "Charisma" };

const char KeyHealthMax[]   = "HealthPointsMax=";
const char KeyHealthCur[]   = "HealthPointsCur=";
const char KeyName[]        = "Name=";
const char KeySpells[]      = "HasSpells=";
const char KeyWeaponType[]  = "WeaponType=";

class NPC {
public:
  long   idNumber;
  char   name[MaxName];
  int    attributes[MaxAttributes];
  float  healthMax;
  float  healthCur;
  bool   hasSpells;
  char   weaponType;

  bool   isModified;

public:
      NPC (long idNum);
      ~NPC ();
  bool LoadNPC ();
  bool SaveNPC ();
  void DisplayNPC (ostream& os);
};
```

The constructor is passed the NPC id number and attempts to load the properties of this NPC from the ini-like file. The bool, isModified, is set to true whenever any properties are altered. One could easily make these properties protected and provide get/set functions. The set functions would then set isModified. However, I purposely kept it simple for this sample. When the destructor function is called, if isModified is true, the properties are re-written back out to the ini-like text file.

NPC.cpp

```cpp
#include "NPC.h"
#include "Script.h"

NPC::NPC (long idNum) {
 idNumber = idNum;
 // try to load this NPC from the ini file
 if (!LoadNPC ()) {
  // here it failed, so leave the object in a stable state
  name[0] = 0;
  for (int i=0; i<MaxAttributes; i++) {
   attributes[i] = 0;
  }
  healthMax = healthCur = 0;
  hasSpells = false;
  weaponType = 'N';
 }
 isModified = false;
}


NPC::~NPC () {
 // if the NPC has been modified, rewrite to the ini file
 if (isModified) SaveNPC ();
}

bool NPC::LoadNPC () {
 bool ok;
 Script s ("NPC.txt", ok);
 if (!ok) return false;

 char idstring[80];
 _ltoa_s (idNumber, idstring, sizeof(idstring), 10);
 if (!s.FindSection (idstring)) return false;

 if (!s.GetKeyWord (KeyName, name, MaxName)) return false;

 char key[MaxAttrLen+1];
 for (int i=0; i<MaxAttributes; i++) {
  strcpy_s (key, sizeof(key), AttrName[i]);
  strcat_s (key, sizeof(key), "=");
  if (!s.GetKeyWord (key, attributes[i])) return false;
```

```
  }

  if (s.GetKeyWord (KeyHealthMax, healthMax) &&
      s.GetKeyWord (KeyHealthCur, healthCur) &&
      s.GetKeyWord (KeySpells, hasSpells) &&
      s.GetKeyWord (KeyWeaponType, weaponType)) {
   return true;
  }
  else return false;
}

bool NPC::SaveNPC () {
 bool ok;
 Script s ("NPC.txt", ok);
 if (!ok) return false;

 char idstring[80];
 _ltoa_s (idNumber, idstring, sizeof(idstring), 10);
 if (!s.PutSection (idstring)) return false;

 s.PutKeyWord (KeyName, name);

 char key[MaxAttrLen+1];
 for (int i=0; i<MaxAttributes; i++) {
  strcpy_s (key, sizeof(key), AttrName[i]);
  strcat_s (key, sizeof(key), "=");
  s.PutKeyWord (key, attributes[i]);
 }

 s.PutKeyWord (KeyHealthMax, healthMax);
 s.PutKeyWord (KeyHealthCur, healthCur);
 s.PutKeyWord (KeySpells, hasSpells);
 s.PutKeyWord (KeyWeaponType, weaponType);
 s.PutEnd ();
 isModified = false;
 return true;
}

void NPC::DisplayNPC (ostream& os) {
 os << fixed << setprecision (1);
 os << "Id Number     " << setw (4) << idNumber << endl;
 os << "Name:         " << name << endl;
 for (int i=0; i<MaxAttributes; i++) {
  os << left << setw(14) << AttrName[i] << right << setw (4)
     << attributes[i] << endl;
 }
```

```
os << "Health Max    " << setw (4) << healthMax << endl;
os << "Health Cur    " << setw (4) << healthCur << endl;
os << "Weapon Type   " << weaponType << endl;
os << "Has Spells    " << setw (4) << (hasSpells ? "Yes" : "No")
   << endl;
}
```

The main program, Pgm07a, just tests these functions. Notice the { } block around the first definition of the NPC instance called ann. This was done so that the destructor would be called, forcing a re-write of ann's data in the file. I then reloaded ann so that we can see the before and after changes.

```
#include <iostream>
#include <iomanip>
using namespace std;
#include "NPC.h"

int main () {

NPC tom (123);
tom.DisplayNPC (cout);
cout << endl << endl;

 {
  NPC ann (124);
  ann.DisplayNPC (cout);
  cout << endl << endl;

  ann.healthCur = 1.1f;
  ann.isModified = true;
 } // force destruction of ann so the data is rewritten

NPC ann (124);          // reloads ann to verify changes
ann.DisplayNPC (cout);
cout << endl << endl;

NPC henry (125);
henry.DisplayNPC (cout);
cout << endl << endl;

return 0;
}
```

Any number of properties of any number of objects can be stored in these ini-like files. It provides a uniform interface for handling I/O at run time between all kinds of objects.

Could a much faster binary file be used? Yes, particularly if all of the objects being stored were of the same length. If so, a single binary read could be used to input a structure containing all of the properties and then individually assigned to each property of the class instance. This is exactly what I do in my WWII game. I have a large binary database of the equipment. Each piece has a unique id number and the I/O interface can then load in all of the properties for a specific piece of equipment with a single read instruction, yielding very fast runtime operations.

Scripts Controlling Game Action

Often, scripts are used to control actual game play. For example, if the opponent is armed with a dagger only or unarmed, the NPC action may be to attack. However, if the opponent is armed with a large sword, the NPC may chose to flee instead. One now can construct as simple or complex a syntax parser as desired.

```
if opponent has sword {
        flee()
}
if opponent has nothing {
        attack()
}
if opponent has dagger {
        attack()
}
```

In the above script, the parser would search for keywords. The "if" triggers a conditional check. "Opponent" and "has" likewise would be search keywords. The "sword," "dagger," and "nothing" keywords, if found, be converted into game items. Opponent would convert into the character approaching the NPC. Finally, the lines with () indicate an action to take. These keywords would be translated into actual function calls based upon the results of the indicated tests performed upon actual game objects.

Here is another programmed script.

```
if wounds > half and opponent wounds < half {
        flee()
}
```

Once parsed into keywords and aligned with the NPC and opponent objects, a check can be made on the number of wounds the NPC has taken compared to his or her opponent. If the condition is met, the NPC would then execute a flee type of function. This adds realism but it also provides a good way to tweak the game. If you hard-code such logic, into the program, it cannot be changed without recoding. However, if a script is used, then one could tweak it and see the overall effect upon game play:

```
if wounds > .9 and opponent wounds < half {
        flee()
}
```

Now the NPC will not break off the attack until very badly wounded.

Yet another use for scripts is the handling of the usual dialog conversations within the game. The script would have two main verb keywords, such as ask or query or question and reply or say or speak or answer. Perhaps one of the most commonly found questions that can be asked is this one. "What is your name?" Assuming our verbs are "Question" and "Answer," the script might be written this way.

Question "What is your name?"

Answer "I am Archmage Alexandro Sustera, the Almighty."

A large text file can be constructed with all of the questions a player or NPC might wish to originate or be asked along with their replies. At the appropriate time within the game, if an NPC is asked a question, simply go through the array of questions looking for a match and then show or speak the reply.

However, there is one huge problem with dialog. While you have total control over the questions to be asked by your NPCs, you are at the mercy of the player who chooses to ask a question. The above often used question could be entered by the player in many other ways.

What name?

WHAT IS YOUR NAME

What's your name?

Sire, what is your name?

Sir, what are you called?

Do you have a name?

Hi there, I am Fred. Who are you?

I well remember playing Infocomm's Hitchiker's Guide to the Galaxy when it came out in the early years of PCs. I tried for three hours to get the game to put the babel fish into my ear (it's a universal language translator). I finally gave up and resorted to the cheat booklet, only to discover I was one small word off from what the program would accept! Grrr.

One cannot handle the situation by comparing for "what is your name?" even if it is a case insensitive compare. This would only recognize two of these. Yes, I have a deaf young nephew just learning to read and write, though he is a terrific game player, who readily beats me. His writing is as simple as possible, "what name?"

To be able to recognize all of these as the same question would require a good deal of parsing keywords. However, the usual approach is to isolate the really relevant keywords and check if those are present. Here, we could check for "what" and "name." If both were found, the game would speak the reply. This alone would handle all of the variations except the last two. If you desired to be a little more forgiving on user input, you could additionally check for "have" and "name" as well as the pair, "who" and "you."

How is a parser constructed? Case must be ruled out. My suggestion is always pass in your constant programmer strings in lower case. Then, only the user's inputted string must be converted to lower case for comparisons. When converting case, do not use a technique that depends upon the ASCII sequence, because your game could not then be as easily ported to other platforms. Use the

Game Programming Theory

built-in C++ functions to convert case.

Here is a simple keyword finder.

```cpp
#include <string>
using namespace std;

const int MaxUserInputLength = 80;

bool IsKeywordPresent (const char* userInput,
                       const char* keyword) {
  char user[MaxUserInputLength];
  strcpy_s (user, sizeof (user), userInput); // copy user's string
  _strlwr_s (user);                          // convert to lower case
  return strstr (user, keyword) != 0;
}
```

The user's input string is copied and converted to lower case, using the _strlwr_s() function. Then, strstr() function looks for the first occurrence of the keyword within the user string. The function returns a char* pointer to the first occurrence of the keyword. If the keyword is not found, then a NULL pointer is returned. Thus, if the function return is != 0, the keyword is present and the function returns true.

If you were always looking for a pair of keywords, then for efficiency, pass in both keywords. This way, the conversion to lower case is not done more than once. Here is the second overloaded version.

```cpp
bool IsKeywordPresent (const char* userInput,
                       const char* keyword1,
                       const char* keyword2) {
  char user[MaxUserInputLength];
  strcpy_s (user, sizeof (user), userInput); // copy user's string
  _strlwr_s (user);                          // convert to lower case
  return strstr (user, keyword1) != 0 &&
         strstr (user, keyword2) != 0;
}
```

Scripting is not something done after the game engine is build. Scripting should be designed into the original specifications of the game. Present from the start, many scripts can be tested and various parameters tweaked as they are developed.

Finite State Machines

A finite state machine is an abstract concept representing a "machine" which has specific, finite states which it knows how to act and perform. Additionally and often, the machine has trigger events to which it can respond by changing from one state into another state.

Finite state machines have been around a long time. Perhaps one of the best know examples is Pac Mac. The ghosts are essentially finite state machines. One state is freely roaming about the playing field. The second and third states are activated by the player eating a "power pill." At this point, they change state and evade the player. When the power boost runs out, they change state back to chasing or roaming.

The finite state machine is diagramed showing the possible states and the trigger mechanism that allows them to change from one state to another. Figure 7-1 shows a finite state machine representation of Pac Man.

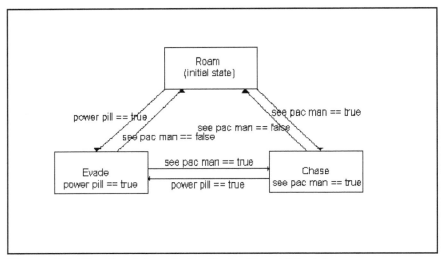

Figure 7-1 The Pac Man Finite State Ghost Machine

Initially all ghosts being in the Roam state. If the ghost sees pac man, it can change state to Chase. As long as the ghost continues to see pac man, it remains in the chase state. If in the Roam state and the power pill is used, the state changes to Evade, which remains in effect as long as the power pill is in effect. In the Chase state, if the power pill is used, the state changes to Evade. However, if in the Chase state and sight of pac man is lost, the ghost reverts back to the Roam state. Thus, a series of simple test conditions trigger the machine to change from one state into another state.

Let's see how a simple finite state machine can be implemented and see the visual effect it can have. Consider a herd of grazing animals and one hunter. Initially, the herd animals will be in

Game Programming Theory

the Grazing State. In this state, they meander about clear terrain tiles. After ten turns of grazing, they become thirsty and move to the nearest water tile. In the Water State, they go to water and drink for three turns. The third state can occur at any time, when the presence of the hunter is detected. A herd animal can detect the presence of the hunter whenever the hunter is within ten tiles from it and it has a clear line of sight to the hunter, not obstructed by a forest tile. In the Flee State, the herd animal moves away from the hunter until more than ten tiles separate it from the hunter. At this point, it reverts back to its previous state to finish off that state.

The Animal class would have then four key state functions: CheckState(), DoFlee(), DoGraze(), and DoWater(). In order to more realistically implement the behaviors, let's use random numbers for directions and locations of the herd.

C++ supports a random number generator called rand(), which returns the next random number. However, the generator requires a seed value from which the series of numbers are created. If the same seed is used from one program execution to the next, the same series of random numbers are presented. Hence, the time of day is often used for this seed value, guaranteeing that a different set of numbers are generated each time the program executes. Here is the Random.h definition. It is a very simple class, allowing for two construction methods. The default constructor is used in production, while the second one allows you to specify the starting seed number so that you can repeat the previous series of random numbers for debugging purposes.

```
#pragma once
/**********************************************************/
/*                                                        */
/* Random: obtain a random number between 1 and the number of  */
/*         die sides passed                               */
/*                                                        */
/**********************************************************/

class Random {

public:
        // seeds the random number generator with current time
        Random ();

        // for debugging, seed with a specific repeatable sequence
        Random (unsigned int x);

        // gets a random number between 1 and num_sides
 unsigned GetRandom (int num_sides) const;

};
```

The header file, ctime, contains the definitions for the time functions, while the random number functions are defined in iostream.

```
#include <ctime>
```

```
#include <iostream> // for the random number functions
using namespace std;
#include "Random.h"

/**************************************************************/
/*                                                          */
/* Random: initialize the random number generator            */
/*         using the current time as the seed value          */
/*                                                          */
/**************************************************************/

        Random::Random () {
 srand ((unsigned) time (0)); // use the current time as the seed
}

/**************************************************************/
/*                                                          */
/* Random: for debugging, use the passed seed value          */
/*                                                          */
/**************************************************************/

        Random::Random (unsigned int x) {
 srand (x); // use the passed repeatable seed value
}

/**************************************************************/
/*                                                          */
/* GetRandom: obtain a random number between 1 and numsides  */
/*                                                          */
/**************************************************************/

unsigned  Random::GetRandom (int num_sides) const {
 return (rand () % num_sides) + 1;
}
```

Because a number of our constant values must be shared between other files, I moved them into a header file called constants.h. Note that I added an array of Point structures to store the locations of the watering holes.

```
#pragma once
#include "Point.h"

const int MaxRows = 24;
const int MaxCols = 80;
const int MaxPathElements = 200;
const int NotOnPath = -1;
const int MaxAnimals = 10;

const int UpArrow = 72;     // the special key codes for the arrow
```

```
operators
const int DownArrow = 80;
const int LeftArrow = 75;
const int RightArrow = 77;

enum TravelDirection {North = 1, NorthEast, East, SouthEast, South,
SouthWest, West, NorthWest};
```

`const Point Water[2] = {Point (38, 21), Point (38, 22)};`

Now let's look at the Animal class definition, which uses the finite state machine. I added an enum to keep track of which state the animal is currently in, along with the color used to display an animal which is in this state.

```
#pragma once
#include <iostream>
using namespace std;
#include "Point.h"
#include "constants.h"
#include "Random.h"
#include "Screen.h"

enum State {Grazing, Watering, Fleeing};
const      Screen::Color      stateColor[3]      =      {Screen::Green,
Screen::BrightAqua, Screen::Red};

const int SeeHunterDistance = 10;
const int MaxTurnsGrazing = 10;
const int MaxTurnsWatering = 3;

class Animal {
public:
 State state;
 State previousState;
 Point loc;

 int  turnsGrazing;
 int  turnsWatering;
 bool foundWater;

  Animal ();
 ~Animal ();

 void CheckState (const Point& hunter);

 void DoFlee (const Point& h, char field[][MaxCols+1]);
```

```
void DoGraze (char field[][MaxCols+1], Random& r);
void DoWater (char field[][MaxCols+1]);
};
```

The previous state is required so that when the animal is done fleeing, it can return to what it was doing before fleeing. When it becomes thirsty, it must go in search of water, which may take a number of turns to get to the watering hole. The turns drinking cannot start until it has reached the water, hence the bool foundWater.

The implementation is actually fairly simple. Examine the CheckState() function. First, the distance between this animal and the hunter is calculated. The worst case scenario is the hunter has gotten too close causing a change to the Fleeing state. Next, check to see if the animal is currently fleeing. If so, see if the animal is now far enough away to feel safe once more, reverting back to its previous state. If neither of these is in effect, then check on the grazing and watering states and handle those changes in state last.

```
#include "Animal.h"

Animal::Animal () {
  state = Grazing;
  previousState = Watering;
  turnsGrazing = turnsWatering = 0;
}

Animal::~Animal () {}

// CheckState: handles state switching
void Animal::CheckState (const Point& hunter) {
  // calculate current hunter distance from this animal
  int dx = abs (hunter.x - loc.x);
  int dy = abs (hunter.y - loc.y);
  int d = dx > dy ? dx : dy;
  // see if it needs to start fleeing
  if (d <= SeeHunterDistance && state != Fleeing) {
    previousState = state;
    state = Fleeing;
  }
  // see if it is done fleeing
  else if (state == Fleeing && d > SeeHunterDistance)
    state = previousState;
  // see if it is done grazing
  else if (state == Grazing && turnsGrazing >= MaxTurnsGrazing) {
    state = Watering;
    turnsWatering = 0;
  }
  // see if it is done watering
```

```
else if (state == Watering && turnsWatering >= MaxTurnsWatering)
{
  state = Grazing;
  turnsGrazing = 0;
 }
}

void Animal::DoFlee (const Point& h, char field[][MaxCols+1]) {
 Point proposed = loc;
 // use crudest method of just going the opposite dir from hunter
 if (h.x > loc.x)
  proposed.x--;
 else if (h.x < loc.x)
  proposed.x++;
 else
  proposed.x++;
 if (h.y > loc.y)
  proposed.y--;
 else if (h.y < loc.y)
  proposed.y++;
 else
  proposed.y++;

 // now check if it went out of range. if so, put it on screen
 if (proposed.x < 1)
  proposed.x = MaxCols-2;
 else if (proposed.x > MaxCols-2)
  proposed.x = 1;
 if (proposed.y < 1)
  proposed.y = MaxRows - 1;
 else if (proposed.y > MaxRows -1)
  proposed.y = 1;

 // now see if new location is obstacle.
 // if so, crudely move animal to a
 // nearby tile by checking adjacent tiles
 if (field[proposed.y][proposed.x] == 'T') {
  if (field[proposed.y][proposed.x-1] != 'T')
   proposed.x--;
  else if (field[proposed.y][proposed.x+1] != 'T')
   proposed.x++;
  else if (field[proposed.y-1][proposed.x] != 'T')
   proposed.y--;
  else if (field[proposed.y+1][proposed.x] != 'T')
   proposed.y++;
 }
```

197

```
 loc = proposed;
 // note: this animal could be on top of another animal
}

void Animal::DoGraze (char field[][MaxCols+1], Random& r) {
 Point proposed;
 bool isValid = false;
 // find a new allowed location to graze, clear tile
 while (!isValid) {
  proposed = loc;
  // pick a random direction to move
  int dir = r.GetRandom (8);
  switch (dir) {
   case 1:
    proposed.y--;
    break;
   case 2:
    proposed.y--;
    proposed.x++;
    break;
   case 3:
    proposed.x++;
    break;
   case 4:
    proposed.y++;
    proposed.x++;
    break;
   case 5:
    proposed.y++;
    break;
   case 6:
    proposed.y++;
    proposed.x--;
    break;
   case 7:
    proposed.x--;
    break;
   case 8:
    proposed.y--;
    proposed.x--;
    break;
  }
  // check if out of bounds, if so, try a new random direction
  if (proposed.x < 1 || proposed.x > MaxCols-2 ||
      proposed.y < 1 || proposed.y > MaxRows -1)
   continue;
```

```cpp
   // see if the proposed tile is clear
   if (field[proposed.y][proposed.x] == ' ')
     isValid = true;
  }
  // note: this animal could be on top of another animal
  loc = proposed;
  turnsGrazing++;
}

void Animal::DoWater (char field[][MaxCols+1]) {
  // if animal is in the water tile, continue drinking
  if (field[loc.y][loc.x] == 'W') {
   turnsWatering++;
   return;
  }
  // here, it is not in the water yet, so move to closest one
  int dx1 = abs (loc.x - Water[0].x);
  int dy1 = abs (loc.y - Water[0].y);
  int dx2 = abs (loc.x - Water[1].x);
  int dy2 = abs (loc.y - Water[1].y);
  int d1 = dx1 > dy1 ? dx1 : dy1;
  int d2 = dx2 > dy2 ? dx2 : dy2;
  // w contains location of closest water tile
  Point w = d1 > d2 ? Water[0] : Water[1];
  // use crudest line of sight method to move there
  Point proposed = loc;
  if (w.x > loc.x)
   proposed.x++;
  else if (w.x < loc.x)
   proposed.x--;
  if (w.y > loc.y)
   proposed.y++;
  else if (w.y < loc.y)
   proposed.y--;
  // if new location is obstacle,
  // attempt to move to neighboring tile
  if (field[proposed.y][proposed.x] == 'T') {
   if (field[proposed.y][proposed.x-1] != 'T')
    proposed.x--;
   else if (field[proposed.y][proposed.x+1] != 'T')
    proposed.x++;
   else if (field[proposed.y-1][proposed.x] != 'T')
    proposed.y--;
   else if (field[proposed.y+1][proposed.x] != 'T')
    proposed.y++;
  }
```

```
// note animal could be on top of another one
loc = proposed;
}
```

Notice how each state has its own algorithm of operation. Admittedly, more than one animal could be in a single tile. Whether or not this is allowed in your game is up to you. While I could have added more coding to restrict "stacking," I chose to keep this as simple as possible to illustrate the finite state machine algorithm.

The main() function runs the simulation. Again, I kept the LoadField() and ShowField() functions used in the previous programs; they are not shown here. I only added a check to show the water tiles in blue. When constructing the random number generator, I used a seed of 42 so that I can get a repeatable sequence for debugging. When this program goes into production, use the default constructor so that the time of day is used.

```
#include <iostream>
#include <fstream>
#include <iomanip>
using namespace std;

#include "Screen.h"
#include "Point.h"
#include "Random.h"
#include "Animal.h"
#include "constants.h"

void LoadField (char field[][MaxCols+1],
                Screen::Color fieldColor[][MaxCols]);
void ShowField (Screen& s, char field[][MaxCols+1],
                Screen::Color fieldColor[][MaxCols]);
void MoveHunter (Screen& s, Point& h, char field[][MaxCols+1]);

int main () {
 Random r (42);
 cin.sync_with_stdio ();  // if you want to use cin
 Screen s (Screen::Blue, Screen::BrightYellow);

 s.SetTitle ("Tile-based Tracing Pathfinding");
 s.DrawBox (0, 0, 24, 79, Screen::Gray, Screen::BrightYellow);

 char          field[MaxRows][MaxCols+1];
 // the playing field
 Screen::Color fieldColor[MaxRows][MaxCols];
 // colors of obstacles

 // load and show the entire field
```

```
LoadField (field, fieldColor);
ShowField (s, field, fieldColor);

// set up and show the hunter
Point hunter (70, 4);
s.GoToXY (hunter.x, hunter.y);
s << 'H';

int i;
Animal a[MaxAnimals]; // the herd of animals

// create the initial location for the herd animals
for (i=0; i<MaxAnimals; i++) {
 // initially all are in the grazing state for various times
 a[i].turnsGrazing = r.GetRandom (15);
 bool isValid = false;
 // obtain an initial location that is allowed for the animal
 while (!isValid) {
  a[i].loc.x = r.GetRandom (10) + 11;
  a[i].loc.y = r.GetRandom (10) + 10;
  if (field[a[i].loc.y][a[i].loc.x] != 'T')
    isValid = true;
 }
 s.OutputUCharWith ('a', a[i].loc.y, a[i].loc.x, Screen::Blue,
                    stateColor[a[i].state]);
}
```

Notice the above loop which assigns each animal to its initial location. I obtain a random number between 1 and 10 and add that to a fixed location in the bottom quadrant of the screen. However, if that location is one that is not allowed, another pair of random numbers are used.

```
// the simulation lasts for 50 hunter turns
Point old;
int count = 50;
while (count) {
 old = hunter; // save hunter's current position
 MoveHunter (s, hunter, field);
 // now remove hunter from old location
 s.OutputUCharWith (field[old.y][old.x], old.y, old.x,
                    Screen::Blue,
                    fieldColor[old.y][old.x]);
 // and display hunter at new location
 s.GoToXY (hunter.x, hunter.y);
 s << 'H';
```

Note that in this simulation, before the object is displayed at its new location, it is removed from its old location by redisplaying the corresponding character from the map.

```
for (i=0; i<MaxAnimals; i++) {
 old = a[i].loc;              // save old location
 a[i].CheckState (hunter);    // handle any state changes
 switch (a[i].state) {        // process the current state
   case Fleeing:
    a[i].DoFlee (hunter, field);
    break;
   case Grazing:
    a[i].DoGraze (field, r);
    break;
   case Watering:
    a[i].DoWater (field);
    break;
 }
 // remove previous image and show new image at new location
 s.OutputUCharWith (field[old.y][old.x], old.y, old.x,
                    Screen::Blue, fieldColor[old.y][old.x]);
 s.OutputUCharWith ('a', a[i].loc.y, a[i].loc.x, Screen::Blue,
                    stateColor[a[i].state]);
 }
 count--;
}

s.GoToXY (0, 24);
s.GetAnyKey ();

return 0;
}

// MoveHunter: use arrow keys to move one tile
void MoveHunter (Screen& s, Point& h, char field[][MaxCols+1]) {
 bool isValid = false;
 Point proposed;
 unsigned char skey, c;
 while (!isValid) {
  c = s.GetSpecialKey (skey);
  proposed = h;
  switch (skey) {
   case UpArrow:
    proposed.y--;
    break;
   case DownArrow:
    proposed.y++;
```

```
      break;
   case LeftArrow:
    proposed.x--;
    break;
   case RightArrow:
    proposed.x++;
    break;
  }
  // make sure this is an allowed tile for the hunter
  if (field[proposed.y][proposed.x] == ' ' ||
      field[proposed.y][proposed.x] == 'R') {
   h = proposed;
   isValid = true;
  }
 }
}
```

Finite state machines add a good deal of realism to games. Herds of animals and flocks of birds are easily simulated this way. The finite state machine is widely used for computer controlled objects.

Notice that we have not yet talked about combat situations. This is because the computer controlled objects are often implemented as finite state machines, initiate combat is one such state.

Programming Problems

Chapter 8 All About Projectiles, Cars, and Boats

What's supposed to happen when the shot is fired? It depends upon the underlying physics of the motion. Is there a difference between the firing of a bullet from a gun at an elevation angle of say 45 degrees with an initial velocity of 100 feet per second and the firing of a pumpkin fired at the same angle and initial velocity? Hint, which is more aerodynamic? What do you suppose air resistance has to do with the two trajectories? True, the pumpkin is vastly heavier than a bullet and mass does enter into the equation of motion. But in which case could you safely ignore air drag and still end up with a reasonable game simulation? How about firing a bird feather and a child's hand made paper airplane. Both weigh about the same, yet there is a terrific difference in their flight paths, try it sometime.

We are going to examine a number of canned situations involving the firing of a projectile. With each, a series of canned solution equations are given. Why? Because a game programmer just needs the formula to apply in a given situation. Later on in game tuning, the programmer must also know what factor can be eliminated to speed the game up without sacrificing significant realism. Game programmers do not need to be physicists, but they do need to have a grasp of a wide number of formulas and how they apply to his or her specific situation they are modeling in their game.

Projectile motion is one of the critical motions in many games. From firing of guns, shotguns, pistols, rifles, bazookas, artillery, bows and arrows, spear guns, baseballs, football passes, thrown objects, ah, the list goes on and on. Knowledge of the formulas for projectiles is fundamental in game programming. What do we know about the projectile problem?

First, a projectile is launched with an initial thrust and at some elevation angle. Once fired or let go, it is then acted on only by external forces of gravity and perhaps air drag. The initial launch is actually an impulse force, a sudden initial thrust acting over a relatively short period of time. Other types of projectiles may have additional capabilities during flight, such as rockets and guided missiles, which have their own propulsion mechanisms and steering or guidance systems onboard. Let's not consider these types just yet. Keep it simple for now.

If we consider the projectile to have been launched on earth, where we can consider the earth to be flat not curved over the distance traveled, we can make some safe assumptions. The trajectory is that of a parabolic curve. By now, you should realize that at an angle of 45 degrees the maximum distance can be traveled. The impact velocity will be the same as the launch velocity, if the landing spot is at the same elevation as the launching spot. At the top of the trajectory, the vertical velocity component is zero for a brief instant, before it begins falling. Further the time required to reach the highest point, its apex, is the same for it to reach the landing point from the apex, if the launching

Game Programming Theory

and landing points are at the same elevation. Finally, if you have not had a basic laboratory physics course, you might not realize this one: the time to fall from its apex to the landing point is the same amount of time that the projectile would take if it was simply dropped from that apex height, falling straight down.

If we fire a simple projectile, four cases arise for our consideration. First, the launching and landing points are at the same level. Second, the launching point is higher than the landing point. Third, the launching point is lower than the landing point. Fourth, the launching point is from a moving object high in the air and the projectile is dropped, ie, a bomb or rocket fired from a plane.

In all these equations, the x axis is along the direction the projectile travels, while the y axis is vertically upwards. I will used the following symbols to represent the various quantities.

D is the total distance traveled along the x asis

T is the total time required to reach the landing point

H is the maximum height the projectile reaches during its flight

v_x and v_y represent the velocities in along the x and y axes

v(t) is the velocity as a function of time

x(t) is the distance traveled along the x axis as a function of time

y(t) is the height traveled along the y axis as a function of time

v(t) is the speed as a function of time (not a vector, only the magnitude)

e is the elevation angle of the launch

v_0 is the launch velocity or muzzle velocity

Case 1: Launching and Landing Points Are at the Same Height

Figure 8-1 shows the situation, in terms of the quantities listed above.

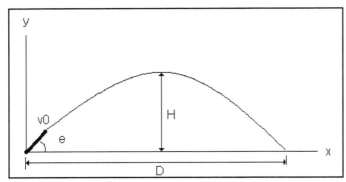

Figure 7-1 Launching and Landing at Same Height

Here are the simplified equations of motion.

$D = v_0 * T * \cos(e)$

$T = 2 * v_0 * \sin(e) / g$

$H = v_0 * v_0 * \sin(e) * \sin(e) / (2 * g)$

$x(t) = (v_0 * \cos(e)) * t$

$y(t) = (v_0 * \sin(e)) * t - g * t * t / 2$

$v(t) = \text{sqrt}(v_0 * v_0 - 2 * g * v_0 * \sin(e) * t + g * g * t * t)$

$v_x(t) = v_0 * \cos(e)$

$v_y(t) = v_0 * \sin(e) - g * t$

where $g = 32.2$ feet per second per second or 9.8 meters per second per second

Case 2: Launching Point Is Higher Than the Landing Point

Figure 8-2 shows the situation, in terms of the quantities listed above. The only difference in the equations is the total time T required to land.

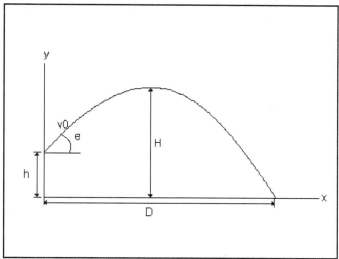

Figure 8-2 Launching Point Is Higher Than Landing

Here are the equations that define this type of shot.

$D = v_0 * T * \cos(e)$

$T = v_0 * \sin(e) / g + \text{sqrt}(2 * H / g)$

$H = h + v_0 * v_0 * \sin(e) * \sin(e) / (2 * g)$

$x(t) = v_0 * \cos(e) * t$

$y(t) = v_0 * \sin(e) * t - g * t * t / 2$

$v(t) = \text{sqrt}(v_0 * v_0 - 2 * g * v_0 * \sin(e) * t + g * g * t * t)$

$v_x(t) = v_0 * \cos(e)$

$v_y(t) = v_0 * \sin(e) - g * t$

Case 3: Launching Point Is Lower Than the Landing Point

Figure 8-3 shows the situation, in terms of the quantities listed above. The only difference in the equations is the total time T required to land.

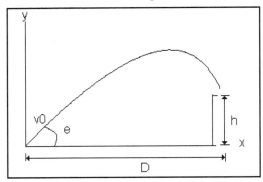

Figure 8-3 Launching Point Is Lower

Here are the equations for this situation.

$D = v_0 * T * \cos (e)$

$T = v_0 * \sin (e) / g + \text{sqrt} ((2 * (H - h)) / g)$

$H = v_0 * v_0 * \sin (e) * \sin (e) / (2 * g)$

$x(t) = v_0 * \cos (e) * t$

$y(t) = v_0 * \sin (e) * t - g * t * t / 2$

$v(t) = \text{sqrt} (v_0 * v_0 - 2 * g * v_0 * \sin (e) * t + g * g * t * t)$

$v_x(t) = v_0 * \cos (e)$

$v_y(t) = v_0 * \sin (e) - g * t$

Case 4: Projectile Is Dropped From a Plane

Figure 8-4 shows the situation, in terms of the quantities listed above.

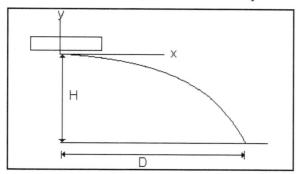

Figure 8-4 Dropped Projectile

Here are the simplified equations for this situation.

$D = v_0 * T$

$T = \text{sqrt} (2 * H / g)$

$H = g * t * t / 2$

$x(t) = v_0 * t$

$y(t) = H - g * t * t / 2$

$v(t) = \text{sqrt} (v_0 * v_0 + g * g * t * t)$

$v_x(t) = v_0$

$v_y(t) = - g * t$

The Impact of Drag on Projectile Motion

Earlier, we examined idealized drag forces, which yielded rather complex equations of motion. Now it's time to examine drag in more detail. The drag force acting on an object is proportional to a number of things: the speed of the object, its size and shape, the density of the fluid, and the viscosity of the fluid.

Undoubtedly you have actually experienced these effects. There is a huge difference in the drag force when you stick your hand outside a car window when it is going at a high rate of speed versus when it is going slowly. That is the speed factor at work. What is the effect of placing your hand vertical against the air flow versus horizontally? Here is the shape making itself felt on the drag force. When you go swimming and move your hands under water, because the water is more dense than air, there is more resistance to your arm motions. Try swimming with your fists in a ball to see the difference shape plays on your overall speed.

How then do we account for all of these variables upon the drag force? By gaining a better understanding of what is involved with drag forces. Consider the flow pattern of a fluid around a spherical steel ball. Out in front of the ball, all flow vectors are moving straight and parallel right at the ball. When they near the ball, some fluid must be displaced, moving around to the sides of the sphere. Yet once they have gone by the sphere, the fluid rejoins. That is, the pressure of the fluid is constant way out in front and way behind the sphere. Bernoulli's equation helps us understand this.

$$P / w + z + V^2 / (2g) = \text{some constant}$$

where P is the pressure, w is the specific weight of the fluid, z is the elevation of the point we are examining, V is the fluid velocity, and g is the gravitational acceleration. Looking at one point, z, then since the whole equation results in some constant, if the pressure increases, then the velocity must decrease so that the equation results stay constant. Conversely, if the velocity increases, the pressure must decrease.

With our steel ball, the pressure will increase at the leading point which is facing the incoming fluid. This out in front point is known as the stagnation point. As the fluid is forced around to the sides, the pressure will decrease for some distance before it increases back to normal at the rear, opposite the leading stagnation point. This is known as the trailing stagnation point. The pressure at the two stagnation points will be the same, but at the top and bottom, the pressure will be lower, because the fluid has an increase in velocity as it is moving out of the space occupied by the steel sphere.

What does this say about drag? If the pressures fore and aft are the same as well as above and below, there is no net pressure on the ball, as each cancels the other out. The pressures balance out. However, in the real world, there is friction to consider, that fluid moving around the ball will encounter friction, a resistance to its movement. As the fluid flows around the steel ball, some of the fluid will stick to the sphere. This sticky zone is known as the boundary layer. At the bottom of the boundary layer, the surface of our steel ball, the velocity of the fluid will be zero, sticking to the ball. Just above that the fluid will have a tiny velocity, increasing steadily until it reaches the boundary layer, after which it is flowing normally. This zone of velocity change transfers momentum to the steel ball and is what gives rise to our frictional drag force!

If the flow around the steel ball is laminar, the sheer between these velocity changes layers produces the frictional drag. However, if the flow becomes turbulent, then the sharp velocity gradients produce the frictional drag. Furthermore, as the velocity increases, on the back side the boundary layer where the fluid tends to stick to the ball increases toward the rear stagnation point. At some point, the fluid will not be able to continue to stick to our steel ball and will at last separate from the ball. This point of separation is called the separation point. Beyond or further to the rear from the separation point, the flow will be turbulent, the turbulent wake. In this wake zone, the pressure is lower than the pressure at the front of the ball and generates a pressure component to the drag forces!

Why do golf balls have small dimples on them instead of being smooth? Because of this effect. If you roughen up the smooth surface with dimples, you will increase the friction drag and the fluid will stick to the ball longer, or further toward the rear stagnation point. This then reduces the size of the turbulent wake, and thus lowers the pressure differential, lowering the pressure drag on the golf ball. Result, the dimpled golf ball has a smaller total drag than a smooth golf ball. Thus, the dimple ball travels significantly farther than a smooth one!

To measure the total drag on an object, often the Reynold's number, R_n, is used. It is a dimensionless number given by the following.

$R_n = v\,L\,/\,vis$, where v is the velocity, L is the length, and vis is the viscosity of the fluid

or $\quad R_n = v\,L\,d\,/\,av$, where d is the fluid mass density and av is the absolute viscosity

The values are normally worked out empirically in an experimental lab. If you want to know the drag coefficients for a new airplane, make a scale model and test it in the lab, determining the parameters experimentally. Then, scale them up to the full sized plane.

In general, a low Rn indicates laminar flow, while a high Rn indicates turbulent flow. One then gets a formula such as this.

$C_d = R_t\,/\,(d\,v^2\,A)$

where C_d is our drag coefficient, R_t is the total resistance, d is the fluid mass density, v is the velocity, and A is the frontal projected area of the object. For our steel ball, the A would be the area of a circle which has the same diameter as the steel ball. In practice, while this is a much better equation to use to find the drag coefficient, it does require knowing more about the object, that is, its total resistance and its fluid mass density.

Drag and Terminal Velocities

Earlier in the battleship's artillery firing, we implemented an idealized drag into the equations. If you recall, the y velocity component at a some time interval later on was given by the following equation.

$$v_{y2} = [\, e^{(-Cd/m)t} \,(C_d\, v_{y1} + m\, g) - m\, g\,]\, /\, C_d$$

Looking at this nasty equation, it is not obvious that as time goes on the velocity ends up at a fixed amount, the terminal velocity. One could plot this function on graph paper and see that it does. However, if we merely drop an object from some height, the equation simplifies because there is no initial velocity component.

$$v_{y2} = (\, e^{(-Cd/m)t} \, m\, g - m\, g\,)\, /\, C_d$$

Now there is only one term dealing with time. As t grows significantly large, the exp term becomes asymptotically small, yielding a terminal velocity.

If one utilizes the previous equations that use the total resistance, then the terminal velocity equation becomes this.

$$V_t = sqrt\,(\, 2 * m * g\, /\, (\, C_d * A * d))$$

where V_t is the terminal velocity, d is the fluid mass density, and A is the total area.
Of course, the challenging part of the equation is to know what value to use for C_d. On earth, the air density, d, near the surface is .00237 slugs/ft^3 when the temperature is sixty degrees Fahrenheit.

However, just looking at the equation, you can see that as the weight or mass of the falling object increases, so does its terminal velocity. As the area of the object increases, the lower the terminal velocity, hence parachutes and gliders.

Game Programming Theory

The Robbins Effect (Magnus Effect)

From real life, we know that objects moving through a fluid are often given a spin. Baseball pitchers do this all the time, especially the strike out kings. Tennis players, ping pong players, even football quarterbacks, all put a spin on their balls. Why? What is the impact of a spin on the object's motion?

If an object is moving through a fluid and if that object is spinning about an axis that goes through its center of mass, it generates a lift force! We normally think of lift as being associated with airplanes, hang gliders, and such, which have an air foil that produces the lift. Yet, a spinning steel sphere also produces lift.

A clockwise spin forces some of the fluid in the downward direction, yielding a lift in the upwards direction. A counter clockwise spin does the opposite, driving the sphere downward.

The magnitude of the Robbins force or Magnus force is proportional to the speed of the object, how fast it is spinning, the fluid density, the size of the object, and the type of fluid flow (laminar or turbulent).

Here are some approximate equations for two commonly found objects, a spinning cylinder and a sphere.
Cylinder:

$$F = 2\,PI\,d\,L\,v\,r^2\,\omega$$

where d is the fluid density, L is the length of the cylinder, v is the velocity, r is its radius, and ω is its angular velocity in radians per second.
Sphere:

$$F = 2\,PI\,d\,v\,r^4\,\omega\,/\,(2\,r)$$

where r is its radius.

Normally, we think of spin in terms of revolutions per minute, or rpm. To find ω, use this equation.

$$\omega = 2\,PI\,n\,/\,60, \text{ where n is its rpm}$$

When we use these in our equations of motion, we usually reduce the formulas to parallel those for drag.

$$F = d\,v^2\,A\,C_L\,/\,2$$

Now we only need to determine or guess what the coefficient of lift is.

In baseball, if the pitcher gives the ball a top spin, the ball tends to drop more than expected. If given a spin to either side, the ball curves in towards or away from the plate. If given a bottom spin, the ball appears to rise.

213

Game Programming Theory

In your game simulations, then, you must be the judge as to whether or not these additional components need to be added to your equations of motion.

Self-propelled Rockets

Self-propelled rockets present another variation on projectile motion. As long as their engines are burning, an additional thrust force is being generated. However, along with the force comes a corresponding decrease in total mass of the rocket, as its fuel is being burned. This gives rise to the variable mass situation in projectile motion.

Two situations arise. First, the consumption of fuel does not add to the absolute velocity of the object, such as a ship steaming across the ocean. In this case, the sum of the forces become altered slightly.

$$F = m \, (dv/dt) + v \, (dm/dt)$$

That was simple, but second is the rocket which burns its fuel so as to increase its absolute velocity. Let u represent the relative velocity of the burning fuel which is being added to the overall speed of the rocket. The sum of the forces acting on the rocket can be expressed this way.

$$F = m \, dv/dt + u \, dm/dt$$

If we let m' be the rate of fuel burn, or mass change, the we get on earth

$$-mg = m \, dv/dt - m' \, u$$

or

$$m' \, u - mg = m \, dv/dt$$

where m' u represents the thrust that is propelling the rocket as it burns its fuel. Normally, fuel is burned at a constant rate. This allows you to calculate the total mass at any point in time this way.

$$m_1 = m_0 - m' \, t$$

All About Cars

Let's examine some specifics of automobiles from the viewpoint of a rigid body that we can use in our simulations. There are four key components to discuss.

Resistance to Motion

If you are driving down the road at some speed and put the car in neutral, the car eventually slows down to a stop. Why? The resistance from the fluid air causes a drag force opposite to the forward movement and there is a mechanical rolling resistance from the various parts of the tires and the drive train.

The total resistance can be expressed this way.
$$R_t = R_{air} + R_{rolling}$$

The air resistance comes from the surface friction with the air as a drag pressure similar to a projectile, although we do not usually think of a rolling car as a projectile. This resistance is given by the following.
$$R_{air} = d\ v^2\ A_f\ C_d\ /\ 2$$
where d is the mass density of the air, v is the velocity of travel, A_f is the frontal area of the car perpendicular to the direction of travel, and C_d is the drag coefficient.

What are typical drag coefficients for cars?

Type of Car	Low C_d	High C_d
Sports Car	.29	.40
Economy Car	.40	.50
Pickup Trucks	.43	.50
Semi-tractor trailers	.60	.90

The low, sleek, streamlined sports cars have the lowest air drag, while the tall semis have the highest.

The rolling resistance comes from the rolling tires and drive train package. The resistance comes from the deformation of the tires as they roll, not from friction, and from the resistance to motion from the drive train.
$$R_{rolling} = C_r\ w$$
where w is the weight supported by the tires. Tire manufacturers usually provide the rolling resistance for their tires.

215

Car tire: C_r are about .015

Truck tires: C_r range from .006 to .01

Assuming the car has four tires on the road, divide the car's total weight by four to get an individual weight for each tire. If you have an 18-wheeler, then use eighteen. To find the total rolling resistance, find the value for one tire and multiply by the number of tires touching the road.

Power to Overcome the Total Rolling Resistance

Power is the amount of work done by a force or a torque over time. We need to calculate how much power is required to overcome the total rolling resistance. The excess power then can move the car. Work is force times distance, expressed as foot-pounds or newton-meters. Power is work per time, or foot-pounds per second or newton-meters per second. However, with cars, power is often expressed as horsepower.

1 horsepower = 550 foot-pounds per second

The horsepower to overcome total resistance is given by this equation.

$H_{pr} = R_t \, v \, / \, 500$

where v is the velocity. Note that R_t is in pounds, v is in feet per second.

However, this power reaches the tires as a torque, rotational force against the pavement. The actual force to move the car is given by this equation.

$F = T \, / \, r$

where F is the force delivered by the tire to the road, T is the torque on the tire, and r is the tire's radius.

Note that you will need more than this minimum to drive the car, because of friction within the drive train and the need to run the alternator, air conditioner, stereo, and so on.

Distance Required to Stop a Car

Stopping a car means braking. How fast it stops depends on how hard one breaks, whether or not the braking turns into a skid, and whether or not the direction of travel is up hill or down hill or level. Perhaps in a snow storm you have been going down hill and had to stop. This can be a nasty situation, because there is little friction with the snowy road surface and the car naturally want to continue on downhill.

The stopping distance can be estimated from this equation, if we ignore air drag resistance.

$$D = v^2 / [2 g (u \cos (i) + \sin (i))]$$

where v is the velocity of travel, u is the coefficient of tire friction on the road, i is the inclination angle. A positive inclination angle means going uphill, while a negative inclination means going downhill.

The wild variable in the equation is the u coefficient of friction. On dry pavement, u is between .4 and .55 typically. However, on wet or snow covered roads, it is a whole lot smaller!

When inserting this into our simulations, the frictional force between a tire and the pavement is given by this.

$$F_f = u \, w$$

where F_f is the frictional force of one tire, u is the coefficient of friction, and w is the weight supported by that tire.

Banking of Curves

When you go around a curve, you typically feel an apparent centrifugal force forcing your body to one side. Yet, this is only an apparent force coming from the inertia of the car attempting to continue in its original direction. The real force is coming from the side to side friction of the tires, the roadway, and any roadway bank. This is the centripetal force or center seeking force that acts on the car. We are experiencing an acceleration due to a change in direction of the velocity vector, unless you are also slowing down or speeding up.

If the car's speed is too great and or the turn too sharp, the tire's side friction is not enough and the car begins to skid sideways. Hence, curves are often banked. The amount of banking of a curve is called super-elevation. The tangent of the super-elevation angle can be found by this equation.

$$\tan (a) = V_t^2 / (\, g\, r\,) - u$$

where V_t is the tangential velocity of the car, r is the radius of the curve, and u is the coefficient of friction between the tires and the road.

Or another way of looking at this, the tangential velocity at which skidding occurs is given by this one.

$$V_t = \text{sqrt} \,[(\tan (a) + u)\, g\, r]$$

All About Boats

Simulating a ship at sea becomes a more complex problem than a projectile or a car. The ship must maintain its buoyancy at all times or it sinks. Let's begin by defining some key terms needed in grasping the physics of motion of ships.

The bow of the ship is its front; the stern, its rear. Port is the left side, while starboard is the right side. The width of the ship is called its beam. When a ship is sitting in the water, part of it is submerged. That part that is under water is called its draft, while the depth refers to the total height from the very bottom of the ship to its main deck. If the draft equals the depth, the water comes in over the side of the ship and it capsizes and sinks. The hull of a ship is the watertight outer shell that supports the ship and displaces the water to keep it afloat. The length of the ship is measured by the overall length of the hull.

The displacement of a ship is that volume of water that is pushed aside or displaced by the ship as it sits in the water. The displacement is totally supported by buoyancy. The force on an object due to buoyancy is a function of the submerged volume of the hull. Archimedes's principle states that the weight of an object floating in a fluid is equal to the weight of the volume of fluid displaced by that object. In other words, the weight of a ship is the amount of water displaced by the ship at any point in time.

The buoyance force is given by this equation.
$$F_b = d \, g \, V_s$$
where d is the density of the fluid, g is gravity, and V_s is the volume of that part which is submerged. As a force, it is a vector and always acts through the center of buoyancy, which not the center of gravity. Rather, the center of buoyancy is the geometric center of the submerged part of the ship.

Now this gives us some key ship design guidelines. The center of buoyancy must be directly **below** the center of gravity, when the ship is at rest. The weight of the ship acts downward through the ship's center of gravity and opposes the force of buoyancy which acts on the center of buoyancy. These two forces are equal when the ship is in equilibrium.

Now suppose the wind hits the ship or a big wave rocks the boat. The ship rolls or pitches, a portion of the hull that is below water changes, causing the center of buoyancy to change to a new location. If the ship rolls to the starboard, the center of buoyancy also moves to the starboard. If the center of gravity is too high, then the ship just continues to roll over, capsizing! If the center of gravity is low, the forces generated tend to pull the ship back to equilibrium, because gravity acting downward pulls the ship back the other way. When it is too high, gravity acting downwards, only adds to the rolling movement started by the wave.

Game Programming Theory

This also applies to submarines and other underwater craft. If the sub's center of gravity is too high, when something tends to rock the ship from its equilibrium point, gravity only adds on to that action, rolling the sub over, ending upside down. Hence, when working with ships, the hardest part will be to calculate the volume that is under water. Hull geometries are often very complex shapes indeed.

Calculating a Ship's Resistance

Ships experience several types of drag resistance, both from the air and the water. In general, they can be lumped together to get an approximate expression.

$$R_t = R_f + R_p + R_w + R_a$$

where R_t is the total resistance to movement, R_f is the resistance due to friction, R_p is the resistance due to pressure, R_w is the resistance due to waves hitting the ship, and R_a is the resistance caused by air striking that portion of the ship that is above water.

In normal ship design, various complex and ship-specific calculations are made. However, we can make some very approximate equations which will work well in simulations that are not too demanding.

The R_f component is due to the friction of the water drag on the under water portion of the hull. It can be approximated this way.

$$R_f = d\ v^2\ S\ C_f\ /\ 2$$

where d is the fluid density of water, v is the velocity, S is the surface area of the hull that is under water, and C_f is the coefficient of friction. Thankfully, the coefficient of friction can also be estimated by the following equation.

$$C_f = .075\ /\ (\log_{10}(R_n) - 2)^2$$

where R_n is the Reynold's number and $\log_{10}$ is the base 10 logarithm, not the natural log.

How can we estimate the surface area of the underwater portion of the hull, S, in the above equation?

$$S = C_{ws}\ \text{sqrt}\ (V_d\ L)$$

where C_{ws} is the coefficient of the wet surface, L is the length of the ship, and V_d is the volume that is being displaced. C_{ws} is a function of the ship's beam to draft ratio and usually ranges between 2.6 to 2.9.

The R_p, pressure drag, is caused by a difference in pressure between the bow and stern caused by its speed. At the stern, we find a somewhat lower pressure. This factor must be computed from a detailed knowledge of the ship's geometry or by performing experimental measurements on a scale model and extrapolating to the full scale ship.

Game Programming Theory

The R_w, resistance due to waves hitting the ship, is also very difficult to determine. Like the pressure drag, it is usually determined experimentally on scale models.

Often, then, the R_w and R_p terms are combined into one experimentally determined value.
$$R_{pw} = d\ v^2\ S\ C_{pw}$$
where d is the fluid density of water, v is the velocity, S is the surface area under water, and C_{pw} is the coefficient. The C_{pw} must be calculated because it is often a function of speed, complicating matters. Roughly, C_{pw} may lie within the range of .001 to .003.

The R_a, resistance drag because of air hitting the above water portion of the ship can be estimated this way.
$$R_a = d\ v^2\ A_{air}\ C_{air}$$
where d is the fluid density, v is the velocity, A_{air} is the surface area tangential to the air flow direction, and C_{air} is the air drag coefficient, which typically ranges from .6 to 1.1. Ships with a low profile tend to have the lower values, while those with a large superstructure tend to have the largest values.

The A_{air} term can be approximated this way.
$$A_{air} = B^2\ /\ 2$$
where B is the beam or width of the ship.

Of course, there can be other sources of resistance to motion. A build up of barnacles on the hull gives rise to more resistance to motion, for example, which is why ships get their hulls cleaned and repainted periodically.

The Virtual Mass of a Ship

There is one additional consideration we must make when simulating a ship. Recall that at the boundary layer, some of the fluid actually sticks to the surface. On an object of such large proportions as a ship, this small build up of sticking water adds appreciable mass to the ship, primarily because near the stern the layer may be nearly three feet thick!

Rather than perform detailed calculations on just how much this extra mass actually is, approximations are used. Typical values of this additional mass range from 4% to 15% of the mass of the ship. However, a good conservative value to use is 20%. That is, when you need the mass of the ship in your calculations, use 1.2 times m instead.

Calculating the Volume of a Ship's Hull

Okay, we now have all we need to begin ship simulations, except for the ability to calculate the critical volume of the ship's hull that is currently under water. We cannot just plug in one number because that volume will change when the ship is loaded down with cargo. There are various algorithms for calculating the volume of complex shapes. However, in games programming, one technique is widely used, far more than all the others, the triangulated polyhedron.

A tetrahedron is a four sided geometric solid, with four vertices, in other words, a pyramidal shape. Figure 8.5 shows a tetrahedron and the four vertices and the three side vectors, a, b, and c, that we need to use to find its volume. Vertex v4 recedes from view or is in back of the vertices v1 through v3.

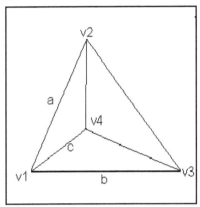

Figure 8-5 Tetrahedron

Notice that all of the four faces are triangles and totally enclose the space. Each edge connects with two vertices. Each edge is shared with only two faces or sides. Further, the following Euler's formula is satisfied.

Number of vertices – number of edges + number of faces = 2
4 – 6 + 4 = 2

Okay, so why have we picked a tetrahedron? The triple scalar product,
a . (**b** x **c**) {read: **a** dot (**b** cross **c**)}
is equal to the volume of the parallelepiped formed from these three vectors. And that volume is precisely 1/6th the volume of the tetrahedron!

Further, the geometric center of the tetrahedron is the average of the four vertices.
d = (**a** + **b** + **c**) / 4
The method so commonly used in games programming is to take the complex shape and divide it

222

up into a large number of tetrahedrons, such that they completely fill the volume of the shape, leaving no gaps or holes or overlaps.

Let's see how this works on something simple, for which we can easily calculate its volume by hand, a cube. Let's say the cube is 4 inches on a side. We divide the cube into four tetrahedrons. See Figure 8-6.

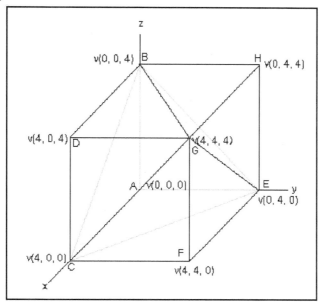

Figure 8-6 Division of a Square into Polyhedrons

Later on when you get to the point where you are going to use DirectX to display objects in 3D, you will be specifying vertices. So it makes sense to input the vertices. However, we need vectors that represent the sides for the algorithm. If an array of vertices are given or input, then we can specify the sides in terms of the subscripts of the vertices array.

The input data consists of the following to define the eight vertices. I added the corresponding subscript so we can follow more readily the definition of the faces, as well as a letter for each vertex.

```
8
0 0 0        [0]      A
0 0 4        [1]      B
4 0 0        [2]      C
4 0 4        [3]      D
0 4 0        [4]      E
4 4 0        [5]      F
4 4 4        [6]      G
0 4 4        [7]      H
```

Next, we enter the three sides, a, b, and c of the four tetrahedrons, being careful to always enter the three values going **counterclockwise** between the vertices that make up the tetrahedron as viewed from its outside, not from inside it. Hence, there are twelve faces to be entered in the correct order.

```
12
2 3 1
2 1 0
4 5 2
4 2 0
6 3 2
6 2 5
6 7 1
6 1 3
6 5 4
6 4 7
1 7 4
1 4 0
```

Pgm08a calculates the volume and center of volume for an arbitrary object of n vertices and m faces. Since we do not know the upper limit of either n or m, I chose to dynamically allocate the array of vertices and faces, based on the runtime contents of n and m. Full error checking is in force as well. The vertices are of type Vector, while I created a Face structure to hold the indexes of the vertices which comprise that face.

Pgm08a.cpp
```cpp
#include <iostream>
#include <iomanip>
#include <fstream>
using namespace std;
#include "Vector.h"

struct Face {
  int a;
  int b;
  int c;
};

void FindVolume (Vector* vertices, int numVertices, Face* faces,
                 int numFaces, double& volume, Vector& center);

int main () {

  ifstream infile ("square.txt");
  if (!infile) {
    cerr << "Error: cannot open input file\n";
    return 1;
  }
```

```
int numVertices;
infile >> numVertices;
if (!infile) {
 cerr << "Error: cannot input number of vertices\n";
 infile.close();
 return 2;
}
if (numVertices < 4) {
 cerr << "Error: number of vertices cannot be less than 4\n";
 infile.close ();
 return 3;
}
```

Note: only continue and allocate the array if numVertices is at least 4.

```
Vector* vertices = new (std::nothrow) Vector [numVertices];
if (!vertices) {
 cerr << "Error: out of memory on vertices\n";
 infile.close ();
 return 4;
}

int i;
for (i=0; i<numVertices; i++) {
 infile >> vertices[i];
}
if (!infile) {
 cerr << "Error: bad vertex data in input file\n";
 infile.close();
 delete [] vertices;
 return 5;
}

int numFaces;
infile >> numFaces;
if (!infile) {
 cerr << "Error: cannot input number of faces\n";
 infile.close();
 delete [] vertices;
 return 6;
}

if (numFaces < 4) {
 cerr << "Error: number of faces must be greater than 4\n";
 infile.close();
 delete [] vertices;
 return 7;
```

```
}
```

Same is true for the faces array, only if there are at least four faces do I attempt to allocate the array.

```
Face* faces = new (std::nothrow) Face [numFaces];
if (!vertices) {
 cerr << "Error: out of memory on faces\n";
 infile.close();
 delete [] vertices;
 return 8;
}

for (i=0; i<numFaces; i++) {
 infile >> faces[i].a >> faces[i].b >> faces[i].c;
}
if (!infile) {
 cerr << "Error: cannot input the faces data\n";
 infile.close();
 delete [] vertices;
 delete [] faces;
 return 9;
}
infile.close ();

double volume;
Vector center;
FindVolume (vertices, numVertices, faces, numFaces, volume,
            center);
cout << "Volume = " << fixed << setprecision (2) << volume
     << endl;
cout << "Center = " << center << endl;

return 0;
}

void FindVolume (Vector* vertices, int numVertices, Face* faces,
                 int numFaces, double& volume, Vector& center) {
 int i;
 volume = 0;
 Vector a, b, c;
 Vector d;
 double partialVol = 0;
 Vector centerSum;
 for (i=0; i<numFaces; i++) {
  a = vertices[faces[i].a];
  b = vertices[faces[i].b];
```

```
c = vertices[faces[i].c];
partialVol = TripleScalarProduct (a, b, c) / 6;
volume += partialVol;
d = (a + b + c) / 4;
centerSum += d * partialVol;
}
center = centerSum / volume;
}
```

The program outputs that the volume is 64.00 and the center is at (2, 2, 2), which we can easily verify (4 x 4 x 4).

The challenging part is to take your ship's hull design in three dimensions and somehow divide it up into rectangular solids of various dimensions which when joined make a reasonable estimation of that shape. Perhaps even more challenging is to then construct the data file of the numerous polyhedrons!

Problems

Problem 8-1 Write a Generic Shoot Function

Ignoring drag effects, write a generic function that calculates whether or not a shot hits the target. The idea is that we write this function once and then insert it into any game which has a projectile being fired or thrown in 2D space. The function should be passed the initial velocity and angle of elevation, along with the height of the shooter above "ground level" and the height of the target, also above "ground level." Also, the function is passed the distance that the object is from the shooter and the height of the target. The function returns true or false, indicating whether or not the projectile hit the target or not.

Thoroughly test the program, using a gun (straight shot, elevation always zero), an artillery type of shooting, and a baseball pitch.

Problem 8-2 Write a WillCarSkid() Function

Write a generic function that can be inserted into any game that involves cars or trucks. As the car or truck approaches a curve in the road, this function is called to see if skidding will occur or if it can safely make the turn going at the velocity that it enters the curve.

You are to determine what parameters the function must be passed so that it can perform its job. The function returns true, skidding will occur, or false. Additionally, it also saves the fastest velocity allowed to safely make this turn in a passed reference variable.

Thoroughly test the program.

Chapter 9 Writing an Airplane Simulator

Writing an airplane simulator is perhaps the most complex situation we are examining in this course, because of the complex interaction of its many parts, because of the wide variety of forces that can act upon it, and because it is inherently a three dimensional problem, not 2D. Let's begin by getting the nomenclature of planes defined, then work out the nature of the forces acting upon it, and finally, work out a simulation model that can be used in a game.

Figure 9-1 shows the key parts of an airplane, from the propeller up front to the rudder in the rear.

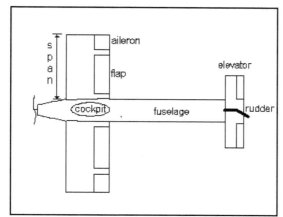

Figure 9-1 Parts of an Airplane

The propeller provides the forward thrust or propulsion. The wings provide the main lifting force. What do the other parts actually do? The flags, when down, create a significantly greater lifting force, needed for take offs and landings. However, to grasp what the ailerons, elevator and rudder do, one should understand the possible motions the plane can have in 3D space. The longer dimension of the main wing is its span, while the shorter dimension is the chord. The aspect ratio, a_r, is given by this equation.

$a_r = \text{span}^2 / \text{wing area}$

For a rectangular wing, the area is span * chord, so the aspect ratio becomes this.

$a_r = \text{span} / \text{chord}$

Assume a plane is flying a level course. The positive z axis is vertically upwards from the plane. The nose coming upwards or downwards, that is a vertical rotation, up or down the z axis, around the center of gravity of the plane, is called **pitch**. The pitch of a plane is controlled by the action of the elevator flaps. When the elevator flaps are lowered, the nose climbs. Conversely, when

229

the elevator flaps are raised upwards, the nose dips downward. This rotation is said to be a rotation about the pitch axis of the plane.

A **roll** is the plane rotating about the centerline running the length of the plane from front to back. In a roll, one wing tip rises while the other falls. The action is again along the z axis and such rotations are about the roll axis. The ailerons control the rolling action of a plane. Note that a 180 degree roll would make the pilot now upside down.

A **yaw** is a rotation about the center of gravity constrained to the x-y plane. In a yaw, the plane changes direction, to the right or left of its original heading. Such rotations are about the yaw axis of the plane. The rudder controls the yaw.

What forces act on the plane? The most important one is the thrust provided by the engines, whether by propeller or by a jet engine, for without it, you can only glide. Drag forces operate as usual directly opposite this thrust. Gravity pulls the plane downward, while the lift force causes the plane to rise. If the lift force ceases, the plane falls. We are already familiar with gravity and can deal with the force provided by the engine. It is the lift and drag estimations that require further study and analysis, in order to obtain a realistic simulation.

To grasp lift and drag, we must take a closer look at the main wings and their design and nomenclature. Figure 9-2 shows a wing cross section with the main terms used to describe the wing.

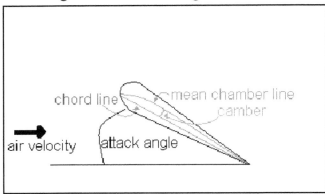

Figure 9-2 Cross Section of Airfoil of Wing

The chord line, shown in blue, is a straight line from the trailing edge of the wing to the leading edge. Note the leading edge is that portion of the wing which first encounters the air flowing at it. The air velocity then pushes up against the underside of the wing which is tilted at some angle, called the attack angle. Next, if you divide the wing into lots of cross sections and draw a curved line through the mid-section of each and then compute the average, that yields the mean chamber line, shown in red. The difference between the mean chamber line and the chord line is called the camber, or curvature of the airfoil.

As the air rushes over the top of the wing, a region of low pressure is formed on the top surface, while a region of higher pressure forms under the wing, giving rise to the lift force. The effect is similar to the spinning steel ball effect. As the incoming air (fluid) reaches the leading edge, it splits into two halves at the stagnation point, part of the air must speed up to go up and over the wing, while the rest of it goes under the wing and is pushed downward by the attack angle. The air flows smoothly across both the top and bottom surfaces and then rejoins at the trailing edge.

In terms of vectors, the forces appear as shown in Figure 9-3, forces.

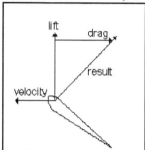

Figure 9-3 Forces

The pressure differential above and below the airfoil also adds some drag force to the situation, which is in the opposite direction from the velocity. Lift and drag forces are perpendicular to each other. Both lift and drag forces are dependent upon speed, air density, viscosity, surface area, angle of attack, and the aspect ratio (wing span / chord).

The formulas for the coefficients of lift and drag are as follows.
$$C_L = L / (d\ v^2\ S\ /\ 2)$$
$$C_d = D / (d\ v^2\ S\ /\ 2)$$
where S is the wing span area (span * chord for a rectangular wing), L is the lift force, d is the air density, v is the speed, and D is the drag force. The coefficients are experimentally determined in wind tunnel experiments. Results are presented as graphs of lift coefficient versus attack angle or drag coefficient versus attack angle. When the flaps are down, additional lift and drag forces are generated. Often these are plotted on the same graphs as the coefficients.

For typical wings, the lift coefficient is zero around an attack angle of –2 degrees, rising in nearly a straight line upwards to 1.5 at an angle of 15 degrees, the optimum lift angle. Immediately after that point, it drops off sharply. With flaps down, the attack angle is –8 degrees downward when lift is zero, peaking at nearly 2.0 at an angle of around 15 degrees. These sharp drops above 15 degrees produce a stall. The optimum amount of lift occurs then at the critical attack angle, usually around 15 degrees.

The engine thrust is given in pounds, but the ratio of thrust to weight is often used to compare relative merits of aircraft. This is the maximum thrust of which the engine is capable divided by the total weight of the plane. Interestingly enough, if the thrust to weight ratio is greater than 1.0, the plane can climb vertically up! I am a WWI biplane buff and the dreaded Fokker D VII could indeed climb vertically, firing its machine guns straight up at the belly of another plane, making them exceedingly dangerous to the allied planes.

Thrust is not constant, however. As the plane gains altitude, the air becomes thinner, less dense, and provides less oxygen for the engine. Often, there will be a maximum altitude that the engines can take the plane.

Additionally, other surfaces add additional drag and lift forces and at various times. The fuselage and other appendages, such as wheels down, add in drag. The elevator is a small wing and adds its lift and drag to the mix. In the Fokker D III, tri-plane, a tiny airfoil was added between the wheels to provide extra lift, hoping to counter the drag of the wheels. The drag forces are expressed similarly as proportional to

$$d \, v^2 \, S \, / \, 2$$

where S is the projected frontal area to the force and d is the air density.

How significant can these additional drag forces be? Landing gear can add a drag coefficient between .25 and .55. External fuel tanks and rockets appended to the exterior can add between .06 and .26, depending upon how streamlined they are. You need to decide whether these extra drag forces are important to your simulation.

Flying the Plane

The flaps are lowered usually to between 30 and 60 degrees during slow speed portions of a flight, during take off and landings. Why? To increase lift, but of course it also slows the speed down while landing and requires greater thrust to overcome the drag during take off. Downward flap deflections are considered positive.

The ailerons are used to control roll or cause it, when rolling over. One aileron goes up while the other goes down to roll the plane over. This causes a lift differential between the two wings. This difference in lift, separated by the length of the wings out to the ailerons, causes a torque which rolls the plane. Usually, it is the flight stick which controls this action.

The elevators control the pitch. Sometimes there are small flaps on the elevators which move, other times, the entire elevator moves. When the elevator goes up, the plane nose rises. When it moves downward, the nose falls. They are used as well to keep the plane flying level.

The center of gravity is usually above the mean quarter-chord line of the wings and in line with the main lifting force of the wings. As fuel is burned, this location can shift, so the elevators are needed to keep the plane flying level.

The rudder is controlled by foot pedals and controls the yaw motion of the plane. Pushing the left pedal causes the plane to yaw or turn to the left; the right pedal, a right yaw. When flying straight, the rudder provides no lift. However, if the plane is flying say with one wing pointing to the ground, the rudder can provide its maximal lift. Thus, when using the rudder, often the ailerons are also used to help compensate for any possible roll.

When you design your plane simulator, cockpit controls should be shown. Commonly, a joystick is used to emulate the plane's stick, with some buttons handling the rudder and brakes, when landing. However, these are all graphical elements to be shown or program inputs and are beyond the scope of this theory course. You can learn about making the graphical elements in the DirectX course.

Constructing the Plane Model

Since we are using the rigid body model, we need to account for all of the forces acting at one moment upon the airplane. This means that we need to break down the model into specific pieces so that we can easily calculate the relevant forces. Here is the sequence to follow.

1. Break the lifting surfaces down into smaller wing sections, each performing its own function.
2. Gather the geometric and air foil performance data to describe each piece.
3. Calculate the relative air velocity over each wing section.
4. Calculate the attack angle for each wing section.
5. Determine the lift and drag coefficents for each piece.
6. Calculate the lift and drag forces acting on the plane at this point in time.
7. Integrate the equations of motion.
8. Update the display.

For this example, let attempt to model the Fokker D VII biplane shown in Figure 9-4.

Figure 9-4 The Fokker D. VII

However, let's modernize the plane and give it both flaps and ailerons so that we can simulate their effects. The original plane had ailerons of an unusual shape at the wing tips of the top wing. Additionally, I do not have accurate data for much of the plane, so we will just use some estimates.

Into what pieces should we divide the plane? Let's create a top wing section that includes the aileron and another that contains the flaps, one pair for each side. The bottom wing is broken into two portions, separated by the fuselage. The elevator is broken into the left and right halves. The rudder will be a single piece. I will lump the fuselage into a heavy forward, motor piece and a light rear piece. I am going to ignore the landing gear.

For each piece, we need its dimensions, weight, and location so that the center of gravity can be calculated. Thus, I drew the plane on a piece of graph paper, placing the location of the coordinate system at the rear end of the plane. From this drawing, I can make reasonable estimates of all values, except mass. The x axis is positive towards the nose. The positive y axis points to the port side, while the positive z axis is upwards.

Each element also has a dihedral angle, which is the angle about the x axis. All of the wings have a zero dihedral angle, except the rudder which is at 90 degrees, vertical. Some plane wings do have dihedral angles of a few degrees, however.

The wings may have an incidence angle, which is a fixed angle from level where the wings are attached to the fuselage. Modern planes have a small angle, of the order of -3.5 degrees for the main wings.

Additionally, we must know the mass moment of inertia for each piece. This can be a bit tricky because of the irregular shapes of all the pieces. What I did was draw the plane on graph paper, adding a coordinate system. Next, for each piece, I estimated the centroid, assuming equally

Game Programming Theory

distributed mass and turning the foils into simple rectangular solids. Then, I can apply the basic formulas for inertia given in the earlier chapter. Each piece then has its centroid and moment of inertia as two data members.

The top wing, located nine feet above ground (z coordinate) is divided into four pieces. The port half is composed of the stylized aileron piece and a fictitious flap section. The entire half has the dimensions of fifteen feet by six feet. I altered the foil shape into a rectangular solid and said the uniform depth was three inches. The aileron piece is the outermost five feet, while the remainder in reality is just wing; here is where I placed the non-existent flap. The leading edge of the wing is at a y distance of twenty feet.

The center of mass will be in the dead center of each piece. For the outer aileron piece, the centroid vector will be (17.5, 12.5, 8.88) or leading edge x position of 20 minus half of its span of 5 feet, 10 feet for the start of the aileron piece plus half of its length of 7 feet, height of wing minus half of the wing's thickness of .25 feet. The starboard side aileron has a centroid vector of (17.5, −12.5, 8.88). The port flap piece has its centroid at (17.5, 5, 8.88); its x coordinate is at 0 plus half its length of ten feet. The starboard flap's centroid is (17.5, −5, 8.88).

We know that the fully loaded weight is 2550 pounds and its empty weight is 1984 pounds. The fuel and pilot and ammunition are in the fuselage, unlike the modern wing tanks, and tends to balance out the forward weight of the engine. I estimated the engine assembly to be 500 pounds and the fuselage loaded at 1200 pounds. The top wing is 250 pounds, while the lower wing is 200 pounds, the elevator assemblage is 100 pounds, and the tail is 30 pounds. Using these total values, I then divided them up into proportional amounts for the different wing pieces. To get the center of gravity to be over the cockpit, I broke the fuselage into a front heavy half and a long, light back half.

Table 9-1 shows the various values I calculated or estimated from my graph paper drawing.

Piece	Center Gravity	Mass (slugs)	Area	Dihedral	Incidence	Span	Chord	Thickness
Starboard Aileron	(17.5, −12.5, 8.88)	1.3	25	0	−3.5	5	5	.25
Starboard Flap	(17.5, −5, 8.88)	2.59	50	0	−3.5	10	5	.25
Port Aileron	(17.5, 12.5, 8.88)	1.3	25	0	−3.5	5	5	.25
Port Flap	(17.5, 5, 8.88)	2.59	50	0	−3.5	10	5	.25
Starboard Bottom	(17, −8.25, 3)	3.11	54	0	−3.5	13.5	4	.25
Port Bottom	(17, 8.25, 3)	3.11	54	0	−3.5	13.5	4	.25
Starboard Elevator	(1.5, −3.1, 7)	1.56	12.5	0	0	5	5	.25
Port Elevator	(1.5, 3.1, 7)	1.56	12.5	0	0	5	5	.25
Tail	(0, 1.5, 7.5)	.93	4.71	90	0	3	.25	3
Fuselage Front	(21.5, 0, 4.5)	47.89	9	0	0	3	3	4
Fuselage Back	(10, 0, 4.5)	10.29	60	0	0	20	3	4

Next, we need the local moments of inertia for all of these pieces. Recall from chapter 2, the following formulas for a rectangular solid whose dimensions are x, y, z in the three corresponding axes. Also, note that the origin of the coordinate system is the center of the object. Later, we'll calculate the moments as a combined plane.

$$Ixx = 1/12 \, m \, (y^2 + z^2)$$
$$Iyy = 1/12 \, m \, (x^2 + z^2)$$
$$Izz = 1/12 \, m \, (x^2 + y^2)$$

Lacking the formula for the strange shaped elevators, I chose to treat them as a rectangular solid and divide by two.

Game Programming Theory

Once we have these basic properties for each piece determined, next we must put the pieces together into the plane as a composite. First, sum the individual masses to find the total mass of the plane. To find the center of gravity for the entire plane, sum up the individual moment of inertia vectors and divide that by the total mass.

```
mass = 0;
Vector moment;
for (i=0; i<numPieces; i++) {
 mass += pieces[i].mass;
 moment += pieces[i].mass * pieces[i].centerGravity;
}
centerOfGravity = moment / mass;
```

Once we know the center of gravity of the plane as a whole, we can go back and calculate the location of each piece with respect to the actual center of gravity, so that each piece is ready for the simulation calculations, based on the plane as a whole.

```
for (i=0; i<numPieces; i++) {
 pieces[i].centerGravityPlane =
                        pieces[i].centerGravity - centerOfGravity;
}
```

Now comes the more difficult part. Since we are in three dimensions, we have to consider rotations in all three planes, which requires a vector for the moment of inertia, actually it is a tensor, a matrix plus a direction. We can calculate the individual components of the inertia.

```
double Ixx = 0, Iyy = 0, Izz = 0, Ixy = 0, Ixz = 0, Iyz = 0;
for (i=0; i<numPieces; i++) {
 Ixx += pieces[i].localInertia.x + pieces[i].mass *
     (pieces[i].centerGravityPlane.y * pieces[i].centerGravityPlane.y +
      pieces[i].centerGravityPlane.z * pieces[i].centerGravityPlane.z);

 Iyy += pieces[i].localInertia.y + pieces[i].mass *
     (pieces[i].centerGravityPlane.z * pieces[i].centerGravityPlane.z +
      pieces[i].centerGravityPlane.x * pieces[i].centerGravityPlane.x);

 Izz += pieces[i].localInertia.z + pieces[i].mass *
    (pieces[i].centerGravityPlane.x * pieces[i].centerGravityPlane.x +
     pieces[i].centerGravityPlane.y*pieces[i].centerGravityPlane.y);

 Ixy += pieces[i].mass * (pieces[i].centerGravityPlane.x *
                      pieces[i].centerGravityPlane.y);

 Ixz += pieces[i].mass * (pieces[i].centerGravityPlane.x *
                      pieces[i].centerGravityPlane.z);

 Iyz += pieces[i].mass * (pieces[i].centerGravityPlane.y *
                      pieces[i].centerGravityPlane.z);
}
```

Game Programming Theory

We can store these parts in a matrix, which is 3x3 in size.

```
inertia = Matrix3D (Ixx, -Ixy, -Ixz,
                    -Ixy,  Iyy, -Iyz,
                    -Ixz, -Iyz,  Izz);
```

Finally, the integration of the equations of motion may require the inverse of the inertia matrix, that is 1/inertia. It makes sense to only calculate this inverse matrix one time and store it as well.

```
inertiaInverse = inertia.Inverse();
```

Thus, we now must deal with matrix math. I have provided a simple Matrix3D class that handles the frequently needed matrix manipulations required in rigid body simulations. But first, let's review a bit about matrix math, which lies at the foundation of three dimensional simulations.

Matrix Algebra

Multiple dimensioned arrays open new vistas in the types of problems that can be solved. Specifically, matrices can be stored in two-dimensional arrays. Matrices form the underpinnings of 3D space simulations. The starting point is a brief review of the rules of Matrix Algebra.

Suppose that we had the following simultaneous equations.

$5x + 4y + 3z = 40$
$9y + 3z + 8x = 10$
$4z + 3x + 6y = 20$

They must be rearranged into the proper format.

$5x + 4y + 3z = 40$
$8x + 9y + 3z = 10$
$3x + 6y + 4z = 20$

In matrix notation, this becomes the following.

$$\begin{pmatrix} 5 & 4 & 3 \\ 8 & 9 & 3 \\ 3 & 6 & 4 \end{pmatrix} x \begin{pmatrix} x \\ y \\ z \end{pmatrix} = \begin{pmatrix} 40 \\ 10 \\ 20 \end{pmatrix}$$

Or $\mathbf{A\ X} = \mathbf{B}$; so the solution is $\mathbf{X} = \mathbf{B/A}$

The normal matrix notation for this case of 3 equations in 3 unknowns is show below.

$$\begin{pmatrix} a11 & a12 & a13 \\ a21 & a22 & a23 \\ a31 & a32 & a33 \end{pmatrix} \cdot \begin{pmatrix} x1 \\ x2 \\ x3 \end{pmatrix} = \begin{pmatrix} b1 \\ b2 \\ b3 \end{pmatrix}$$

Notice that the math matrix notation parallels C++ subscripts, but begins with subscript 1 not 0. Always remember to subtract 1 from the matrix math indices to get a C++ array subscript.

In this example, the **a** matrix is composed of 3 rows or row vectors, and 3 columns or column vectors. In general a matrix is said to be an **m** by **n** matrix, **m** rows and **n** columns. When **m** = **n**, it is called a **square** matrix. A matrix with only one row is a **row** matrix; one with only one column is a **column** matrix. The **x** and **b** matrices are both column matrices.

Matrix Math Operations Summary

1. Two matrices are said to be equal if and only if they have the same dimensions and all corresponding elements are equal.

$a_{ij} = b_{ij}$ for all $i=1,m$ and $j=1,n$

2. Addition and Subtraction operations require that the matrices involved have the same number of rows and columns. To compute $C = A + B$ or $C = A - B$, simply add or subtract all corresponding elements. This can be implemented in C++ as follows.

```
for (int I=0; I<M; I++) {
  for (int J=0; J<N; J++) {
    C(I,J) = A(I,J) + B(I,J);
  }
}
```

3. Multiplication of a matrix by a number is commutative. That is, **rA** is the same as **Ar.** The result is given by **r** times each element.

```
for (int I=0; I<M; I++) {
  for (int J=0; J<N; J++) {
    A(I,J) = A(I,J) * r;
  }
}
```

For example, assume **A** is defined to be the following.

$$A = \begin{pmatrix} 2.7 & -1.8 \\ 0.9 & 3.6 \end{pmatrix}$$

Then 2**A** would be

$$A = \begin{pmatrix} 5.4 & -3.6 \\ 1.8 & 7.2 \end{pmatrix}$$

and 10/9**A** would be

$$A = \begin{pmatrix} 3 & -2 \\ 1 & 4 \end{pmatrix}$$

4. A **diagonal** matrix is one whose elements above and below the principal diagonal are 0: namely **aij=0** for all **i!=j**

$$diagonal \quad \begin{pmatrix} 3 & 0 & 0 \\ 0 & 4 & 0 \\ 0 & 0 & 5 \end{pmatrix}$$

5. An **identity** matrix is a diagonal matrix whose principal diagonal elements are all 1.

$$identity \quad \begin{pmatrix} 1 & 0 & 0 \\ 0 & 1 & 0 \\ 0 & 0 & 1 \end{pmatrix}$$

6. Matrix multiplication says that the product of a square matrix times a column matrix is another column matrix. It is computed as follows: for each row in the square matrix, sum the products of each element in the square matrix's row by the corresponding element in the column matrix's column.

$$\begin{pmatrix} a11 & a12 & a13 \\ a21 & a22 & a23 \\ a31 & a32 & a33 \end{pmatrix} \begin{pmatrix} b1 \\ b2 \\ b3 \end{pmatrix} = \begin{pmatrix} a11*b1 + a12*b2 + a13*b3 \\ a21*b1 + a22*b2 + a23*b3 \\ a31*b1 + a32*b2 + a33*b3 \end{pmatrix}$$

For a square matrix times a square matrix, the result is a square matrix of the same dimensions, each element of the result is the sum of the products of each element of the corresponding row of one matrix times each element of the corresponding column of the other matrix

C = A * B

where **Cij** = ith row of **A** * jth column of **B** or in coding

```
for (int I=0; I<3; I++) {
  for (int J=0; J<3; J++) {
    C(I,J) = 0;
    for (int K=0; K<3; K++) {
      C(I,J) = C(I,J) + A(I,K)*B(K,J);
    }
  }
}
```

7. Determinants form a crucial aspect in solving systems of equations. What we are after is the ability to solve: **A*X = B** so that we can solve it as **X = B/A**. However, matrix division is a real problem and really is not needed because there is a simpler method. A determinant can be pictorially thought of as rather like a "greatest common denominator."

If we had this simple two equations in two unknowns problem
```
a11x1 + a12x2 = b1
a21x1 + a22x2 = b2
```
then the long hand solution would be
```
x1 = (b1a22 - b2a12)        x2 = (b2a11 - b1a12)
     ---------------             ---------------
     (a11a22 - a21a12)           (a11a22 - a21a12)
```
assuming the denominator, called the **determinant**, is not zero; Note that the determinant is a single number. Notice that the determinant can be considered as the sum of the right slanted diagonals — sum of the left slanted diagonals.

It is notated as |**a**|, the determinant of **a**. For a 3x3 matrix, the determinant is given by the following number.
```
   a11a22a33 + a12a23a31 + a13a32a21
 - a11a23a32 - a21a12a33 - a31a22a13
```
For a larger matrix, that is, the general case, the Cofactor Matrix concept is used. Consult a matrix math text for details. Normally another approach is used when the number of dimensions becomes four or more.

8. The inverse of a matrix satisfies the following, where M is the matrix, M^{-1} is the inverse matrix, and I is the identity matrix.

$$M\,M^{-1} = I$$

Mathematical Theorems of Determinants

The following summarize the rules that apply to working with determinants. We will apply these to the problem of solving simultaneous equations shortly.

1. The value of a determinant is not altered if its rows are written as columns in the same order.

$$\begin{pmatrix} 1 & 3 & 0 \\ 2 & 6 & 4 \\ -1 & 0 & 2 \end{pmatrix} = \begin{pmatrix} 1 & 2 & -1 \\ 3 & 6 & 0 \\ 0 & 4 & 2 \end{pmatrix} = -12$$

2. If all the elements of one row (or one column) of a determinant are multiplied by the same factor **k**, the value of the determinant is **k** times the value of the determinant. Notice the difference between **k|D|** and **kA**, where **|D|** is a determinant and **A** is a matrix. The operation **k|D|** multiplies just one row or column by **k** but **kA** multiplies all elements by **k**.

3. If all elements of a row or column of a determinant are zero, the value of the determinant is zero.

4. If any one row is proportional to another row (or one column is proportional to another column), then the determinant is zero.

5. If the elements of any one row are identical (in the same order) to another row, the determinant is zero. Likewise for columns.

6. Any two rows or columns may be interchanged, and the determinant just changes sign.

7. The value of a determinant is unchanged if the elements of a row (or column) are altered by adding to them any constant multiple of the corresponding elements in any other row (or column).

Constructing a Matrix Class for Game Simulations

We could store our matrix as a 2D array. For example, we might start off this way.

```
class Matrix3D {
public:
  double m[3][3];

Matrix3D::Matrix3D () {
  for (int row=0; row<3; row++) {
   for (int col=0; col<3; col++) {
    m[row][col] = 0;
    }
   }
}

Matrix3D::Matrix3D (const Matrix3D& x) {
  for (int row=0; row<3; row++) {
   for (int col=0; col<3; col++) {
    m[row][col] = x.m[row][col];
    }
   }
}
```

While this looks promising, the method has a very serious drawback: speed of execution. Recall from your previous programming classes that every time there is a subscript access, of the order of 33 clock cycles are consumed by the multiplication of the subscript in order to find the offset from the start of the array to the specified element. With the above coding, we have two subscripts for each element access. There is a way around this degradation. Suppose that we coded these this way.

```
Matrix3D::Matrix3D () {
  m[0][0] = m[0][1] = m[0][2] = 0;
  m[1][0] = m[1][1] = m[1][2] = 0;
  m[2][0] = m[2][1] = m[2][2] = 0;
}

Matrix3D::Matrix3D (const Matrix3D& x) {
  m[0][0] = x.m[0][0];
  m[0][1] = x.m[0][1];
  m[0][2] = x.m[0][2];
  m[1][0] = x.m[1][0];
  m[1][1] = x.m[1][1];
  m[1][2] = x.m[1][2];
  m[2][0] = x.m[2][0];
  m[2][1] = x.m[2][1];
  m[2][2] = x.m[2][2];
}
```

I am hard-coding the subscripts. Now, at compile time, the compiler works out all of the constant offsets. The generated code is now as fast as if we had stored nine independent doubles! Thus, we lose no execution speed with this class.

The Matrix3D class definition is as follows. An instance can be inputted or outputted as well, for debugging purposes, primarily.

```
#pragma once
#include <iostream>
#include <iomanip>
using namespace std;
#include "Vector.h"

class Matrix3D {
public:
  double m[3][3];

    Matrix3D ();
    Matrix3D (const Matrix3D& x);
    Matrix3D (double m00, double m01, double m02,
              double m10, double m11, double m12,
              double m20, double m21, double m22);
  ~Matrix3D () {}
```

```
double     Determinant () const;
Matrix3D   Transpose () const;
Matrix3D   Inverse () const;

Matrix3D& operator+= (const Matrix3D& x);
Matrix3D& operator-= (const Matrix3D& x);
Matrix3D& operator*= (double s);
Matrix3D& operator/= (double s);

Matrix3D   operator+ (const Matrix3D& x) const;
Matrix3D   operator- (const Matrix3D& x) const;
Matrix3D   operator/ (double s) const;
Matrix3D   operator* (const Matrix3D& x) const;
Matrix3D   operator* (double s) const;
Vector     operator* (Vector v) const;

friend Vector     operator* (Vector v, const Matrix3D& x);
friend Matrix3D   operator* (double s, const Matrix3D& x);
friend istream&   operator>> (istream& is, Matrix3D x);
friend ostream&   operator<< (ostream& os, const Matrix3D& x);
};
```

Here is the hard-coded, efficient version of the class.
```
#include "Matrix3D.h"

Matrix3D::Matrix3D () {
 m[0][0] = m[0][1] = m[0][2] = 0;
 m[1][0] = m[1][1] = m[1][2] = 0;
 m[2][0] = m[2][1] = m[2][2] = 0;
}

Matrix3D::Matrix3D (const Matrix3D& x) {
 m[0][0] = x.m[0][0];
 m[0][1] = x.m[0][1];
 m[0][2] = x.m[0][2];
 m[1][0] = x.m[1][0];
 m[1][1] = x.m[1][1];
 m[1][2] = x.m[1][2];
 m[2][0] = x.m[2][0];
 m[2][1] = x.m[2][1];
 m[2][2] = x.m[2][2];
}

Matrix3D::Matrix3D (double m00, double m01, double m02,
            double m10, double m11, double m12,
            double m20, double m21, double m22) {
```

```
m[0][0] = m00;
m[0][1] = m01;
m[0][2] = m02;
m[1][0] = m10;
m[1][1] = m11;
m[1][2] = m12;
m[2][0] = m20;
m[2][1] = m21;
m[2][2] = m22;
}

double    Matrix3D::Determinant () const {
 return m[0][0] * m[1][1] * m[2][2] -
        m[0][0] * m[2][1] * m[1][2] +
        m[1][0] * m[2][1] * m[0][2] -
        m[1][0] * m[0][1] * m[2][2] +
        m[2][0] * m[0][1] * m[1][2] -
        m[2][0] * m[1][1] * m[0][2];
}

Matrix3D  Matrix3D::Transpose () const {
 return Matrix3D (m[0][0], m[1][0], m[2][0],
                  m[0][1], m[1][1], m[2][1],
                  m[0][2], m[1][2], m[2][2]);
}

Matrix3D  Matrix3D::Inverse () const {
 double d = Determinant ();
 if (fabs (d) < EPS) d = 1; // avoid division by 0
 return Matrix3D ( (m[1][1] * m[2][2] - m[1][2] * m[2][1]) / d,
                  -(m[0][1] * m[2][2] - m[0][2] * m[2][1]) / d,
                   (m[0][1] * m[1][2] - m[0][2] * m[1][1]) / d,
                  -(m[1][0] * m[2][2] - m[1][2] * m[2][0]) / d,
                   (m[0][0] * m[2][2] - m[0][2] * m[2][0]) / d,
                  -(m[0][0] * m[1][2] - m[0][2] * m[1][0]) / d,
                   (m[1][0] * m[2][1] - m[1][1] * m[2][0]) / d,
                  -(m[0][0] * m[2][1] - m[0][1] * m[2][0]) / d,
                   (m[0][0] * m[1][1] - m[0][1] * m[1][0]) / d
                  );
}

Matrix3D& Matrix3D::operator+= (const Matrix3D& x) {
 m[0][0] += x.m[0][0];
 m[0][1] += x.m[0][1];
 m[0][2] += x.m[0][2];
 m[1][0] += x.m[1][0];
```

```
m[1][1] += x.m[1][1];
m[1][2] += x.m[1][2];
m[2][0] += x.m[2][0];
m[2][1] += x.m[2][1];
m[2][2] += x.m[2][2];
return *this;
}

Matrix3D& Matrix3D::operator-= (const Matrix3D& x) {
m[0][0] -= x.m[0][0];
m[0][1] -= x.m[0][1];
m[0][2] -= x.m[0][2];
m[1][0] -= x.m[1][0];
m[1][1] -= x.m[1][1];
m[1][2] -= x.m[1][2];
m[2][0] -= x.m[2][0];
m[2][1] -= x.m[2][1];
m[2][2] -= x.m[2][2];
return *this;
}


Matrix3D& Matrix3D::operator*= (double s) {
m[0][0] *= s;
m[0][1] *= s;
m[0][2] *= s;
m[1][0] *= s;
m[1][1] *= s;
m[1][2] *= s;
m[2][0] *= s;
m[2][1] *= s;
m[2][2] *= s;
return *this;
}

Matrix3D& Matrix3D::operator/= (double s) {
m[0][0] /= s;
m[0][1] /= s;
m[0][2] /= s;
m[1][0] /= s;
m[1][1] /= s;
m[1][2] /= s;
m[2][0] /= s;
m[2][1] /= s;
m[2][2] /= s;
return *this;
```

```
}

Matrix3D  Matrix3D::operator+ (const Matrix3D& x) const {
  return Matrix3D (
    m[0][0] + x.m[0][0], m[0][1] + x.m[0][1], m[0][2] + x.m[0][2],
    m[1][0] + x.m[1][0], m[1][1] + x.m[1][1], m[1][2] + x.m[1][2],
    m[2][0] + x.m[2][0], m[2][1] + x.m[2][1], m[2][2] + x.m[2][2]
                );
}

Matrix3D  Matrix3D::operator- (const Matrix3D& x) const {
  return Matrix3D (
    m[0][0] - x.m[0][0], m[0][1] - x.m[0][1], m[0][2] - x.m[0][2],
    m[1][0] - x.m[1][0], m[1][1] - x.m[1][1], m[1][2] - x.m[1][2],
    m[2][0] - x.m[2][0], m[2][1] - x.m[2][1], m[2][2] - x.m[2][2]
                );
}

Matrix3D  Matrix3D::operator/ (double s) const {
  return Matrix3D (m[0][0] / s, m[0][1] / s, m[0][2] / s,
                   m[1][0] / s, m[1][1] / s, m[1][2] / s,
                   m[2][0] / s, m[2][1] / s, m[2][2] / s
                );
}

Matrix3D  Matrix3D::operator* (const Matrix3D& x) const {
  return Matrix3D (
  m[0][0] * x.m[0][0] + m[0][1] * x.m[1][0] + m[0][2] * x.m[2][0],
  m[0][0] * x.m[0][1] + m[0][1] * x.m[1][1] + m[0][2] * x.m[2][1],
  m[0][0] * x.m[0][2] + m[0][1] * x.m[1][2] + m[0][2] * x.m[2][2],
  m[1][0] * x.m[0][0] + m[1][1] * x.m[1][0] + m[1][2] * x.m[2][0],
  m[1][0] * x.m[0][1] + m[1][1] * x.m[1][1] + m[1][2] * x.m[2][1],
  m[1][0] * x.m[0][2] + m[1][1] * x.m[1][2] + m[1][2] * x.m[2][2],
  m[2][0] * x.m[0][0] + m[2][1] * x.m[1][0] + m[2][2] * x.m[2][0],
  m[2][0] * x.m[0][1] + m[2][1] * x.m[1][1] + m[2][2] * x.m[2][1],
  m[2][0] * x.m[0][2] + m[2][1] * x.m[1][2] + m[2][2] * x.m[2][2]
                );
}

Matrix3D  Matrix3D::operator* (double s) const {
  return Matrix3D (m[0][0] * s, m[0][1] * s, m[0][2] * s,
                   m[1][0] * s, m[1][1] * s, m[1][2] * s,
                   m[2][0] * s, m[2][1] * s, m[2][2] * s
                );
}
```

```
Vector      Matrix3D::operator* (Vector v) const {
  return Vector (m[0][0] * v.x + m[0][1] * v.y + m[0][2] * v.z,
                 m[1][0] * v.x + m[1][1] * v.y + m[1][2] * v.z,
                 m[2][0] * v.x + m[2][1] * v.y + m[2][2] * v.z);
}

Vector      operator* (Vector v, const Matrix3D& x) {
  return Vector (
                 v.x * x.m[0][0] + v.y * x.m[1][0] + v.z * x.m[2][0],
                 v.x * x.m[0][1] + v.y * x.m[1][1] + v.z * x.m[2][1],
                 v.x * x.m[0][2] + v.y * x.m[1][2] + v.z * x.m[2][2]
                 );
}

Matrix3D  operator* (double s, const Matrix3D& x) {
    return Matrix3D (x.m[0][0] * s, x.m[0][1] * s, x.m[0][2] * s,
                     x.m[1][0] * s, x.m[1][1] * s, x.m[1][2] * s,
                     x.m[2][0] * s, x.m[2][1] * s, x.m[2][2] * s
                     );
}

istream&  operator>> (istream& is, Matrix3D x) {
  is >> x.m[0][0] >> x.m[0][1] >> x.m[0][2]
     >> x.m[1][0] >> x.m[1][1] >> x.m[1][2]
     >> x.m[2][0] >> x.m[2][1] >> x.m[2][2];
  return is;
}

ostream&  operator<< (ostream& os, const Matrix3D& x) {
  os << fixed << setprecision (2);
  os << '{'
    << setw (10) << x.m[0][0] << setw (10) << x.m[0][1]
    << setw (10) << x.m[0][2] << endl
    << setw (10) << x.m[1][0] << setw (10) << x.m[1][1]
    << setw (10) << x.m[1][2] << endl
    << setw (10) << x.m[2][0] << setw (10) << x.m[2][1]
    << setw (10) << x.m[2][2]
    << "}\n";
  return os;
}
```

The Plane Classes Thus Far

Before we tackle the most complex portion of the simulation, the calculation of the forces upon the plane at any instant in time, let's examine the classes thus far. I created a Piece class that encapsulates the specific data needed to define a part of the plane. An enum helps to identify each piece and the name of each piece is useful for debugging purposes.

The enum FlapsSet is going to be used when responding to user input to adjust the plane's flaps, ailerons, or elevator. If we store the state of the flaps as an integer, whose initial value is zero indicating the flaps are in a level position, then by adding the values FlapsUp or FlapsDown to the integer state, we can easily adjust them.

Plane.h
```
#pragma once
#include "stdafx.h"
#include "Vector.h"
#include "Matrix3D.h"
#include "Quaternion.h"

const int PieceName = 19;

class Piece {
public:
  enum PieceType {Aileron, Flap, Wing, Elevator, Rudder,Fuselage};
  enum FlapsSet   {NoFlaps, FlapsDown = 1, FlapsUp = -1};

  PieceType type;
  int       flapSet;

  char    name[PieceName];
  Vector  centerGravity;
  double  mass;
  double  area;
  double  dihedral;
  double  incidence;
  double  span;
  double  chord;
  double  thickness;

  Vector  localInertia;

  Vector  normalVector; // relative air velocity for lift and drag
  Vector  centerGravityPlane;
```

```
// debugging fields
```

To facilitate the debugging of a plane simulation, I've added a number of intermediate variables that are used in the calculations. When not debugging, these variables are not filled in. They only have values when debugging is turned on.

```
Vector   thisAngularVelocity;
Vector   thisLocalVelocity;
double   thisLocalSpeed;
Vector   thisLocalDragDirection;
Vector   thisLocalLiftDirection;
double   thisLocalAttackAngle;
double   thisLift;
double   thisDrag;
Vector   thisLiftDrag;
Vector   thisThisMoment;

  Piece ();
 ~Piece ();

friend istream& operator>> (istream& is, Piece& p);
void CalcMomentOfInertia ();
void CalcNormalVector ();
};
```

Each piece is capable of inputting itself from the text file, one line per piece. The Plane consists of a dynamically allocated array of Piece instances. Let's examine the Piece first.

Piece.cpp

```
#include "stdafx.h"
#include <fstream>
#include <iomanip>
#include <cctype>
#include <cmath>
using namespace std;

const      double RHO = 0.0023769;   // density of air at sea
                                     // level, slugs/ft^3
const double Gravity = -32.147;      // ft/s^2 downward

#include "Plane.h"

Piece::Piece () {
 name[0] = 0;
 mass = area = dihedral = incidence = span = chord = thickness=0;
 flapSet = NoFlaps;
```

```
 type = Wing;
 thisLocalSpeed = thisLocalAttackAngle = thisLift = thisDrag = 0;
}


Piece::~Piece () { }
```

Notice that I input the data items of a piece into temporary variables, and only if the entire input is successful are they then assigned into the actual instance members.

```
istream& operator>> (istream& is, Piece& p) {
 char n[PieceName];
 double m, a, d, i, s, c, t, x, y, z;
 char j;
 is >> ws;
 is.get (n, sizeof(n));
 is >> j >> x >> j >> y >> j >> z >> j >> m >> a >> d >> i >> s
    >> c >> t >> j;
 if (!is) return is;
 strcpy_s (p.name, sizeof(p.name), n);
 p.centerGravity = Vector (x, y, z);
 p.mass = m;
 p.area = a;
 p.dihedral = d;
 p.incidence = i;
 p.span = s;
 p.chord = c;
 p.thickness = t;
 j = toupper (j);
 switch (j) {
  case 'A':
   p.type = Piece::Aileron; break;
  case 'F':
   p.type = Piece::Flap; break;
  case 'W':
   p.type = Piece::Wing; break;
  case 'E':
   p.type = Piece::Elevator; break;
  case 'R':
   p.type = Piece::Rudder; break;
  case 'G':
   p.type = Piece::Fuselage; break;
  default:
   cerr << "Error: unknown piece type: " << j << endl;
 }
 p.localInertia = p.normalVector = Vector (0, 0, 0);
 p.flapSet = Piece::NoFlaps;
 p.CalcMomentOfInertia ();
```

```
 p.CalcNormalVector ();
 return is;
}

void Piece::CalcMomentOfInertia () {
 double d = mass / 12;
 double x2 = chord * chord;
 double y2 = span * span;
 double z2 = thickness * thickness;
 double ix0 = d * (y2 + z2);
 double iy0 = d * (x2 + z2);
 double iz0 = d * (x2 + y2);
 localInertia.x = ix0;
 localInertia.y = iy0;
 localInertia.z = iz0;
 if (type == Elevator) {
  localInertia.x = ix0 / 2;
  localInertia.y = iy0 / 2;
  localInertia.z = iz0 / 2;
 }
}

void Piece::CalcNormalVector () {
 double radInc = DegreesToRadians (incidence);
 double radDih = DegreesToRadians (dihedral);
 normalVector = Vector (sin (radInc),
                        cos (radInc) * sin (radDih),
                        cos (radInc) * cos (radDih));
 normalVector.Normalize ();
}
```

Next, let's see how the Plane class puts the pieces together into a plane object. The constructor calls LoadPieces() to get the pieces inputted and then BuildPlane() to put them together into the package. However, during operations, we must know the subscripts of the various pieces. Hence, I adhere to a strict order of entry of the pieces. The first line of the data file contains a lengthy (here, line wrapped) column headings so that you can tell the meaning of each number. For pieces of the same type, starboard comes before port. The ailerons are first, followed by the flaps, the elevator, the rudder, the lower wing, and finally the fuselage.

```
Piece (starboard then port) Center Gravity Mass (slugs) Area
Dihedral Incidence Span Chord Thickness Type
11
Starboard Aileron    (17.5, -12.5, 8.88) 1.30  25 0 -3.5 5 5 .25 A
Port Aileron         (17.5, 12.5, 8.88) 1.30 25 0 -3.5 5 5 .25 A
Starboard Flap       (17.5, -5, 8.88) 2.59 50 0 -3.5 10 5 .25 F
Port Flap            (17.5, 5, 8.88) 2.59 50 0 -3.5 10 5 .25 F
```

```
Starboard Elevator    (1.5, -3.1, 7)  1.56 12.5 0 0 5 5 .25 E
Port Elevator         (1.5, 3.1, 7)   1.56 12.5 0 0 5 5 .25 E
Tail                  (0, 1.5, 7.5)   .93 4.71 90 0 3 .25 3 R
Starboard Bottom      (17, -8.25, 3)  3.11 54 0 -3.5 13.5 4 .25 W
Port Bottom           (17, 8.25, 3)   3.11 54 0 -3.5 13.5 4 .25 W
Fuselage Front        (21.5, 0, 4.5)  47.89 9 0 0 3 3 4 G
Fuselage Back         (10, 0, 4.5)    10.29 60 0 0 20 3 4 G
```

Given this prelude, what does the Plane class look like? Notice that once again, enums are handy. This time I use them as subscripts into the array of pieces so that we can directly access each piece as needed. For example, the user wishes to raise the elevator to make the plane climb. By using the two indices, ElevatorSIdx and ElevatorPIdx, we can directly set the flaps on the elevator pieces.

Plane.h

```
#pragma once
#include "stdafx.h"
#include "Piece.h"

class Plane {
public:
 enum Index { AileronSIdx, AileronPIdx, FlapSIdx, FlapPIdx,
              ElevatorSIdx, ElevatorPIdx, RudderIdx};
 Piece*    pieces;
 int       numPieces;

 double    mass;
 Vector    centerOfGravity;    // body coordinates
 Matrix3D  inertia;            // body coordinates
 Matrix3D  inertiaInverse;     // body coordinates

 Vector       velocityBody;    // velocity in body coordinates
 Vector       angularVelocity; // angular velocity in body coords
 Vector       eulerAngles;     // Euler angles in body coordinates
                               // (roll, pitch, yaw)
 double       speed;           // speed (magnitude of the velocity)

 Vector       position;        // position in earth coordinates
 Vector       velocity;        // velocity in earth coordinates
 Quaternion   orientation;     // in earth coordinates
 Vector       thrust;          // current thrust vector
 double       thrustForce;     // current engine thrust output

 Vector       forces;          // total force on body
 Vector       moments;         // total moment (torque) on body
 Vector       acceleration;    // acceleration total of plane
```

```
bool        isStalling;      // true when the plane is stalling

bool        debug;
Vector      totalLocalForceLessGravity;
```

Notice that the member, debug, is part of the Plane class. When set, it causes all of the intermediate calculation results to be stored for each piece. Additionally, the total force acting on the plane, less gravity, is also stored here in the Plane instance.

LoadPieces() and BuildPlane() are called to input the pieces and perform the initial plane initialization, done once. For the simulation physics, we have the usual CalculatePlaneLoads() which finds the current operational forces acting upon the plane. As part of this calculation, the lift and drag coefficients must be found, based upon the attack angle of each piece. The rudder is done separately. MakeAngularVelocityMatrix() is called to make the 3x3 matrix that defines the current angular velocity acting upon the plane. Finally, IntegrateEuler() is called by the simulation code for each interval of time.

A simple user interface must also be provided so that the plane can be "flown." These functions consist of controlling the flaps, elevator, ailerons, and rudder. Additionally, some means of adjusting the throttle or thrust is provided.

```
public:
  Plane (const char* filename);
  ~Plane ();

protected:
  bool LoadPieces (const char* filename);
  void BuildPlane ();

public:
  void   CalculatePlaneLoads ();
  double FindRudderLiftCoefficient (double angle);
  double FindRudderDragCoefficient (double angle);
  double FindLiftCoefficient (double angle, int flaps);
  double FindDragCoefficient (double angle, int flaps);
  void   IntegrateEuler (double dt);

  Matrix3D MakeAngularVelocityMatrix ();

  void   ZeroRudder ();
  void   ZeroElevators ();
  void   ZeroAilerons ();
  void   ZeroFlaps ();
  void   MoveFlaps (Piece::FlapsSet type);
  void   MoveAilerons  (bool rollLeft);
```

```
void      MoveElevators (Piece::FlapsSet type);
void      MoveRudder (double angle);
void      ChangeThrottle (double amount);
double GetPercentThrottle () const;
};
```

The implementation ranges from the simple to the very complex. Let's take it a step at a time. First, let's just get the pieces loaded and the initialization done.

```
#include "stdafx.h"
#include <fstream>
#include <iomanip>
#include <cctype>
#include <cmath>
using namespace std;

const double RHO = 0.0023769;    // desity of air at sea level
                                 // slugs/ft^3
const double Gravity = -32.147; // ft/s^2 downward

#include "Plane.h"

Plane::Plane (const char* filename) {
 debug = false;
 pieces = 0;
 numPieces = 0;
 if (!LoadPieces (filename)) {
  exit (1);
 }
 BuildPlane ();
 thrustForce = 0;   // current amount of engine thrust
 thrust.x = 1;      // thrust acts in x direction only
 speed = 0;
 isStalling = false;
 orientation = MakeQFromEulerAngles (
                 eulerAngles.x, eulerAngles.y, eulerAngles.z);
}

bool Plane::LoadPieces (const char* filename) {
 char x[200];
 ifstream infile (filename);
 if (!infile) {
  cerr << "Error: cannot open plane file: " << filename << endl;
  return false;
 }
 // input caption line
 infile.getline (x, sizeof(x));
```

256

```
 // input the number of pieces that follow
 infile >> numPieces;
 if (!infile || numPieces < 1) {
  cerr << "Error: unable to input plane and pieces: " << filename
      << endl;
  infile.close ();
  return false;
 }

 // allocate the array of pieces
 pieces = new (std::nothrow) Piece [numPieces];
 if (!numPieces) {
  cerr << "Error: out of memory loading pieces of plane: "
      << filename << endl;
  infile.close ();
  return false;
 }

 int i;

 // input all the pieces
 for (i=0; i<numPieces; i++) {
  infile >> pieces[i];
 }

 // file should still be in the good state
 if (!infile) {
  cerr << "Error: during loading pieces of plane: " << filename
      << endl;
  infile.close ();
  delete [] pieces;
  return false;
 }

 infile.close ();
 return true;
}

void Plane::BuildPlane () {
 // Calculate total mass and combined center of gravity location
 int i;
 mass = 0;
 Vector moment;
 for (i=0; i<numPieces; i++) {
  mass += pieces[i].mass;
  moment += pieces[i].mass * pieces[i].centerGravity;
```

```
}
centerOfGravity = moment / mass;

// calculate each piece's location from the center of gravity
// the of plane
for (i=0; i<numPieces; i++) {
 pieces[i].centerGravityPlane =
                      pieces[i].centerGravity - centerOfGravity;
}

// Calculate the moments and products of inertia for the
// combined elements, creating an inertia matrix
// (which is a tensor) that is in body coordinates
double Ixx = 0, Iyy = 0, Izz = 0, Ixy = 0, Ixz = 0, Iyz = 0;
for (i=0; i<numPieces; i++) {
 Ixx += pieces[i].localInertia.x + pieces[i].mass *
        (pieces[i].centerGravityPlane.y *
         pieces[i].centerGravityPlane.y +
         pieces[i].centerGravityPlane.z *
         pieces[i].centerGravityPlane.z);
 Iyy += pieces[i].localInertia.y + pieces[i].mass *
        (pieces[i].centerGravityPlane.z *
         pieces[i].centerGravityPlane.z +
         pieces[i].centerGravityPlane.x *
         pieces[i].centerGravityPlane.x);
 Izz += pieces[i].localInertia.z + pieces[i].mass *
        (pieces[i].centerGravityPlane.x *
         pieces[i].centerGravityPlane.x +
         pieces[i].centerGravityPlane.y *
         pieces[i].centerGravityPlane.y);
 Ixy += pieces[i].mass * (pieces[i].centerGravityPlane.x *
        pieces[i].centerGravityPlane.y);
 Ixz += pieces[i].mass * (pieces[i].centerGravityPlane.x *
        pieces[i].centerGravityPlane.z);
 Iyz += pieces[i].mass * (pieces[i].centerGravityPlane.y *
        pieces[i].centerGravityPlane.z);
}

// Store these in the plane's inertia matrix and find the inverse
of the inertia matrix
 inertia = Matrix3D (Ixx, -Ixy, -Ixz,
                     -Ixy,  Iyy, -Iyz,
                     -Ixz, -Iyz,  Izz);
 inertiaInverse = inertia.Inverse();
}
```

```
Plane::~Plane () {
  if (pieces)
    delete [] pieces;
}
```

Dealing with Rotations in 3D Space

When an object is rotating in 3D space, it can be rotating about either of the three axes: x, y, or z. Worse yet, it could be rotating about an arbitrary axis that is not either of these three! Normally, we think of pitch, roll, and yaw, the three Euler angles. Here, the plane's nose may pitch up or down, as it climbs or dives. It may roll or bank left or right. It may turn left or right, the yaw.

You might be thinking that this is all that we need for our 3D simulation. However, a numerical problem arises when you use these Euler angles in a 3D simulation. Suppose that the pitch angle becomes 90 degrees, either straight up or down. When a plane is in this position, roll and yaw become ambiguous to say the least, since either are creating the same effect! However confusing this may be, computationally, the equations of motion involve a cosine of the pitch angle. If the pitch is 90 degrees, the cosine is 0 and a division by zero error crashes the program!

There are two different approaches that can be used: rotational matrices and quaternions, which is essentially a vector plus a scalar in combination.

Rotation Matrices

Definition: a rotational matrix is a 3x3 matrix. If this matrix is multiplied by a point or a vector, it results in the rotation of that point or vector around some axis and gives you the new coordinates. Even more importantly, the matrix converts points from one coordinate system to another, given that one is rotated relative to the other: conversion from body or local coordinates to world or global coordinates. This latter is precisely what we face in 3D rigid body simulations, conversion to and from local and global coordinate systems.

Typical usage of the rotation matrix $\mathbf{R}$ is the following equation, where vector $\mathbf{v}_1$ is rotated about some axis, giving the result, $\mathbf{v}_2$.
$$\mathbf{v}_2 = \mathbf{R}\,\mathbf{v}_1$$

If you have multiple rotations that are sequential in nature, one after the other, then they can be combined by matrix multiplication. Assuming the rotational matrices are in global coordinates, they can be combined this way.
$$\mathbf{R}_c = \mathbf{R}_1\,\mathbf{R}_2$$
However, if the coordinates are in local coordinates, not global, the multiplication is reversed.

Game Programming Theory

$$R_c = R_2 R_1$$

Let's examine a simpler case first. Consider an object rotating solely around the z axis. It has some angular rotational change, a, in the x-y plane, from x_1, y_1 to x_2, y_2. Knowing the angle, a, we desire to calculate the coordinates x_2, y_2. We know the formulas to calculate this are these.

$x_2 = x_1 \cos(a) + y_1 \sin(a)$
$y_2 = -x_1 \sin(a) + y_1 \cos(a)$
$z_2 = z_1$

The z coordinate does not change, since this is the axis of rotation.

Now how do we put this into matrix notation. Let $\mathbf{v_1}$ be (x_1, y_1, z_1) and $\mathbf{v_2}$ be (x_2, y_2, z_2) be the rotated result. Then, the rotational matrix, $\mathbf{R}$, would be this.

```
|cos(a_z)   -sin(a_z)  0|
|sin(a_z)    cos(a_z)  0|
|  0           0       1|
```

Now we can write the rotation as this.

$$\mathbf{v_2} = \mathbf{R} \, \mathbf{v_1}$$

Now, we can also rotate solely around the x axis, that is in the y-z plane. Here the rotation matrix would be this.

```
|1      0          0     |
|0   cos(a_x)  -sin(a_x)|
|0   sin(a_x)   cos(a_x)|
```

We can rotate solely around the y axis, that is in the x-z plane. Here the rotation matrix would be this.

```
|cos(a_y)   0   sin(a_y)|
|   0       1      0     |
|-sin(a_y)  0   cos(a_y)|
```

Now that we have the normal rotation matrices for pitch, roll, and yaw, we can combine them to find the total rotation matrix by using matrix multiplication of these three. Just be sure you use the correct order of term multiplication depending upon whether you are in local or global coordinate systems.

In our rigid body simulations, we use the rotation matrices to keep track of our orientation. If the matrix is applied to our local coordinates, it will rotate it to resemble the body's current orientation in global coordinates. That is, this rotation matrix is going to be a function of time. In our simulations, once we set up the initial orientation angle and the corresponding matrix, as time progresses, various forces, lift, drag, and thrust, will make small changes in the angular velocity about the axes, which will in turn alter the orientation and angles. Hence, we need a way to relate the rotation matrix to the angular velocity so that we can update the orientation appropriately. The formula is this.

$$dR/dt = \Omega\, R$$
where Ω is built from the angular velocity vector this way.
$$
\begin{vmatrix}
0 & -\omega_z & \omega_y) \\
\omega_z & 0 & -\omega_x \\
-\omega_y & \omega_x & 0
\end{vmatrix}
$$

In our simulations, you know the initial rotation matrix at the very start. At each increment of time, you calculate the new angular velocity vector. Then, you can easily update the rotation and orientation, by multiplying the original rotation matrix by Ω. This then avoids the division by zero problem and it avoids numerous calls to the high overhead trig functions. There is, however, an additional problem beyond requiring nine values each time.

This rotation matrix must be orthogonal and have a determinant of 1. Since you will be calculating it numerous times, small roundoff errors accumulate over time. We must apply the constraints periodically. The constraint is that it represents a unit vector and that they are all at right angles to each other.
$$R^T\, R = I$$
where R is the rotation matrix, R^T is the transpose of R, and I is the identity matrix. Failure to do this often enough can result in a scaling of the object, larger or smaller in size, or a translation of the object to a different location than it is supposed to be. Quaternions offer an easier approach.

Quaternions

Quaternions were invented by William Hamilton for his complex number mathematics. Think of a quaternion as a vector plus a scalar. It is usually written this way.
$$\mathbf{q} = q_0 + q_x\mathbf{i} + q_y\mathbf{j} + q_z\mathbf{k}$$
In handling rotation and our orientation, the unit or normalized quaternion is most valuable.
$$q_0^2 + q_x^2 + q_y^2 + q_{z2} = 1$$

To implement a quaternion, use a vector plus a scalar. For rotation of angle a about an arbitrary axis represented by vector $\mathbf{v}$, the quaternion to represent this is given by this.
$$\mathbf{q} = [\cos(a/2),\ \sin(a/2)\,\mathbf{v}]$$

To use them in our simulations, we must setup the initial quaternion that represents the initial orientation of the object. Next, at the small time intervals later on, we use
$$d\mathbf{q}/dt = \omega_q\, \mathbf{q}\, /\, 2$$
where we must write the angular velocity as a quaternion
$$\omega_q = [0,\ \omega]$$

Game Programming Theory

To rotate vectors from one coordinate system to another, use this.

$$\mathbf{v_2} = \mathbf{q}\ \mathbf{v_1}\ \mathbf{q}^*$$

where $\mathbf{q}^*$ is the conjugate

$$\mathbf{q}^* = q_0 - q_x\mathbf{i} - q_y\mathbf{j} - q_z\mathbf{k}$$

We will use this to convert from body coordinates to global coordinates, after we have applied all of the forces to the body in local coordinates. Sometimes you need to convert the object's velocity in global coordinates back into local coordinates as well. Hence, we need a quaternion class.

The Quaternion Class

Again, I have provided a Quaternion class for our use. It stores a double scalar and a vector as the data members. The default constructor sets everything to zero, the overloaded constructor allows us to build a Quaternion from four doubles. The math operation we are likely to need are +=, -=, *=, /=, along with various forms of +, -, *, and /. The conjugate function is the ~ operator. Additionally, the QGetAngle() and QGetAxis() functions return the angle of rotation around the axis of rotation which this instance is storing and a unit vector along that axis, respectively. The QRotate() function rotates the quaternion q_1 by q_2. Similarly, QVRotate() rotates the vector **v** by **q**. For orientation situations, the two functions MakeQFromEulerAngles() and MakeEulerAnglesFromQ() create a quaternion from the pitch, roll, and yaw angles and create the pitch, roll, and yaw angles from the quaternion. Also, the insertion and extraction operators allow us to input and output a quaternion, primarily for debugging purposes.

```cpp
#pragma once
#include "Vector.h"

class Quaternion {
public:
 double s; // scalar portion
 Vector v; // vector portion

  Quaternion ();
  Quaternion (double q0, double q1, double q2, double q3);
 ~Quaternion ();

 double Magnitude () const;
 Vector GetVector () const;
 double GetScalar () const;

 Quaternion& operator+= (const Quaternion& q);
 Quaternion& operator-= (const Quaternion& q);
 Quaternion& operator*= (double x);
 Quaternion& operator/= (double x);
 Quaternion  operator~ () const;

 Quaternion operator+ (const Quaternion& q) const;
 Quaternion operator- (const Quaternion& q) const;
 Quaternion operator* (const Quaternion& q) const;
 Quaternion operator* (double x) const;
 friend Quaternion operator* (double x, const Quaternion& q);
 Quaternion operator* (Vector v) const;
 friend Quaternion operator* (Vector v, const Quaternion& q);
 Quaternion operator/ (double x) const;
```

```
double QGetAngle () const;
Vector QGetAxis () const;

friend Quaternion QRotate (const Quaternion& q1,
                           const Quaternion& q2);
friend Vector    QVRotate (const Quaternion& q, Vector v);

friend Quaternion MakeQFromEulerAngles (double rollAngle,
                                        double pitchAngle,
                                        double yawAngle);
Vector MakeEulerAnglesFromQ () const;

friend istream& operator>> (istream& is, Quaternion& q);
friend ostream& operator<< (ostream& os, const Quaternion& q);
};
```

Some of the functions are straightforward and obvious, while others are quite complex. Some are even beyond the scope of this course. The Magnitude() function returns the square root of the sum of the squares of the four components. The addition and subtraction of two quaternions is just the addition and subtraction of the four components. Similarly the multiplication and division of a quaternion and a double is the multiplication and division of each component by the double. The conjugate (operator~) returns a new quaternion whose vector components are the negative of the original vector. For the multiplication of a vector by a quaternion or vice-versa, consult a math text.

```
Quaternion::Quaternion () {
  s = 0; // v's ctor already set it to 0
}

Quaternion::~Quaternion () { }

Quaternion::Quaternion (double q0, double q1, double q2, double q3)
{
  s = q0;
  v = Vector (q1, q2, q3);
}

double Quaternion::Magnitude () const {
  return sqrt (s * s + v.x * v.x + v.y * v.y + v.z * v.z);
}

Vector Quaternion::GetVector () const {
  return v;
}

double Quaternion::GetScalar () const {
  return s;
```

```
}

Quaternion& Quaternion::operator+= (const Quaternion& q) {
  s += q.s;
  v.x += q.v.x;
  v.y += q.v.y;
  v.z += q.v.z;
  return *this;
}

Quaternion& Quaternion::operator-= (const Quaternion& q) {
  s -= q.s;
  v.x -= q.v.x;
  v.y -= q.v.y;
  v.z -= q.v.z;
  return *this;
}

Quaternion& Quaternion::operator*= (double x) {
  s *= x;
  v.x *= x;
  v.y *= x;
  v.z *= x;
  return *this;
}

Quaternion& Quaternion::operator/= (double x) {
  s /= x;
  v.x /= x;
  v.y /= x;
  v.z /= x;
  return *this;
}

Quaternion  Quaternion::operator~ () const {
  return Quaternion (s, -v.x, -v.y, -v.z);
}

Quaternion Quaternion::operator+ (const Quaternion& q) const {
  return Quaternion (s + q.s, v.x + q.v.x, v.y + q.v.y, v.z +
q.v.z);
}

Quaternion Quaternion::operator- (const Quaternion& q) const {
  return Quaternion ( s - q.s, v.x - q.v.x, v.y - q.v.y, v.z -
q.v.z);
```

```
}

Quaternion Quaternion::operator* (const Quaternion& q) const {
 return Quaternion (s * q.s - v.x * q.v.x - v.y * q.v.y - v.z *
q.v.z,
                    s * q.v.x + v.x * q.s + v.y * q.v.z - v.z *
q.v.y,
                    s * q.v.y + v.y * q.s + v.z * q.v.x - v.x *
q.v.z,
                    s * q.v.z + v.z * q.s + v.x * q.v.y - v.y *
q.v.x);
}

Quaternion Quaternion::operator* (double x) const {
 return Quaternion (s*x, v.x * x, v.y * x, v.z * x);
}

Quaternion operator* (double x, const Quaternion& q) {
return Quaternion (q.s * x, q.v.x * x, q.v.y * x, q.v.z * x);
}

Quaternion Quaternion::operator* (const Vector& u) const {
 return Quaternion (-(v.x * u.x + v.y * u.y + v.z * u.z),
                    s * u.x + v.y * u.z - v.z * u.y,
                    s * u.y + v.z * u.x - v.x * u.z,
                    s * u.z + v.x * u.y - v.y * u.x);
}

Quaternion operator* (const Vector& u, const Quaternion& q) {
 return Quaternion (-(q.v.x * u.x + q.v.y * u.y + q.v.z * u.z),
                    q.s * u.x + q.v.z * u.y - q.v.y * u.z,
                    q.s * u.y + q.v.x * u.z - q.v.z * u.x,
                    q.s * u.z + q.v.y * u.x - q.v.x * u.y);
}

Quaternion Quaternion::operator/ (double x) const {
 return Quaternion (s / x, v.x / x, v.y / x, v.z / x);
}

double Quaternion::QGetAngle () const {
 return 2. * acos (s);
}

Vector Quaternion::QGetAxis () const {
 Vector u = v;
 double mag = u.Magnitude();
```

```
if (mag <= EPS)
  return Vector (0,0,0);
else
  return u / mag;
}



Quaternion QRotate (const Quaternion& q1, const Quaternion& q2) {
  return q1 * q2 * (~q1);
}

Vector QVRotate (const Quaternion& q, const Vector& v) {
  Quaternion temp = q * v * (~q);
  return temp.GetVector();
}

istream& operator>> (istream& is, Quaternion& q) {
  double q0, q1, q2, q3;
  is >> q0 >> q1 >> q2 >> q3;
  if (!is) return is;
  q = Quaternion (q0, q1, q2, q3);
  return is;
}

ostream& operator<< (ostream& os, const Quaternion& q) {
  os << fixed << setprecision (2);
  os << "[" << setw(10) << q.s << ", " << q.v << "]";
  return os;
}
```

Given the pitch angle about the y axis, the yaw angle about the z axis, and the roll angle about the x axis, the quaternion is constructed. Similarly, the vector which holds the angles made from a quaternion are (roll, pitch, yaw), that is (x, y, z). Again, consult a math text if you desire to know how this process is done. It is beyond this beginning course. I will point out that there is an alternative tangent function, atan2() which is passed two sides instead of the single value. The atan2() function does the division for us and utilizes the signs of the two parameters to help determine the quadrant of the angle being returned.

```
Quaternion   MakeQFromEulerAngles   (double   rollAngle,   double
pitchAngle, double yawAngle) {
  double roll  = DegreesToRadians (rollAngle);
  double pitch = DegreesToRadians (pitchAngle);
  double yaw   = DegreesToRadians (yawAngle);

  double cosyaw, cospitch, cosroll, sinyaw, sinpitch, sinroll;
```

```
double cosyaw_cospitch, sinyaw_sinpitch, cosyaw_sinpitch,
        sinyaw_cospitch;

cosyaw   = cos (.5 * yaw);
cospitch = cos (.5 * pitch);
cosroll  = cos (.5 * roll);
sinyaw   = sin (.5 * yaw);
sinpitch = sin (.5 * pitch);
sinroll  = sin (.5 * roll);

cosyaw_cospitch = cosyaw * cospitch;
sinyaw_sinpitch = sinyaw * sinpitch;
cosyaw_sinpitch = cosyaw * sinpitch;
sinyaw_cospitch = sinyaw * cospitch;

Quaternion q (
        cosyaw_cospitch * cosroll + sinyaw_sinpitch * sinroll,
        cosyaw_cospitch * sinroll - sinyaw_sinpitch * cosroll,
        cosyaw_sinpitch * cosroll + sinyaw_cospitch * sinroll,
        sinyaw_cospitch * cosroll - cosyaw_sinpitch * sinroll
           );
 return q;
}

Vector Quaternion::MakeEulerAnglesFromQ () const {
 double x11, x12, x13;
 double x21;
 double x31, x32, x33;
 double q00, q11, q22, q33;
 double temp;
 Vector u;

 q00 = s * s;
 q11 = v.x * v.x;
 q22 = v.y * v.y;
 q33 = v.z * v.z;

 x11 = q00 + q11 - q22 - q33;
 x21 = 2 * (v.x * v.y + s * v.z);
 x31 = 2 * (v.x * v.z - s * v.y);
 x32 = 2 * (v.y * v.z + s * v.x);
 x33 = q00 - q11 - q22 + q33;

 temp = fabs (x31);
 if(temp > 0.999999) {
  x12 = 2 * (v.x * v.y - s * v.z);
```

```
    x13 = 2 * (v.x * v.z + s * v.y);
    u.x = RadiansToDegrees (0.);                           // roll
    u.y = RadiansToDegrees (- PI / 2 * x31 / temp);     // pitch
    u.z = RadiansToDegrees (atan2 (-x12, -x31 * x13));  // yaw
    return u;
  }
  u.x = RadiansToDegrees (atan2 (x32, x33));   // roll
  u.y = RadiansToDegrees (asin (-x31));        // pitch
  u.z = RadiansToDegrees (atan2 (x21, x11));   // yaw
  return u;
}
```

Armed with this class, we can add a quaternion member to the Plane class to store our plane's orientation.

Building the Rigid Body 3D Plane Simulator

Now we are ready to build the plane simulator. What additional variables do we need to add to out Plane class? Just as we did with the 2D rigid body simulator, we must add the following variables to track the current velocity, position, orientation, total forces, total moments, and angular velocity acting upon the plane. Let's see how the loads are found for each piece.

```
void Plane::CalculatePlaneLoads () {
  isStalling = false; // reset isStalling

  // reset forces and moments:
  forces = moments = thrust = Vector (0, 0, 0);

  // set new thrust force
  thrust.x = 1;
  thrust *= thrustForce;

  // First, find the forces and moments in body space

  Vector localVelocity; // local velocity in body space of piece
  double localSpeed = 0;    // magnitude of the local velocity
  Vector dragVector;
  Vector liftVector;
  double attackAngle = 0;
  double d;
  Vector result;
  Vector temp;
  int    i;
```

```
Vector totalForce;
Vector totalMoments;

// loop through all lifting pieces, except the fuselage
// you could also add in its impact as well
for (i=0; i<numPieces; i++) {
 if (pieces[i].type == Piece::Fuselage) continue;

 // handle rudder separately, it rotates, which means the normal
 // vector must be recalculated each time
 if (pieces[i].type == Piece::Rudder) {
  double incidence, dihedral;
  incidence = DegreesToRadians (pieces[i].incidence);
  dihedral  = DegreesToRadians (pieces[i].dihedral);
  pieces[i].normalVector = Vector (sin(incidence),
                             cos(incidence) * sin(dihedral),
                             cos(incidence) * cos(dihedral));
  pieces[i].normalVector.Normalize();
 }

 // Find the local velocity at this element which includes
 // velocity due to linear motion of the airplane plus the
 // velocity at each element due to the rotation of the airplane
 temp = angularVelocity ^ pieces[i].centerGravityPlane;
 localVelocity = velocityBody + temp;
 localSpeed = localVelocity.Magnitude(); // the local air speed

 // Find the direction of the drag force
 if (localSpeed > 1.) {
  dragVector = -localVelocity / localSpeed;
 }

 // Find the direction of the lift force, which is always
 // perpendicular to the drag force
 liftVector =
            (dragVector ^ pieces[i].normalVector) ^ dragVector;
 liftVector.Normalize();
```

Notice that if debug is true, I save a copy of these intermediate results in the various members of the Piece instance.

```
 if (debug) {
  pieces[i].thisAngularVelocity = temp;
  pieces[i].thisLocalVelocity = localVelocity;
  pieces[i].thisLocalSpeed = localSpeed;
  pieces[i].thisLocalDragDirection = dragVector;
  pieces[i].thisLocalLiftDirection = liftVector;
```

```
}

// Find the angle of attack which is the angle between the lift
// vector and the element's normal vector
// Interesting property:
// sin (attack angle) = cos (angle between drag vector and
// normal vector)
d = dragVector * pieces[i].normalVector;
// force it into range -1 to 1
d = d > 1 ? 1 : (d < -1 ? -1 : d);
attackAngle = RadiansToDegrees (asin (d));
if (debug) {
 pieces[i].thisLocalAttackAngle = attackAngle;
}

// Determine the resultant force (lift and drag) on the element
d = 0.5 * RHO * localSpeed * localSpeed * pieces[i].area;

if (pieces[i].type == Piece::Rudder) {
 double rLift = FindRudderLiftCoefficient (attackAngle);
 double rDrag = FindRudderDragCoefficient (attackAngle);
 result = (liftVector * rLift + dragVector * rDrag) * d;
 if (debug) {
  pieces[i].thisLift = rLift;
  pieces[i].thisDrag = rDrag;
  pieces[i].thisLiftDrag = result;
 }
}
else {
 // save lift for stalling check
 double liftC = FindLiftCoefficient (
                          attackAngle, pieces[i].flapSet);
 double dragC = FindDragCoefficient (
                          attackAngle, pieces[i].flapSet);
 result = (liftVector * liftC + dragVector * dragC) * d;
 if (debug) {
  pieces[i].thisLift = liftC;
  pieces[i].thisDrag = dragC;
  pieces[i].thisLiftDrag = result;
 }

 // check for stalling: lift coefficient is zero
 if (pieces[i].type < Piece::Elevator) {
  if (fabs (liftC) <= EPS) isStalling = true;
 }
}
```

```
// accumulate the total forces acting on plane
totalForce += result;

// Calculate the moment about the CG of this element's force
temp = pieces[i].centerGravityPlane ^ result;
if (debug) {
  pieces[i].thisThisMoment = temp;
}
// accumulate total moments acting on plane
totalMoments += temp;
}

// finally, add in the thrust force
totalForce += thrust;
if (debug) {
  totalLocalForceLessGravity = totalForce;
}

// Convert forces from body space to global space
forces = QVRotate (orientation, totalForce);

// add in the force of gravity
forces.z += Gravity * mass;

moments += totalMoments;
}
```

Finding the lift and drag coefficients requires two actions. The first is at design time. One must ascertain the lift and drag coefficients that are representative of your plane's inherent design. Here, I used those provided by the text, <u>Physics for Game Developers</u>, David M. Bourg. The second action is to handle the interpolation between two points. For example, the rudder lift coefficient is known for angles of 0 and 4 degrees. If our angle is now 2 degrees, we must pass a straight line between the two points and find the appropriate lift. Recall the equation of a straight line is

$$y - y_1 = m (x - x_1)$$
$$m = (y_1 - y_0) / (x_1 - x_0)$$

Hence the expression
```
(liftCoef[i] - liftCoef[i+1]) / (angles[i] - angles[i+1])
```
gives the total amount of change of lift over this interval. If we multiply this by the amount the angle we are looking for is from the left end, we get the proportional amount to be added to the lift.
```
// Find rudder's lift coefficient for a symmetric (no camber)
// airfoil without flaps
double Plane::FindRudderLiftCoefficient (double angle) {
```

```
const double liftCoef[7] =
                {0.16, 0.456, 0.736, 0.968, 1.144, 1.12, 0.8};
const double angles[7]    =
                {0.0,   4.0,    8.0,    12.0,   16.0,   20.0,   24.0};
double liftCoefficient = 0;
double absAngle = fabs (angle);
for (int i=0; i<6; i++) {
 if (absAngle >= angles[i] && absAngle < angles[i+1]) {
  // interpolate the value
  liftCoefficient = liftCoef[i] - (angles[i] - absAngle) *
      (liftCoef[i] - liftCoef[i+1]) / (angles[i] - angles[i+1]);
  if (angle < 0)
   liftCoefficient = -liftCoefficient;
  break;
 }
}
return liftCoefficient;
}


// Find rudder's drag coefficient for a symmetric (no camber)
// airfoil without flaps
double Plane::FindRudderDragCoefficient (double angle) {
 const double dragCoef[7] =
          {0.0032, 0.0072, 0.0104, 0.0184, 0.04, 0.096, 0.168};
 const double angles[7]    =
          {0.0,    4.0,    8.0,    12.0,   16.0,   20.0,   24.0};
 double dragCoefficient = .5;
 double absAngle = fabs (angle);
 for (int i=0; i<6; i++) {
  if (absAngle >= angles[i] && absAngle < angles[i+1]) {
   dragCoefficient = dragCoef[i] - (angles[i] - absAngle) *
      (dragCoef[i] - dragCoef[i+1]) / (angles[i] - angles[i+1]);

   break;
  }
 }
 return dragCoefficient;
}


// Find the lift coefficient given attack angle and the status of
// the flaps for a cambered airfoil with a plain trailing edge
// flap
double Plane::FindLiftCoefficient (double angle, int flaps) {
 const double liftCoefNoFlaps[9] =
        {-0.54, -0.2, 0.2,  0.57, 0.92, 1.21, 1.43,  1.4,   1.0};
```

```
const double liftCoefFlapsDown[9] =
     {0.0,   0.45, 0.85, 1.02, 1.39, 1.65, 1.75,  1.38,  1.17};
const double liftCoefFlapsUp[9] =
     {-0.74, -0.4, 0.0,  0.27, 0.63, 0.92, 1.03,  1.1,   0.78};
const double angles[9] =
     {-8.0,  -4.0, 0.0,  4.0,  8.0,  12.0, 16.0,  20.0,  24.0};
double liftCoefficient = 0;
for (int i=0; i<8; i++) {
 if (angle >= angles[i] && angle < angles[i+1]) {
  switch (flaps) {
   case Piece::NoFlaps:
    liftCoefficient = liftCoefNoFlaps[i] - (angles[i] - angle) *
       (liftCoefNoFlaps[i] - liftCoefNoFlaps[i+1]) /
       (angles[i] - angles[i+1]);
    break;
   case Piece::FlapsDown:
    liftCoefficient = liftCoefFlapsDown[i] -
        (angles[i] - angle) *
        (liftCoefFlapsDown[i] - liftCoefFlapsDown[i+1]) /
        (angles[i] - angles[i+1]);
    break;
   case Piece::FlapsUp:
    liftCoefficient = liftCoefFlapsUp[i] - (angles[i] - angle) *
         (liftCoefFlapsUp[i] - liftCoefFlapsUp[i+1]) /
         (angles[i] - angles[i+1]);
    break;
  }
  break; // out of loop
 }
}
 return liftCoefficient;
}

// Find the drag coefficient, given attack angle and the status
// of the flaps for a cambered airfoil with a plain trailing edge
// flap (+/- 15 degree deflection)
double Plane::FindDragCoefficient (double angle, int flaps) {
 const double dragCoefNoFlap[9] =
              {0.01,   0.0074, 0.004,  0.009,  0.013,  0.023,
0.05, 0.12,  0.21};
 const double dragCoefFlapDown[9] =
              {0.0065, 0.0043, 0.0055, 0.0153, 0.0221, 0.0391,
0.1,  0.195, 0.3};
 const double dragCoefFlapUp[9] =
              {0.005,  0.0043, 0.0055, 0.02601, 0.03757, 0.06647,
0.13, 0.18,  0.25};
```

```
const double angles[9]  =
            {-8.0,   -4.0,    0.0,    4.0,     8.0,      12.0,
16.,   20.,    24.};
double dragCoefficient = .5;
for (int i=0; i<8; i++) {
 if (angle >= angles[i] && angle < angles[i+1]) {
  switch (flaps) {
   case Piece::NoFlaps:
    dragCoefficient = dragCoefNoFlap[i] - (angles[i] - angle) *
        (dragCoefNoFlap[i] - dragCoefNoFlap[i+1]) /
        (angles[i] - angles[i+1]);
    break;
   case Piece::FlapsDown:
    dragCoefficient = dragCoefFlapDown[i] -
        (angles[i] - angle) *
        (dragCoefFlapDown[i] - dragCoefFlapDown[i+1]) /
        (angles[i] - angles[i+1]);
    break;
   case Piece::FlapsUp:
    dragCoefficient = dragCoefFlapUp[i] - (angles[i] - angle) *
        (dragCoefFlapUp[i] - dragCoefFlapUp[i+1]) /
        (angles[i] - angles[i+1]);
    break;
  }
  break;
 }
}
return dragCoefficient;
}
```

In comparison, the actual integration is fairly simple. Calculate the forces, then find the acceleration, which then yields the new velocity. From that, the new position is found. Then, the angular velocity, which rotates the plane, is found and the new orientation found. Finally, the three Euler angles, roll, pitch, and yaw, are found.

```
void Plane::IntegrateEuler (double dt) {
 // calculate all of the forces and moments on the airplane:
 CalculatePlaneLoads();

 // calculate the acceleration of the airplane in earth space
 acceleration = forces / mass;

 // calculate the velocity of the airplane in earth space
 velocity += acceleration * dt;

 // calculate the position of the airplane in earth space
```

```
position += velocity * dt;

//Vector av = angularVelocity; //save

// Now handle the rotations by calculating the angular velocity
// in body space

// the following could be used, but seems to give wrong results
// angularVelocity +=
//      inertiaInverse *
//(moments - angularVelocity ^ (inertia * angularVelocity)) * dt;

Matrix3D mAngularVelocity = MakeAngularVelocityMatrix ();
angularVelocity += inertiaInverse *
  (moments - mAngularVelocity * inertia * angularVelocity) * dt;

// Calculate the new rotation quaternion:
orientation += (orientation * angularVelocity) * 0.5f * dt;

// Normalize the orientation quaternion:
double mag = orientation.Magnitude ();
if (mag != 0) orientation /= mag;

// Calculate velocity in body space
velocityBody = QVRotate (~orientation, velocity);

// calculate the air speed
speed = velocity.Magnitude ();

// Find the Euler angles for our information
eulerAngles = orientation.MakeEulerAnglesFromQ ();
}
```

The functions for the user controls are simple, in contrast. Various functions zero out any flaps or rudder angles, giving a fast reset.

```
void Plane::ZeroRudder () {
 pieces[RudderIdx].incidence = 0;
}

void Plane::ZeroElevators () {
 pieces[ElevatorSIdx].flapSet = Piece::NoFlaps;
 pieces[ElevatorPIdx].flapSet = Piece::NoFlaps;
}

void Plane::ZeroAilerons () {
 pieces[AileronPIdx].flapSet = Piece::NoFlaps;
```

```
  pieces[AileronSIdx].flapSet = Piece::NoFlaps;
}

void Plane::ZeroFlaps () {
 pieces[FlapSIdx].flapSet = Piece::NoFlaps;
 pieces[FlapPIdx].flapSet = Piece::NoFlaps;
}
```

The use of the FlapsSet enum can be seen in the handling of a user request to change them. The enum is added to the current setting, and forced back into range between −1 and +1.

```
void Plane::MoveFlaps (Piece::FlapsSet type) {
 const double MaxAngle = 30; // degrees
 pieces[FlapSIdx].flapSet += type;
 pieces[FlapPIdx].flapSet += type;
 if (pieces[FlapSIdx].flapSet > Piece::FlapsDown) {
  pieces[FlapSIdx].flapSet = Piece::FlapsDown;
  pieces[FlapPIdx].flapSet = Piece::FlapsDown;
 }
 else if (pieces[FlapSIdx].flapSet < Piece::FlapsUp) {
  pieces[FlapSIdx].flapSet = Piece::FlapsUp;
  pieces[FlapPIdx].flapSet = Piece::FlapsUp;
 }
}

void Plane::MoveAilerons  (bool rollLeft) {
 const double MaxAngle = 30; // degrees
 if (rollLeft) {
  if (pieces[AileronPIdx].flapSet == Piece::FlapsUp)
   return;
  pieces[AileronPIdx].flapSet--;
  pieces[AileronSIdx].flapSet++;
 }
 else {
  if (pieces[AileronPIdx].flapSet == Piece::FlapsDown)
   return;
  pieces[AileronPIdx].flapSet++;
  pieces[AileronSIdx].flapSet--;
 }
}

void Plane::MoveElevators (Piece::FlapsSet type) {
 pieces[ElevatorSIdx].flapSet += type;
 pieces[ElevatorPIdx].flapSet += type;
 if (pieces[ElevatorSIdx].flapSet > Piece::FlapsDown) {
  pieces[ElevatorSIdx].flapSet = Piece::FlapsDown;
  pieces[ElevatorPIdx].flapSet = Piece::FlapsDown;
```

```
  }
  else if (pieces[ElevatorSIdx].flapSet < Piece::FlapsUp) {
    pieces[ElevatorSIdx].flapSet = Piece::FlapsUp;
    pieces[ElevatorPIdx].flapSet = Piece::FlapsUp;
  }
}

void Plane::MoveRudder (double angle) {
  const double MaxAngle = 30; // degrees max movement
  double a = pieces[RudderIdx].incidence + angle;
  if (a > 30) a = 30;
  else if (a < -30) a = -30;
  pieces[RudderIdx].incidence = a;
}

Matrix3D Plane::MakeAngularVelocityMatrix () {
  const Vector& v = angularVelocity;
  return Matrix3D (0.0, -v.z, v.y,
                   v.z, 0.0, -v.x,
                   -v.y, v.x, 0.0);
}
```

The last section deals with the thrust force. The maximum speed of the Fokker DVII was 149 mph, which can be converted into the simulation units of feet per second. The horsepower of the engine is 185. Recall that horsepower * 550 gives ft-lbs/sec.

```
const double MaxSpeed = 149; // mph
const double MaxSpeedFtPerSec = MaxSpeed * 5280 / 3600;
const double MaxHorsePower = 185;
const double MaxThrottle = MaxHorsePower * 550; // ft-lbs/sec

void Plane::ChangeThrottle (double amount) {
  double x = thrustForce + amount;
  if (x > MaxThrottle)
    x = MaxThrottle;
  thrustForce = x;
}

double Plane::GetPercentThrottle () const {
  return thrustForce / MaxThrottle * 100;
}
```

To test the simulation, Pgm09a, a Windows application, sets the timer to one second. Each time a second has elapsed, the integration is done, using a delta time of .1 seconds. The results, including the debugging fields are then displayed on the screen. Caution: I am using a screen resolution of 1280x1024. If your screen size is smaller, some of the debug results may be truncated.

278

Figure 9.5 shows the screen at one point during the simulation.

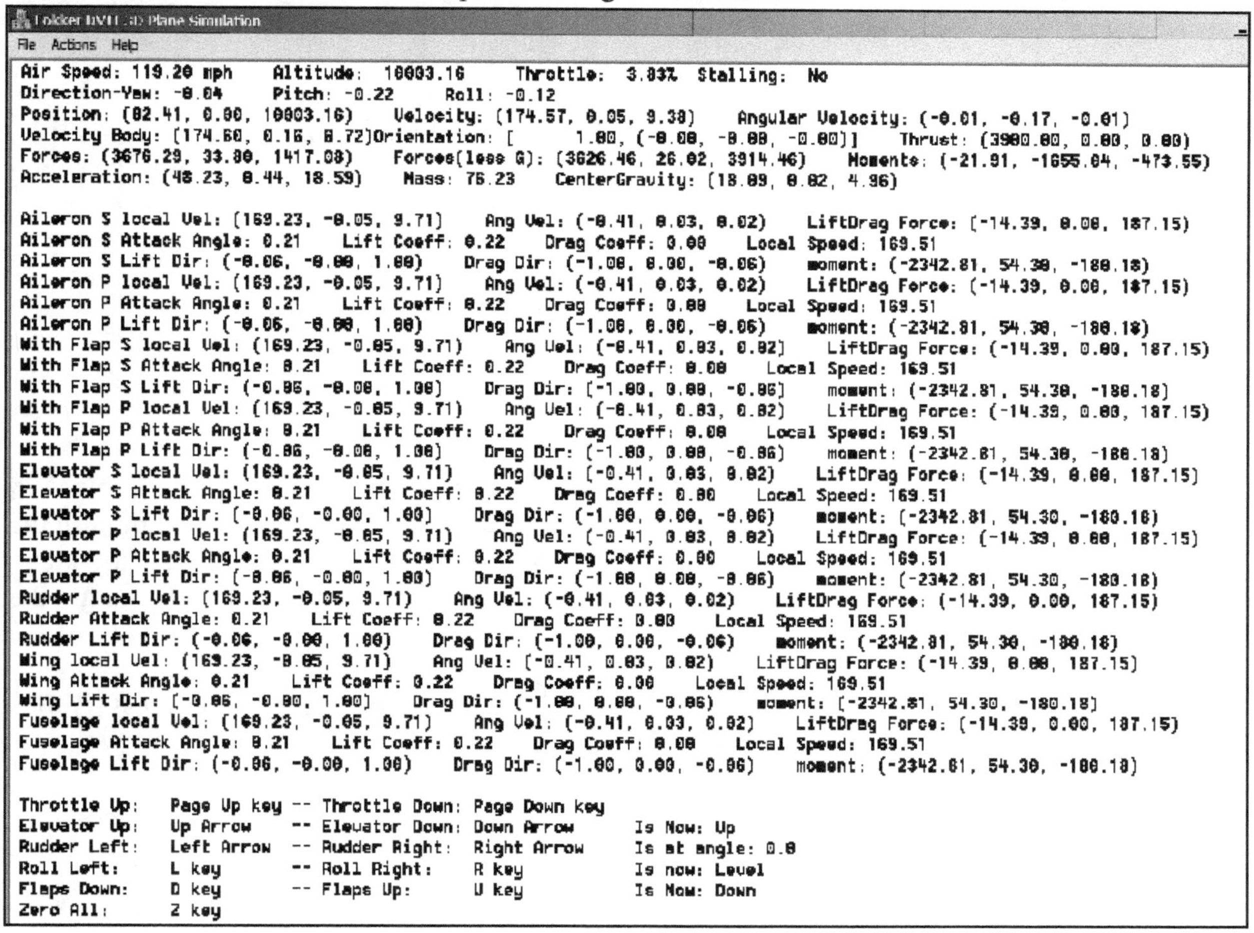

Figure 9.5 The Fokker DVII in Flight

If you observe the simulation and/or experiment with it a bit, you will notice numerous deficiencies. It is virtually impossible to fly the plane in a stable manner. Only the rudder has enough control to make it workable, changing in one degree increments. The elevator and ailerons are supposed to allow fine tuning and control of the plane. However, as they are implemented, the are full up, full down, or level.

To make a more realistic simulation, we need to extract just the elevator section that moves along with the flaps and ailerons. Then implement them as separate pieces. Further, we need to allow for small changes in their movements.

However, breaking the wing sections down into these smaller pieces will present additional problems, primarily in calculating the moments of inertia of irregular shape. Consider the moment of inertia of the wing section where the aileron section has been removed from its geometry. To do

279

the plane simulation justice, one must become an expert at calculating moments of inertia of more unusual shapes.

Next, a means of handling take-off and landings must be implemented. During takeoff, we must add in a substantial drag force with the ground, especially with a biplane. When the tail lifts, the drag force changes significantly with these early planes. Finally, braking forces must be added during landing operations. So yes, this example is a greatly simplified one indeed.

Problems

Problem 9-1 A Model of Your Favorite Plane

Create a flying simulation of your favorite airplane. If you don't have one, pick some airplane to model. Search the Internet and/or libraries to find the needed facts on the plane. Then modify the FokkerDVII.txt file to insert your own plane's data. Note, you may need to also modify the Plane class if the plane is not a biplane or is a tri-plane. However, you probably do not need to modify the Windows classes, such as MainFrame.

When your simulation is operational, is it more stable than mine? Turn in all necessary files so that your instructor can "fly" your plane.

Chapter 10 Fuzzy Logic and Probability

We have arrived at a key junction in your education about inserting AI into the games that you create, a critical junction. This chapter, while simple compared to the plane simulation, is extremely important, because this chapter allows you to insert realism into your computer controlled game elements. Let me set the stage.

The player's party of six, strong, unwounded characters, having just defeated some monsters guarding the entrance of an underground dungeon, now enter the next chamber. Having heard the noise, the four evil NPC's who reside in this, until now well protected chamber, look at the player's party, who are looking back at them. The evil NPC's are currently minus their four, powerful fighters, who are out hunting for food at the moment. Because the denizens of this chamber have heard the players' fighting the monsters, they could be ready to strike the first blow. The four, relatively weak NPCs, thieves and wizards, attack the party, knowing that they are about to be overpowered and slain. Not realistic you say? Quite true.

Or perhaps a troll, badly wounded with an encounter with a stone giant, runs into the player's strong party. It attacks with wild abandon. Hardly likely! Or six infantry platoons guarding a small road bridge spies an armored column of a dozen tanks with supporting infantry and artillery making its way to their bridge. As the first tank begins to cross the bridge, the infantry platoons open fire with their rifles. Not realistic? You bet.

Let's put six German 88 antitank guns hidden in concealed positions along with several long range artillery guns supporting the six platoons. Now as the lead tank begins to cross the bridge, the 88's open fire. Quite realistic indeed.

With all of these situations, what is the common thread? Based upon an intuitive estimate of their strengths and weaknesses and their best guess of the enemy, the opponents must decide what action to take, whether it is an attack, defend and hold on, quietly slip away, flee, our perhaps even surrender. Okay, if you are dealing with one person versus one person, a relatively lengthy series of decisions could permit the game program to ascertain a realistic reaction. However, what happens when the numbers involved increase? Trying to work out what action a platoon of men should take, let alone a regiment, becomes almost undoable. All to often, the game programmer's reaction is to have them always attack, even at ridiculously poor odds.

Now let's take a look at how a human player might size up these same situations. The four evil NPCs, having heard the strong party defeat their monsters who were guarding their entrance, might reason this way. We are minus our fighters; these opponents outnumber us; we are relatively weak and they are strong. Action taken, quietly retreat deeper into the dungeon and head for a secret exit to go find their other party members and then return to attack the player's party.

The wounded troll, seeing the player's party, reasons this way. I am badly hurt, they are strong and unwounded. Although I am bigger and stronger than anyone of them, I am hurting badly. Action taken, troll flees.

The six platoons of infantry guarding the bridge alone, upon seeing the vastly superior force, including much armor, against which they have little to no attack or defense, decide to quietly move away from the bridge and allow this regiment to cross unhindered. They relay the news to their commanders. Once the entire column has crossed, they will retake the bridge and perhaps blow it up so that the column cannot receive reenforcements later on.

The six platoons with anti-tank gun and artillery support decide that they are strong and are facing a strong opponent. They have surprise on their side. A tank moves onto to the bridge. If that tank can be disabled, the entire enemy column comes to a screeching halt, well within their anti-tank guns and artillery range. They attack wholeheartedly.

What is going on with these examples is similar to human reasoning power. We have the power to size up a situation, make a reasonable estimate, a reasonable guess about the problem facing us. For example:
I am WEAK and they are STRONG
I am WOUNDED and they have NO WOUNDS
my attacks have NO EFFECT on them and their attacks EFFECT me
we are STRONG and they are STRONG but we have SURPRISE

We are dealing with a computer and a computer program which deals only with true/false, absolutes. Either it is or it is not. However, what does one mean when they say I am STRONG and they are WEAK? What number represents STRONG or WEAK? These are relative terms at best. Enter fuzzy logic to our rescue.

Fuzzy Logic

Fuzzy logic was created in 1965 by Lofti Zadeh, who described it as "fuzzy logic is a means of presenting problems to computers in a way akin to the way humans solve them." Fuzzy logic is simply a matter of degree, an imprecise analysis.

For example, you are a major league pitcher with the game on the line. Up comes a strong, tall, home run hitter. How do you pitch to him? This batter is a home run threat, so no fast balls. I know that he likes to get around on inside pitches so I will pitch him curve balls and sliders, low and on the outside of the plate. I'll gamble that he cannot drive one of them to the opposite field. Okay, you could begin the analysis by looking at his batting statistics, especially his batting average and the number of home runs he has hit thus far in the season. However, the rest of the analysis is fuzzy. What is "low" and "outside?" Why not a fastball low and outside?

Here's another example, you are doing a one on one mortal combat simulation. You are tall, thin, and wiry while your opponent is short, very heavyset, and well muscled. Your style of combat is fast and full of throws, while his is one of an embracing crush. Do you take on this opponent or choose to pass on this one?

What is tall? What is thin? What is short? What is very heavyset? Again, these are all imprecise terms, yet we make such determinations daily, especially when we walk down a street and see other people. Of course, we might also add in, pretty, cute, and/or handsome to the mix.

In the wider world of programming, fuzzy logic is used to control heating and air conditioning systems, robotic manufacturing systems, rail and even subway systems. In game programming we can use fuzzy logic in many situations, such as controlling the flight of a ship, making assessments of potential threats, and even classification of attributes from which intelligent, sensible decisions can be made.

The fuzzy inference process involves three steps.
1. Fuzzification, which takes crisp input and outputs fuzzy input
2. Fuzzy rules, which uses the fuzzy input to make fuzzy output
3. Defuzzification, which takes fuzzy output and makes crisp results

Fizzification takes real numbers as input, called crisp data, such as the player has 120 hit points, or a strength of 17, or has hit 50 home runs this season, and turns that factual information into fuzzy data. Fuzzy data might be "very hard to kill, very strong, many home runs. Given the fuzzy input, now you can apply the fuzzy rules to that input. If NPC is hard to kill then retreat. If NPC is at least moderately strong, then avoid combat. If batter has hit few home runs, pitch him in the strike zone. While sometimes the fuzzy output is sufficient for the game to utilize the results directly, often it is not. How fast does the NPC retreat? How should combat be avoided? What kind of pitches should be made in the strike zone? The defuzzification process takes these generalities and turns them into specific actions. For example, the NPC runs away at top speed, or the NPC decides to parley with the strong fighter, or pitch curve balls in the strike zone, but fast balls out of the zone.

The Fuzzification Process

The fuzzification process consists of taking factual, crisp, real numbers and turning them into qualitative fuzzy sets. The functions that do this are called membership functions or characteristic functions. Such functions map input data into a degree of membership within a fuzzy set, a real number between 0.0 and 1.0. For example, we might map a character's strength this way: a strength of 5 or less becomes *really weak*, while a strength of 17 or above becomes *very strong*. Or based upon the number of wounds that a person or creature can still absorb, place them into sets: *weak*, *normal*, or *hard*.

We place them into these sets based upon some form of membership function. Let's examine the normal boolean function, shown in Figure 10.1.

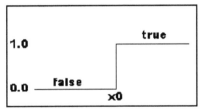

Figure 10.1 Boolean Function

Here, until x_0 is reached, the result is always false or 0.0. From point x_0 onward, the result is always true, 1.0. While this type of membership function can sometimes be used, frequently, this all or nothing approach is not sufficient.

Consider a graded membership function shown in Figure 10.2 next.

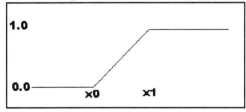

Figure 10.2 Graded Membership Function

From x=0 up to x0, the result is 0.0. From x1 onward, the result is 1.0. However, between x_0 and x_1, the result gradually increases from 0.0 to 1.0. We can determine the y value anywhere along the sloping line from x_0 to x_1 using the point slope form of the equation of a straight line.

$$y - y_0 = m\,(x - x_0)$$

where m, the slope is

$$(y_1 - y_0) / (x_1 - x_0)$$

Substituting 0 for y0, 1 for y_1, we get

$$y = (x - x_0) / (x_1 - x_0)$$

or

$$y = x / (x_1 - x_0) - x_0 / (x_1 - x_0)$$

Thus we can say that the member function produces the following results.

$$F(x) = \begin{cases} = & 0 \text{ if x is less than or equal to } x_0 \\ = & 1 \text{ if x is greater than or equal to } x_1 \\ = & x / (x_1 - x_0) - x_0 / (x_1 - x_0) \text{ if x is greater than } x_0 \text{ and less than } x_1 \end{cases}$$

Let's use the strength of a character or monster for example. If the strength is 5 or less, it is classified as *weak*, so x_0 is then 5. If the strength is 17, x_1, it is classified as *strong*. Say we have a strength of 14. Plugging the numbers into the equation, we can say that this one is classified as strong to the degree of .75.

Consider the strength attribute of characters and monsters. We could classify them as *weak*, *normal*, or *strong*. Figure 10.3 shows a triangular member function arrangement. A good rule of thumb is to have the three categories overlap about 25%.

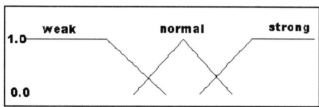

Figure 10.3 Strength Attribute as a Triangle
Member Function

In this situation, we need three functions, one for weak, one for normal, and one for strong. These are expressed this way.

Weak: (x_0 is the point where the slanting line begins downward from 1.0 and x_1 is where it becomes 0.0)

$$f(x) = \begin{cases} = & 1 \text{ if x is less than or equal to } x_0 \\ = & 0 \text{ if x is greater than or equal to } x_1 \\ = & -x / (x_1 - x_0) + x_1 / (x_1 - x_0) \text{ if x is greater than } x_0 \text{ and less than } x_1 \end{cases}$$

Strong: (x_0 is the point where the slanting line begins upward from 0.0 and x_1 is where it becomes

Game Programming Theory

1.0)

$f(x) = 0$ if x is less than or equal to x_0

$= 1$ if x is greater than or equal to x_1

$= x / (x_1 - x_0) - x_0 / (x_1 - x_0)$ if x is greater than x_0 and less than x_1

Normal: (x_0 is the left point where it is 0.0, x_1 is at the peak where it is 1.0, and x_2 is where it becomes 0.0 once more)

$f(x) = 0$ if x is less than or equal to x_0

$= 1$ if x is equal to x_1

$= x / (x_1 - x_0) - x_0 / (x_1 - x_0)$ if x is greater than x_0 and less than x_1

$= - x / (x_2 - x_1) + x_2 / (x_2 - x_1)$ if x is greater than x_1 and less than x_2

The next common fuzzy function is that of a trapezoid, shown in Figure 10.4. The trapezoid is a very useful one as we shall shortly see.

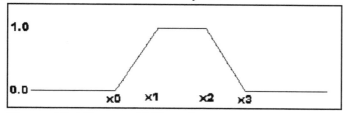

Figure 10.4 Trapezoid Function

The equations are a bit more complex.

$f(x) = 0$ if x is less than or equal to x_0

$= x / (x_1 - x_0) - x_0 / (x_1 - x_0)$ if x is greater than x_0 and less than x_1

$= 1$ if x is greater than or equal to x_1 and less than or equal to x_2

$= -x / (x_3 - x_2) + x_3 / (x_3 - x_2)$ if x is greater than x_2 and less than x_3

$= 0$ if x is greater than x_3

Now how do we put the trapezoid concept to use? Figure 10.5 shows a seven fuzzy setup.

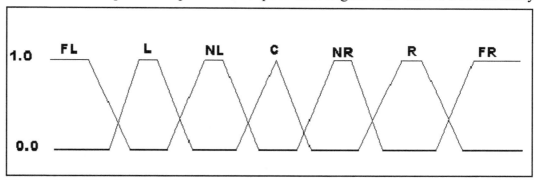

Figure 10.5 The Standard Seven Fuzzy Sets

The seven sets are know as far left, left, near left, center, near right, right, and far right. These can be used to represent anything. Let's continue with our strength attribute situation. The strength can range from 3 to say 21, where strengths beyond 18 are near godlike. We could create the following fuzzy sets that correspond to the seven sets shown in Figure 10.5 above: very weak, weak, below average, average, strong, very strong, super strong. Next, we pick the beginning and ending x values for each set, keeping in mind it is wise to allow about a 25% overlap between sets. The exact numbers can be tweaked for your game to provide the best workability. For example, very weak could range from 3 to 5, where the function becomes 0. Weak could begin its upward slope at 4, peaking at 5, holding level through 6, and then descending to 0 at 7. Below average could begin its upward climb at say 6, peaking at 7 through 8, descending to 9. Average could begin at 8, peak at 9, and descend to 10.

Game Programming Theory

If we do this, the when an NPC party encounters the player's party, a good estimate of their strength can be made, using these categories. For example, a below average strength wizard could encounter a strong fighter. Perhaps it is an average strength thief that encounters a weak wizard, or a strong fighter faces a very strong opponent. Now we are able to cast the problem into terms with which we are more comfortable dealing.

Similarly, we could setup sets for sets that categorize wounds or lack of them. Categories might be near death's door, critically wounded, very badly wounded, badly wounded, slightly wounded, unwounded. Next, we need to join these together, such as if not badly wounded and the opponent's strength is average or less, attack! This leads us at once to the fuzzy logic rules.

Fuzzy Logic Rules

Fuzzy logic parallels the compound joiners of C++. Recall that in C++ we have the AND (&&) operator, the OR (||) operator, and the NOT (!) operators. These are paralleled in fuzzy logic, only we no longer have such a simple true or false absolute result. Instead, we have a continuous range of real numbers from 0.0 to 1.0.

To handle the range of possible values, we can use the MAX and MIN functions, which return the larger or smaller of two real numbers.

Disjunction (fuzzy logic's OR) = MAX (A, B)
Conjunction (fuzzy logic's AND) = MIN (A, B)
Negation (fuzzy logic's NOT) = 1.0 – A
All results will be a real number somewhere between 0.0 and 1.0.

Now we can write expressions such as:
average strength AND unwounded which would be MIN (strength, health)
average strength OR unwounded which would be MAX (strength, health)
NOT unwounded which would be 1.0 - health

Of course, all these fuzzy logic rules result not in an int, true or false, but in a real number lying in the range of 0.0 to 1.0. As such, they imply a fuzzy result, often stored in a double. To make this more interesting, let's add in a third aspect, the distance separating the two opponents, often divided into three sets: melee, missiles, out of range. Now we can write expressions such as:
        if (average strength AND unwounded) {
                if (NOT out of range) then attack
                else do nothing
        }
        else flee

Game Programming Theory

This is looking quite promising indeed!

In order to implement these tests, we need to find a value for the degree of attack, the degree of do nothing, and the degree of fleeing. A better way to rephrase these tests would be as follows.

degree of attack = average strength AND unwounded AND in melee range

degree of do nothing = NOT in melee range AND unwounded

degree of flee = NOT out of range AND NOT unwounded AND NOT average strength

Let's put some numbers up for these test conditions. Let's say that the opponent's strength is average of degree .6 and the character is unwounded of degree .9 and that the opponent is in melee range of degree .4.

The degree of attack would be equal to MIN (MIN (.6, .9), .4) or just .4, while the degree of do nothing would be MIN (1.0 – .4, .9) or .6, and the degree of flee would be MIN (1.0 – .4, MIN (1.0 – .9, 1.0 – .6)) or MIN (.6, MIN (.1, .4)) or just .1. The results thus far yield:

degree of attack = .4

degree of do nothing = .6

degree of flee = .1

However, these results are fuzzy. Precisely what is meant by fleeing? Do we just turn around and walk away, trot away, run away, or drop everything and run at top speed? Even attack could be fuzzy, especially if the character is a barbarian who are known to sometimes go berserk, or a ranger who is facing their nemesis.

Defuzzification Rules

The defuzzification process is used when you need to get back precise values from a fuzzy system of logic. Take the results for fleeing. Precisely how do we flee? An output function is needed to defuzzy the result. Figure 10.6 shows a possible output defuzzification function.

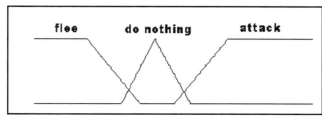

Figure 10.6 Defuzzification Function

In our example above, we found the three results as the degree of attack = .4, the degree of do nothing = .6, and the degree of flee = .1. Using these values, our resultant output function would appear as shown in Figure 10.7.

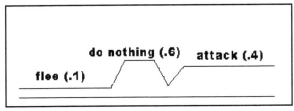

Figure 10.7 Defuzzification Results

Here, I have combined the three output results into a single function. To obtain the crisp output, several methods can be used. We could determine the geometric centroid of the area under the combined function, using the horizontal component of that point as our answer, which represents a weighted average of the three results. However, this means that you have to integrate the function to find the area under the curve and that is computationally expensive, since this action in all likelihood need to be done many, many times during game play. An alternative is to use polygons to compute the area.

However, an even better method is available, the singleton output membership function. This method requires that we assign a numerical value to the possible outcomes. For example, we could assign –10 for fleeing, 1 for do nothing, and +10 for attacking. Given these values, then the preset result for fleeing would be the value times the degree of fleeing, or .1 * (–10) or –1.0. The preset result for attacking would be .4 * 10 or 4.0. The preset result for doing nothing would be .6 * 1 or 0.6.

The singleton output is the sum of the preset results divided by the sum of the degrees. In equation form, if d_i is the degree of the ith result and x_i is the value assigned to the ith result, we have

$$outputnumber = \frac{\sum_{i=1}^{n} d_i x_i}{\sum_{i=1}^{n} d_i}$$

In this example, we would obtain the following result.
$(-1.0 + 4.0 + 0.6) / (0.1 + 0.4 + 0.6) = 3.6 / 1.1 = 3.27$
Thus, the output result says to attack, since 1 is do nothing, but it would be a moderate attack. A result of 10.0 would be an all out assault, berserk attack.

Now we have the keys to the kingdom in our hands. It is very easy to add AI decision making to games. We only need to implement these simple functions.

A Practical Example: Pgm10a

To illustrate these principles, let's examine a portion of my WWII game. Given a list of counters that are available to fire upon each other this turn, determine who fires at whom. At first, this seems quite challenging because of the wide variety of weapons and their ranges and effectiveness versus specific targets. For example, armor piercing rounds fired at close range against an armored target do twice as much damage as when fired at longer ranges, but only half as much damage when fired at non-armored targets. Some howitzers have a large HE value (high explosive), while others, small. Infantry, mortars and gun crews, as well as trucks are very susceptible to HE shells, while armored vehicles are not. So given a line of opponent units, what should a specific attacking unit attack?

The test data file has a small US group attacking a mobile, defensive German group. The fields are as follows. Attacking strength, the type of attack (A for armor piercing, H for HE, I for small arms fire, M for mortars), the range of the fire, the defensive strength, the amount of movement, a character symbol to represent it on the screen, the type of target (A for armored, N for non-armored), its initial x and y coordinate locations on the screen, and its descriptive name. Here are the twenty-six US counters and the twenty German ones.

```
11 A 8  8  8   O A 15 5 Sherman
11 A 8  8  8   O A 15 6 Sherman
11 A 8  8  8   O A 15 4 Sherman
5  A 5  5  11  a A 15 7 Stuart A/C
5  A 5  5  11  a A 15 3 Stuart A/C
4  I 2  10 1   I N 14 6 Arm Infantry
4  I 2  10 1   I N 14 7 Arm Infantry
2  I 2  6  1   i N 16 4 Infantry
2  I 2  6  1   i N 16 5 Infantry
2  I 2  6  1   i N 16 6 Infantry
2  I 2  6  1   i N 16 7 Infantry
2  I 2  6  1   i N 16 8 Infantry
3  M 12 3  1   m N 17 5 81mm Mortar
3  M 12 3  1   m N 17 6 81mm Mortar
2  I 2  3  12  h A 19 5 Halftrack
2  I 2  3  12  h A 19 6 Halftrack
2  I 2  3  12  h A 17 7 Halftrack
2  I 2  3  12  h A 17 8 Halftrack
2  I 2  3  12  h A 17 9 Halftrack
2  I 2  3  12  h A 17 4 Halftrack
2  I 2  3  12  h A 17 3 Halftrack
2  I 2  3  12  h A 18 3 Halftrack
2  I 2  3  12  h A 18 5 Halftrack
2  I 2  3  12  h A 18 6 Halftrack
8  H 12 1  0   H N 16 3 AA Gun
40 H 32 6  8   H A 32 5 How Priest
12 A 8     8 8 O A 9  5 Stug III
```

```
40 H 32 6 10  H A 0 5 Wiespe
20 A 20 1 0   A N 8 4 88mm ATG
13 A 6  2 0   A N 10 3 76mm ATG
14 H 10 1 0   H N 8 6 AA Gun
3 I 2 8 1     I N 10 5 Infantry
3 I 2 8 1     I N 10 6 Infantry
3 I 2 8 1     I N 10 7 Infantry
3 I 2 8 1     I N 10 8 Infantry
3 I 2 8 1     I N 10 4 Infantry
3 M 12 3 1    m N 8 5 81mm Mortar
0 I 0 1 10    t N 8 3 Truck
0 I 0 1 10    t N 9 4 Truck
0 I 0 1 10    t N 7 6 Truck
0 I 0 1 10    t N 9 6 Truck
0 I 0 1 10    t N 8 7 Truck
0 I 0 1 10    t N 8 8 Truck
0 I 0 1 10    t N 9 3 Truck
0 I 0 1 10    t N 7 5 Truck
0 I 0 1 10    t N 9 8 Truck
```

The starting point is to define a class to hold these data, Counter. I defined a pair of enums to track the attack and defense types. This class is merely a container for all data concerning a counter. Further, I added a number of data members that will hold the intermediate calculation results when attempting to determine who fires at whom.

Counter.h

```
#pragma once

enum DefenseType { Armor, NonArmor };
enum AttackType  { AP, HE, I, Mortar };

const int NAMELEN = 21;

class Counter {
public:
double      attackStrength;
AttackType  atype;
double      range;

double      defenseStrength;
DefenseType dtype;

char        name[NAMELEN];
char        symbol;

int         xPosition;
```

```
int         yPosition;
int         movement;

// fields for the opponent's firing calculations
double      distance;
double      odds;
double      cumulativeOdds;
double      fuzzyOdds;
double      criticalness;
double      relativeCriticalness;
double      degreeOfAttack;

    Counter ();
void InitCtr (double atk, AttackType at, double rang, double def,
              char sym, DefenseType dt, const char nam[],
              int xpos, int ypos, int move);
    ~Counter ();
istream& Input (istream& in);
};
```

The implementation is also simple. The constructor sets the key members to zero. InitCtr() initializes all the members to a specific counter's values. This way, we can make an array of Counter objects and then assign them their values. The input function will extract this counter from the text file of counters above. Notice how the letter codes are converted into the appropriate enum values.
Counter.cpp

```
#include <iostream>
#include <iomanip>
#include <string>
#include <cctype>
using namespace std;
#include "Counter.h"

Counter::Counter () {
 attackStrength = 0;
 atype = I;
 range = 0;
 defenseStrength = 0;
 dtype = NonArmor;
 name[0] = 0;
 xPosition = 0;
 yPosition = 0;
 movement = 0;
 symbol = ' ';
}
```

```cpp
void Counter::InitCtr (double atk, AttackType at, double rang,
                       double def, char sym, DefenseType dt,
                       const char nam[], int xpos, int ypos,
                       int move) {
  attackStrength = atk;
  atype = at;
  range = rang;
  defenseStrength = def;
  dtype = dt;
  symbol = sym;
  strcpy_s (name, sizeof (name), nam);
  xPosition = xpos;
  yPosition = ypos;
  movement = move;
}

Counter::~Counter() { }

istream& Counter::Input (istream& in) {
  char a, d, s;
  in >> attackStrength >> a >> range >> defenseStrength
     >> movement >> s >> d >> xPosition >> yPosition >> ws;
  if (!in) return in;
  in.get (name, sizeof (name));
  if (!in) return in;
  a = toupper (a);
  if (a == 'A') atype = AP;
  else if (a == 'H') atype = HE;
  else if (a == 'I') atype = I;
  else if (a == 'M') atype = Mortar;
  else {
   cerr << "Error: invalid attack type. It was " << a
        << " for item " << name << endl;
   exit (3);
  }
  d = toupper (d);
  if (d == 'A') dtype = Armor;
  else if (d == 'N') dtype = NonArmor;
  else {
   cerr << "Error: invalid defense type. It was " << d
        << " for item " << name << endl;
   exit (3);
  }
  symbol = s;
  return in;
}
```

Game Programming Theory

The Game class encapsulates the firing process. The objective is to have the computer make logical decisions about which units attack which units. To simplify the process, I have hard coded two arrays of counters, one for the German units and one for the US units that are available at the start of this turn.

Ah, but this key word brings up another concept, units that are available this turn. As the game progresses, units become not available due to casualties, equipment failure, surrenders, and so on. Thus, at the start of a turn, a list must be made of the currently available units that can potentially attack. Also, in the real simulation, if a unit has moved, normally, is cannot then fire in that same turn, but they could be fired upon. Ideally, then, one would have two separate lists, one of those units that can fire and those that cannot fire or one could have a flag indicating a unit's potential to fire yet this turn.

A list is a data structure or a container class that can hold a series of items. Unlike an array, the list has no specific order, cannot be accessed using subscripts. Instead, pointers are used. Each item in the list is held in a node, which consists of a pointer that points forward to the next node in the list, a back pointer that points to the previous node, and a data pointer pointing in this case to the counter being stored. The container class has four members, a head pointer which points to the first node in the list, a tail pointer which points to the last node, a count of the number of items in the list, and a current pointer which points to the next node as one iterates through the list, visiting each node or counter in turn.

To iterate through the list, one calls ResetToHead() which sets the current pointer to the first node. GetCurrentNode() then returns the data pointer being stored in that node. We must type cast the void* back to a Counter* to use it. The Next() function moves the current pointer on to the next node in the list. When the end of the list is reached, GetCurrentNode() returns a NULL or 0 pointer, which we use to control the looping process.

The initial counters that are available are stored in two fixed-sized arrays. At the start of the turn, the available counters are added to the two lists, one for the German units and one for the US units. The function AddAtTail() is used so that the units remain in the same order as they appear in the array. Only the memory address or pointer of the counter is actually passed to the add function, it stores only the memory address of the counter in the node. Hence, the list is a very frugal data structure, in terms of memory requirements.

Game.h
```
#pragma once
#include "Counter.h"
#include "Screen.h"
#include "DoubleLinkedList.h"
#include "FuzzyLogic.h"
```

```
const int US = 26;
const int GER = 20;

class Game {
public:
 Counter us[US];
 Counter ger[GER];
 Screen s;
 DoubleLinkedList usAvailable;
 DoubleLinkedList gerAvailable;

 int line;

  Game ();
 ~Game ();

 void    FireGer ();
 void    FireUS ();

 void    WhatIsToBeAttacked (DoubleLinkedList& attacker,
                             DoubleLinkedList& defender,
                             const char* who);
 void    ClearFiringResults (DoubleLinkedList& list);
 double  GetBasicCriticalness (Counter& c);
 double  GetOdds (Counter& ctr, Counter& usCtr, double distance);
 double  GetFuzzyOdds (double odds);
 double  GetRelativeCriticalness (Counter& attacker,
                                  Counter& defender);
 double  GetDegreeOfAttack (double critical, double odds,
                            double relative);
};
```

Before we dive into the details, let's examine some of the game firing rules. First, if a unit is firing AP (armor piercing) rounds, then two situations modify the attacking strength. If the target is non-armor, the attack factor is halved. If the target is armored, then if the attacker is at half range or less, it's attack factor is doubled. Second, if a unit is firing HE (high explosive) shells, then if the target is armored, the attack factor is halved. Mortar units are handled the same way, halved against armored targets. Third, infantry weapons have no effect upon armored units.

Target destroyed occurs most frequently when the attack factor is at least 4 to 1 over the defense strength. Hence, when firing, attempts to obtain 4-1 odds is preferred. Several units may combine their attacks on the same target thereby increasing the odds.

Game Programming Theory

On the other hand, while sitting on the battlefield, a specific attacking unit may greatly fear one or more units, which have the capability of wiping them out with a single shot. Thus, when attacking, if the attacking unit has the opportunity to attack one of the defending units which it greatly fears, it would like to do so.

Finally, when analyzing which units to attack first, tactically, there is great benefit in going after specific units of the opposing force which pose the greatest overall threats. In general these are the large HE artillery units, followed by armored tanks and self-propelled guns, then large attack factor mortars. In close combat situations, larger infantry attack factors become important. Thus, there ought to be a standard pecking order for the criticalness of units to be attacked.

However, this basic criticalness ought to be allowed to be overridden. Perhaps, the goal of the attacker is to eliminate as many of the vehicular transport counters, such as trucks and halftracks, as possible, thereby drastically slowing down that groups ability to move over large distances. Perhaps, the overall strategy is to eliminate as many infantry units as possible, so that the smaller numbers of armored vehicles have no support. Strategically, there can be many specific goals that could be employed. Hence, this basic function, GetBasicCriticalness(), can be replaced with other implementations which assign the highest importance to other strategically vital targets. However, for this first simulation, I will stick to the basic military significances, going after the large HE weapons and mortars and larger armored vehicles first.

When a side fires, each potential attacking unit is examined. The defender units are examined for basic criticalness. If that unit can attack the defender, the combat odds are calculated, which will be needed if that defender is the one chosen to be attacked. However, to choose the optimum target, this crisp number must be fuzzied, which is the function of GetFuzzyOdds().

Next, GetRelativeCriticalness() is called to find out how much the attacker is threatened by this defending unit.

Finally, GetDegreeOfAttack() is called which obtains a fuzzy result consisting of ANDing together criticalness, the fuzzy odds, and the relative criticalness. The defending unit that has the highest, reasonable degree is then attacked.

Game.cpp

```cpp
#include <fstream>
#include <iostream>
#include <cmath>
#include <strstream>
#include <iomanip>
using namespace std;

#include "Game.h"

Game::Game () {
```

```
ifstream infile ("army.txt");
if (!infile) {
 cerr << "Error: cannot open army.txt\n";
 exit (1);
}
int i;
for (i=0; i<US && infile; i++) {
 us[i].Input (infile);
 usAvailable.AddAtTail (&us[i]);
}
for (i=0; i<GER && infile; i++) {
 ger[i].Input (infile);
 gerAvailable.AddAtTail (&ger[i]);
}
if (!infile) {
 cerr << "Error: unable to input the army counters properly\n";
 infile.close ();
 exit (2);
}
infile.close ();
s.SetColor (Screen::Blue, Screen::BrightYellow);
s.ClearScreen ();
s.SetTitle ("WWII Attacking");
s.SetHighlightColor (Screen::Green, Screen::BrightRed);
for (i=0; i<US; i++) {
 s.OutputUCharWith (us[i].symbol, us[i].yPosition,
                    us[i].xPosition,
                    Screen::Blue, Screen::BrightGreen);
}
for (i=0; i<GER; i++) {
 s.OutputUCharWith (ger[i].symbol, ger[i].yPosition,
                    ger[i].xPosition,
                    Screen::Blue, Screen::BrightYellow);
}
 line = 11;
}
```

The constructor loads in the text file of counters and gets the units displayed. The lower portion of the screen shows the results, assuming that the two sides fire simultaneously. Figure 10.8 shows the output of the program.

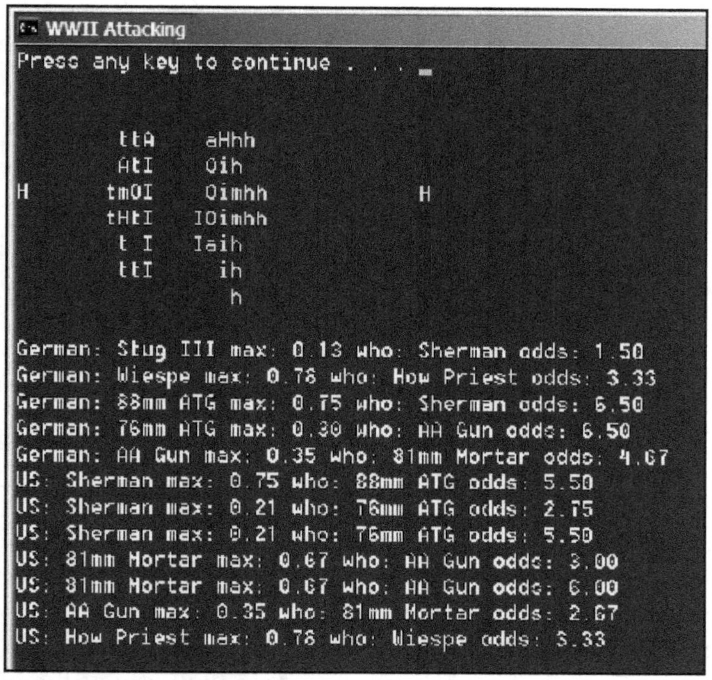

Figure 10.8 Firing Results

```
Game::~Game () {
 usAvailable.EmptyList ();
 gerAvailable.EmptyList ();
}
```

The destructor calls the EmptyList() function to delete all of the nodes in the two containers. The two operational functions, FireGer() and FireUS(), merely call the WhatIsToBeAttacked() function, passing the appropriate two lists, attacker then defender, and a character string to help identify the output.

```
void Game::FireGer () {
 WhatIsToBeAttacked (gerAvailable, usAvailable, "German");
}

void Game::FireUS () {
 WhatIsToBeAttacked (usAvailable, gerAvailable, "US");
}

void Game::ClearFiringResults (DoubleLinkedList& list) {
 list.ResetToHead();
 Counter* ptrctr = (Counter*) list.GetCurrentNode ();
 while (ptrctr != 0) {
  Counter& ctr = *ptrctr;
```

299

```
ctr.distance = ctr.odds = ctr.fuzzyOdds = ctr.criticalness = 0;
ctr.relativeCriticalness = ctr.degreeOfAttack = 0;
ctr.cumulativeOdds = 0;
list.Next ();
ptrctr = (Counter*) list.GetCurrentNode ();
  }
}
```

The ClearFiringResults() function sets all of the intermediate fields back to zero. However, it also illustrates how to iterate through a list container. First, the list's current pointer is set back to the first node in the list, ResetToHead(). Next, the Counter* that is stored in that node is retrieved via GetCurrentNode(). Notice the typecast to change from a void* to a Counter*. The loop is controlled by this pointer. When we have gotten to the end of the list, the GetCurrentNode() returns zero, and our processing loop ends.

However, since we are going to make extensive use of this counter instance, I do not want to have to continually use pointer notation to access member data, such as ptrctr->odds. Instead, I converted the pointer to the Counter back into a reference to a Counter,

```
Counter& ctr = *ptrctr;
```

This defines a temporary reference variable, whose scope is just within the body of the loop. By dereferencing the pointer, the compiler takes over ownership of the memory address and handles all of the details for us, making it simpler to use in our coding and less error prone.

At the end of the loop, Next() is called to move the current pointer of the list to the next node and the pointer stored there is then retrieved. Thus, when the while test condition then activates, it can determine whether or not the end of the list has been reached. This same sequence will be used in the following functions.

WhatIsToBeAttacked() has a nested loop. The outer loop examines each attacker unit to determine what, if anything, it is to attack. The inner loop, performed for each attacker unit, handles finding out what it should attack.

```
void Game::WhatIsToBeAttacked (DoubleLinkedList& attacker,
                               DoubleLinkedList& defender,
                               const char* who) {
  ClearFiringResults (defender);
  attacker.ResetToHead ();
  Counter* ptratkctr = (Counter*) attacker.GetCurrentNode ();
  while (ptratkctr != 0) {
    Counter& ctrAtk = *ptratkctr;
    double myX = ctrAtk.xPosition;
    double myY = ctrAtk.yPosition;
    defender.ResetToHead();
    double max = 0;
    Counter* ptrwho = 0;
```

300

```
Counter* ptrdef = (Counter*) defender.GetCurrentNode ();
while (ptrdef != 0) {
 Counter& ctrDef = *ptrdef;
 if (ctrDef.cumulativeOdds < 4) {
  double x = myX - ctrDef.xPosition;
  double y = myY - ctrDef.yPosition;
  ctrDef.distance = sqrt (x * x + y * y);
```

First, the distance to the target is found. If it is out of range, it is skipped and cannot be attacked. If it is within range of the attacker's weapons, then the situation is analyzed. The basic criticalness is found, the precise combat odds are found and then fuzzied, and the relative threat to this attacker is found. The degree of attack is then found by the fuzzy AND operations. Lastly, the final result is compared to the current "best" shot. If this defending unit is a better target, this one is installed as the currently best shot. Notice that max is updated with this new larger degree of attack result and also the pointer to this defender counter is saved so that we can actually implement the attack on that unit subsequently.

```
  if (ctrDef.distance <= ctrAtk.range) {
   ctrDef.criticalness = GetBasicCriticalness (ctrDef);
   ctrDef.odds = GetOdds (ctrAtk, ctrDef, ctrDef.distance);
   ctrDef.fuzzyOdds = GetFuzzyOdds (ctrDef.odds);
   ctrDef.relativeCriticalness =
                    GetRelativeCriticalness (ctrAtk, ctrDef);
   ctrDef.degreeOfAttack =
                    GetDegreeOfAttack (ctrDef.criticalness,
                                       ctrDef.fuzzyOdds,
                              ctrDef.relativeCriticalness);
   if (ctrDef.degreeOfAttack > max) { // save best shot
    max = ctrDef.degreeOfAttack;
    ptrwho = ptrdef;
   }
  }
 }
 defender.Next ();
 ptrdef = (Counter*) defender.GetCurrentNode ();
}
if (max > 0) { // indicate who should be attacked
 ptrwho->cumulativeOdds += ptrwho->odds;
 char msg [100];
 ostrstream os (msg, sizeof(msg));
 os << fixed << setprecision(2);
 os << who << ": " << ctrAtk.name << " max: " << max <<" who: "
    << ptrwho->name << " odds: " << ptrwho->cumulativeOdds
    << ends;
 s.OutputAt (msg, line++, 0);
}
```

```
  attacker.Next ();
  ptratkctr = (Counter*) attacker.GetCurrentNode ();
  }
}
```

The GetBasicCriticalness() function returns a value between 0.0 and 1.0, where 1.0 means this one is very critical indeed. Notice that large attack factor HE weapons are the top priority, followed by large attack factor AP units. This function can be replaced with another that places higher weights on other strategic units, such as wiping out all trucks and halftracks.

```
double Game::GetBasicCriticalness (Counter& c) {
 if (c.atype == HE) {
  if (c.attackStrength > 8)
   return 1.0;
  else
   return .3;
 }
 else if (c.atype == AP) {
  if (c.attackStrength > 8)
   return .75;
  else
   return .4;
 }
 else if (c.atype == Mortar) {
  if (c.attackStrength > 8)
   return .85;
  else
   return .35;
 }
 else if (c.atype == I) {
  if (c.attackStrength > 1)
   return .5;
  else
   return .2;
 }
 return 0;
}
```

GetOdds() calculates the attacking odds if this counter were to be attacked by this unit. As such, all of the attacking rules must be implemented here. However, to keep it simple, I ignore close assault tactics which allow infantry units to melee or to attack an armored vehicle, which normally they would not be able to damage.

```
double Game::GetOdds (Counter& attacker, Counter& defender, double
distance) {
 double strength = attacker.attackStrength;
 if (strength == 0)
```

```
   return 0;
 if (attacker.atype == AP) {
  if (defender.dtype == Armor) {
   if (distance < .5 * attacker.range)
    strength *= 2;
  }
  else
   strength = strength / 2;
 }
 else if (attacker.atype == HE || attacker.atype == Mortar) {
  if (defender.dtype == Armor)
   strength = strength / 2;
 }
 else if (attacker.atype == I) {
  if (defender.dtype == Armor)
   strength = 0;                    // ignoring close assault tactics
 }
 return strength / defender.defenseStrength;
}
```

GetFuzzyOdds() converts the crisp attack factor or odds into a fuzzy result, using a simple grade from 1.0 to 4.0.

```
double Game::GetFuzzyOdds (double odds) {
 return FuzzyGrade (odds, 1.0, 4.0);
}
```

GetRelativeCriticalness() does the reverse. It calculates the odds that the defender would have should it attack the attacker. That result is then fuzzied and returned.

```
double Game::GetRelativeCriticalness (Counter& attacker, Counter&
defender) {
 double odds = GetOdds (defender, attacker, defender.distance);
 return FuzzyGrade (odds, 1.0, 4.0);
}
```

Finally, GetDegreeOfAttack() fuzzy ANDs all three together to produce the final degree of attack, again a number between 0.0 and 1.0.

```
double Game::GetDegreeOfAttack (double critical, double odds,
                                double relative) {
 return AND (critical, AND (odds, relative));
}
```

The main() program consists of three lines.

```
Game g;
g.FireGer ();
g.FireUS ();
```

As you look over this program, notice how well it does predict which units should attack which. When a player is playing the WWII game, the computer will likely be controlling one side of the battle. Hence, it is imperative that the computer be able to pick optimum targets. Can you see just how important this entire topic of fuzzy logic is for game programming?

Probability Theory

In role playing games, probabilities are used for "to hit" rolls, for determining character attributes, for determining chance encounters, and so on. For example, a fighter character may have a 75% chance or probability of hitting his or her opponent with a long sword. A chance encounter with a dragon may yield a 50% chance of its attacking the party, 25% chance that it will attempt a conversation with them, and a 25% chance that it will completely ignore them. In my WWII game, in heavy mud conditions, a truck has an 80% chance that it will become stuck in the mud should it attempt to drive off of the road, but only a 20% chance if it stays on the road. In the bitter cold of a Russian winter, an armored vehicle has only a 20% chance of being able to start its motor, if it has not been running and is "cold." In a baseball game, a pitcher has equal probabilities of throwing a curve ball, a slider, or a fastball. Which is pitched on his or her next pitch?

The list is endless, probabilities or chances form an integral part of most games. How can we handle probabilities in our game programming? The C++ language has a random number generator, which, given an initial "seed" value, creates an endless supply of seemingly random numbers. However, they are not actually "random," they just can seem to be so. If you use the same seed each time the game starts, the same series of random numbers is generated, one after the other. The function is rand(), and takes no parameters.

To obtain a random number between 1 and 6, you could code
```
int number = rand () % 6 + 1;
```
To obtain a random number between 1 and 100, code
```
int number = rand () % 100 + 1;
```

To ensure that a different series of random numbers is generated each time the game starts, the current clock ticks time is often used to seed the generator. At the beginning, code
```
srand ((unsigned) time (0));
```
The header files needed are <iostream> and <ctime>. Note, in the next course in the games programming sequence, Non-graphical Games Programming, we will develop a robust random number generator that can easily be used in all games.

For example, consider the pitcher situation discussed above. To determine the next pitch, call the rand() function as just shown, to obtain a number between 1 and 100. Alternatively, you could

code
```
int number = rand () % 3 + 1;
```
to get a number between 1 and 3. Then test the result. If it is between say 1 and 33, or just 1, throw a curve ball. If it is between 34 and 67, or just 2, throw a slider, and so on.

Using the random number generator, one can easily handle situations where probability arises. However, we should examine probability theory. There are several interpretations of just what probability actually consists.

Theory of Probability

One view of probability, the classical probability, refers to outcomes, events, and possibilities. The classic case is throwing a six-sided die. In simple terms the probability of an event occurring is given by

probability = number of ways it can occur / total possible ways

If we ask what is the probability of throwing a 6, there is only one way to obtain it on a single die and there are six sides possible. Thus, the probability of throwing a 6 is 1 / 6 or .1667 or 16.67%.

The reverse statement, what is the probability of not throwing a 6 would be given by

probability of failure = 1 − probability of success

In this case,

probability of not throwing a 6 is 1 − .167 or .833 or 83.3%.

When you add in a second dice and ask the same question, what is the probability of throwing a total of 6, we have to determine how many different combinations of the two dice will yield a total of 6. There are 36 possible different rolls (6 sides taken 2 at a time or 6^2), only a few yield 6: 1+5, 5+1, 2+4, 4+2, 3+3

So the resultant probability is 5/36 or 13.9%.

Another viewpoint of probability comes from sampling events or experiments. This is called relative frequency or frequency interpretation. An experiment is done N times and if the desired event occurs n times, then the probability of the event n occurring is

probability = n / N

Bear in mind that the experiment must be done a sufficiently large number of times. The classic example of this one is tossing a penny to see whether heads or tails comes up and how frequently they appear. In this case, since there are two sides, one would expect each to appear half the time.

One might use this interpretation of probability in a lengthy, ongoing campaign game. The enemy leader orders a specific type of attack on the player. He keeps track of the outcome each time. Soon, the leader can make a probability analysis of the effectiveness that this form of attack has on the player. In other words, you can have your computer controlled enemy leader learn from his mistakes or successes.

Another interpretation of probability is that of a subjective probability, a subjective measure of a person's belief that some event will occur. This version is particularly useful when the situation cannot be repeated a large number of times. "It will snow tomorrow." "I think that Sea Biscuit will win in the third race." "The bus will arrive on time." "This player is planning to attack me within a week." All of these are subjective probabilities.

Often, subjective probabilities are backed up by a declaration of "odds." "2 to 1, I will win the next card hand." If we express the odds in favor as a to b, then this can be converted into a probability formula:

probability of winning = a / (a + b)

We can also go the other way. In the die example of rolling a 6, we saw the probability of rolling a 6 was 1 / 6 and the probability of not succeeding was 1 – 1 / 6. Thus the "odds" of rolling a 6 would be

odds = probability of success to probability of not success = 1/ 6 to 5 / 6 = 1 to 5

A Summary of the Rules of Probability

1. Probability is a number between 0 and 1, where 0 means total failure and 1 means total success. There cannot be a negative probability. (You can multiply the fraction by 100 to convert it into a percentage, of course.)

2. If X represents the entire sample, then it's probability is 1, since it encompasses all possible outcomes.

3. The probability of a event not occurring is 1 – probability of the event occurring.

4. If two events, X and Y, are mutually exclusive, then only one of them can occur at a time. Your fighter either has a long sword in his hand or he does not. You are wounded or you are not wounded. You are under an invisibility spell or you are not.

The probability of either X **or** Y occurring =

probability of X occurring + probability of Y occurring

The probability of one of N mutually exclusive actions occurring is then the sum of the probability of each one occurring.

Game Programming Theory

5. If two events, X and Y, are not mutually exclusive, then either one or both can occur at a time. Your fighter has a sword and/or your fighter is facing a troll. These are not mutually exclusive and either one or both could occur.

> The probability of both event X and Y occurring =
> > probability of X occurring +
> > probability of Y occurring –
> > probability of neither X or Y occurs

6. If two events, X and Y, are independent of each other, the probability of **both** occurring at the same time is given by the product of the two probabilities.

> The probability of both X and Y occurring =
> > probability of X occurring * probability of Y occurring

7. If the event Y depends upon event X occurring first, we have now a conditional probability.
> probability of X occurring = probability of both occurring / probability of Y occurring
> probability of Y occurring = probability of both occurring / probability of X occurring
> probability of both occurring = probability of X occurring * probability of Y occuring

or

> probability of Y occurring =
> probability of Y occurring * probability of X occurring before Y / probability of X occurring

Programming Problems

Problem 10-1 The Evil NPC Party Attacks!

The player's party consists of two fighters, a ranger, a wizard, a cleric or priest, and a thief. The NPC party consists of three fighters, a priest, a wizard, and a thief. As the two parties meet, assume that a pair of fighters from both sides are within melee distance from each other. The evil thief is armed with a short bow. Having taken the player's party slightly by surprise, the evil party gets to attack first.

Write a program that identifies who attacks whom, using fuzzy logic to help reach that decision. Use Pgm10a as your shell and model and starting point. Input a file with the various characters' data and display each on the screen as is done in Pgm10a.

You get to decide what the various criteria might be to help reach a decision upon attacking. Here are some possible ideas to help you get started thinking about the situation: you might consider the relative maximum potential amount of damage each could do, the current number of wounds they have, the remaining number of wounds they could take before succumbing. For the spell casters, assume that the spell they might use has some potential maximum damage as you see fit. Be creative and try to make the set of rules you devise be what you might do if you were in their shoes, so to speak. After all, a wizard does not often go in for hand to hand combat with a fighter; neither do thieves, for that matter, but this evil thief does have a short bow (hint). Think about which character(s) present the greatest threat to the evil party.

Once you've determined the attacks, output the results similar to the way that Pgm10a does.

Chapter 11 All About Collisions

The handling of collisions between two objects breaks down into two subjects. First, we must detect that a collision is occurring. Second, we must handle the physics of that collision, whether simple or complex.

Detecting a Collision in 3D

Perhaps the simplest and fastest method for checking whether two objects have collided is to use the **bounding sphere method**. Imagine your object, the biplane, the sailing ship, the race car, any object, is surrounded by a sphere, such that its surface just touches the outermost portion of the object thereby enclosing the whole object. The center of the sphere is the center of the object and the radius of the sphere is the maximum distance from the center to any portion of the object.

Now place a second sphere around that with which the object could collide and determine its radius. To check for a collision, compute the distance separating the two centers and compare that to the sum of the two radii. If the distance is less than the sum, the objects have collided.

Computationally, the center of each object can be calculated at initialization time, along with the radius of the surrounding sphere. At run time, one only needs to compute the distances between objects and compare to the sum of the two radii.

How does one find this bounding sphere? Imagine a large box drawn around the object such that it just encompasses the object's most extreme edges. These end points are often called the vertexes of the object. We begin by knowing the eight vertex values in 3D space. If you are dealing with 2D space, omit the Z axis value and deal with a bounding circle instead of a sphere.

Imagine a line going from the box's back side, top right corner or vertex, diagonally to the front side's bottom left corner. The midpoint of this line will be the center of the bounding sphere. The formula for the midpoint of a line going from point a to point b is given by the following.
Vector center = Vector ((a.x + b.x) / 2, (a.y + b.y) / 2, (a.z + b.z) / 2));

Given the center now located along with an array of the eight vertexes, the radius of the bounding sphere can be calculated. Loop through each vertex in the array and compute the distance between the center and that vertex. Compare that distance to the current maximum distance so far found. If this new one is larger, replace the current maximum with this larger value. When the loop is done, the maximum distance is the radius of the bounding sphere.

For computational efficiency, let's store and compare the square of the distance. Why? The distance between two points is given by this equation.

$$dist = \sqrt{(a.x - b.x)^2 + (a.y - b.y)^2 + (a.z - b.z)^2}$$

Avoid taking the square root eight times. Instead, let's keep track of the square of the distances until we have the maximum found and then one time take the square root.

Assume that the eight vertexes are stored in the array bounds. The coding to find the center and the radius is as follows, using the Vector class.

```
        const int MaxVertex = 8;
        Vector bounds[MaxVertex]; // filled with the bounding box
// assume the diagonal line to find the center goes from element
// 0 (back side top right) to element 6 (front side bottom left)
        Vector center = Vector (
                (bounds[0].x + bounds[6].x) / 2,
                (bounds[0].y + bounds[6].y) / 2,
                (bounds[0].z + bounds[6].z) / 2);
        double max = 0;
        for (int i=0; i<MaxVertex; i++) {
          double x = center.x - bounds[i].x;
          double y = center.y - bounds[i].y;
          double z = center.z - bounds[i].z;
          double d = x * x + y * y + z * z;
          if (d > max)
            max = d;
        }
        double radius = sqrt (max);
```

These calculations are done once at initialization time for each object and saved as member data. At run time, we only need to compute the distance between the two centers and compare that to the sum of the two radii. Computationally, we will be needing to use the same formula as found in the loop above to compute the distance between the two objects at run time, many, many times. Hence, we ought to make an easy to use function for this. While we are at it, why not do so for the formula to find the midpoint of a line between two points.

```
        Vector MidPoint (const Vector& a, const Vector& b) {
            return Vector ((a.x + b.x) / 2,
                           (a.y + b.y) / 2,
                           (a.z + b.z) / 2
```

```
                         );
    }

    double DistanceSquared (const Vector& a, const Vector& b) {
        double x = a.x - b.x;
        double y = a.y - b.y;
        double z = a.z - b.z;
        return x * x + y * y + z * z;
    }

    const int MaxVertex = 8;
    Vector bounds[MaxVertex]; // filled with the bounding box
// assume the diagonal line to find the center goes from element
// 0 (back side top right) to element 6 (front side bottom left)
    Vector center = MidPoint (bounds[0], bounds[6]);
    double max = 0;
    for (int i=0; i<MaxVertex; i++) {
        double d = DistanceSquared (center, bounds[i]);
        if (d > max)
            max = d;
    }
    double radius = sqrt (max);
```

Let's see how this works out for a couple of examples. Consider first the Fokker DVII biplane. It's length was 23 feet, wing span was about 30 feet, height was 9 feet. So the x coordinates run from 0 at the plane's rear to +23. The z axis goes from 0 on the ground to +9. The y axis split the plane in half, so it ranges from -15 to +15. We can now construct the bounding box's vertices, remembering to enter them into the array so that element 0 and element 6 form the proper diagonal from which to find the center point.

```
    Vector bounds[MaxVertex] = {
        Vector (0, -15, 0), Vector (0, -15, 9),
        Vector (0, +15, 9), Vector (0, +15, 0),

        Vector (23, -15, 0), Vector (23, -15, 9),
        Vector (23, +15, 9), Vector (23, +15, 0) };
```

Pgm11a computes these values for the biplane. It's output is

```
Center of biplane:         (11.50, 0.00, 4.50)
Bounding Sphere's radius: 19.43
```

We can now add a function to check on possible collisions.

```
bool    DetectCollision (const Vector& a, double aRadius,
                         const Vector& b, double bRadius) {
    double distance = sqrt (DistanceSquared (a, b));
    return distance < aRadius + bRadius;
```

```
}
```

I tested the function assuming two Fokker DVII planes were flying together.

```
Vector position1 (10, 20, 3000);
Vector position2 (12, 23, 2975);
if (DetectCollision (position1, radius, position2, radius))
  cout << "Collision detected\n";
else
  cout << "No collision detected\n";
```

A collision was detected.

There is only one complication. The positions we store in our rigid body simulations is the location of the center of gravity or center of mass of the object, not it's geometrical center. However, since we know the vector location of the center of gravity, the object's vector position, and the geometrical center of the object, we can compute the object's position with respect to the center of gravity for collision detection.

```
Vector position;
Vector centerOfGravity;
Vector geometricalCenter;
Vector geoPosition =
            position - centerOfGravity + geometricalCenter;
```

While this method is simplistic, it is fast to calculate. If there are many objects involved, this collision detection process does not slow down the game. There are other, more accurate methods, but require more math and a whole lot more computing power to detect collisions. One of the better methods is known as the triangle to triangle method. See *Games Programming Gems*, Mark DeLoura, Charles River Media, 2000.

Collision Response

When two objects collide, various things can happen. One or more of the objects might disintegrate, such as a solid object hitting a comet made of ice and dust or a meteor hitting a plane or space shuttle. On the other hand, one might just deform, being crushed utterly by the force of impact, such as a compact car colliding with a tractor trailer rig. However, let's deal with the more usual results, such as a cue ball striking the nine ball in a pool game.

We are dealing primarily with objects that can be considered rigid bodies. If two rigid bodies collide, then there can be a linear motion reaction as well as an angular motion result. Consider two cars traveling slowly, one behind the other. The rear car bumps into the one in front of it. Naturally, we would expect that the force of impact would "push" the front car more forward, having transferred some momentum or acceleration to the front car. This is the linear component in action. Now consider what happens if the cars strike each other's front ends at a 45 degree angle, both now have an angular momentum component of acceleration and often begin to spin in opposite directions. Let's examine each of these situations, with regard to rigid body collisions.

The first thing to realize about a collision is that the forces are acting over a very small interval of time. Impulse is defined as a force that acts over a tiny amount of time. Imagine a ball hitting a bat, a tennis ball hitting a racket, a foot kicking a soccer ball, all forces are delivered in a very small amount of time. The impulse-momentum principle says that the impulse delivered is equal to the change in momentum. This can be expressed in equation form. Let t_0 be the moment in time just before the collision and t_1 be the moment in time just after the collision.

$$Linear\, impulse = \int_{t_0}^{t_1} F\, dt = m(v_1 - v_0)$$

$$Angular\, impulse = \int_{t_0}^{t_1} M\, dt = I(\omega_1 - \omega_0)$$

where both **F** and **v** are vectors, as are **M**, **I**, and **ω**. Here **M** is the impulse torque or moment.

From these, we get the average impulse force and the average torque..
F = m (**v₁** – **v₀**) / (t₁ – t₀)
M = **I** (**ω₁** – **ω₂**) / (t₁ – t₀)

Suppose we shoot a 45 caliber Winchester rifle, whose muzzle velocity is 2470 feet/sec. The bullet weighs 350 grains or about .024 slugs. Let's assume that it takes only .008 seconds for the bullet to travel the length of the rifle barrel. Average impulse force = .024 * 2470 / .008 = 7,406 pounds. Impressive?

The impulse forces applied during collisions can be very high indeed. Fortunately, the time over which the force acts is very small. When two objects collide, each one applies a force to the other equal in magnitude, but opposite in direction. This is Newton's third law. With the rifle, the opposite direction force is known as the rifle's kick back.

Impact

Newton's principle of conservation of momentum states that momentum is conserved. That is, the momentum before the collision must be equal to the momentum after the collision. If two rigid bodies, a and b, collide, this means that the following must be true.

$$m_a \, v_{a0} + m_b \, v_{b0} = m_a \, v_{a1} + m_b \, v_{b1}$$

where m is the mass and v is the velocity.

A critical assumption is being made here and that is that during the duration of the impact, no other forces are acting on the two objects. Since the time interval is so small, this approximation can be safely made.

A further assumption is also made and that is that the objects do not change their shapes during the collision. In the real world, we know that this is often not the case. Take two cars, for example, that collide at ten miles per hour. Fenders dent and bend, deformation invariable occurs along with expensive body repair work. In this case, kinetic energy is being converted into a deformation or strain energy required to alter the shape of the car's sides. If the deformation does not immediately undo itself and the deformation remains permanent, energy is lost and is not conserved.

The formula for kinetic energy in a linear form is

$$K_e = \tfrac{1}{2} \, m \, v^2$$

This is the energy needed to accelerate the object from rest to its current speed or the energy required to bring the object to zero velocity or a stop.

The formula for angular kinetic energy (rotational) is

$$K_a = \tfrac{1}{2} \, I \, \omega^2$$

where I is the inertia and ω is its angular velocity.

When a collision does not result in the loss of any kinetic energy or momentum, the collision is said to be elastic. However, when energy or momentum is lost, the collision is said to be inelastic or plastic. Automobile manufacturers are going to great lengths to make their vehicles absorb a great

Game Programming Theory

deal of kinetic energy delivered during impacts, greatly reducing the potential damage to the vehicle's occupants. Not only do fenders crumple, but also bumpers absorb shocks, and the frames twist and give, softening the blow to the occupants.

Since most collisions are not perfectly elastic, we need a way to represent this for our rigid body simulations. We can define the coefficient of elasticity as being given by this equation.

$$e = -\left(v_{a1} - v_{b1}\right) / \left(v_{a0} - v_{b0}\right)$$

The coefficient of elasticity is governed by the object's geometry, material, and the way it is built. These are determined experimentally in a lab. If a collision is perfectly elastic, the coefficient is 1, but for perfectly inelastic collisions, it is 0. However, the velocities in the equation must be along the line of action of the collision only, such as two pool balls hitting each other square on.

This gives us two types of collisions. The line of action is a line between the two centers fo gravity or mass of the colliding objects at the point of impact. More precisely, the line of action is a perpendicular line (normal) to the colliding surfaces. When the velocities of the objects are both along the line of action, the collision is said to be a direct impact. When one or more of the velocities do not lie 100% along the line of action, the collision is said to be an oblique impact.

The Equations for Linear and Angular Impulse

The equations break down into two scenarios. If the collisions are between particles or spheres, then only linear impulse must be considered. If the collisions are between rigid bodies that can rotate, the angular impulse must also be considered. Finally, these equations assume that there are no frictional components to the collision.

The mechanics of a collision between particles or spheres is shown in Figure 11.1.

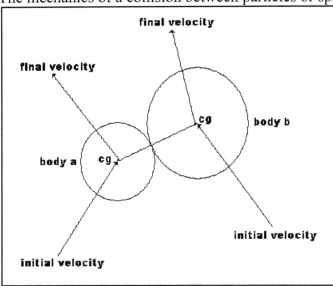

Figure 11.1 Collision of Two Spheres or Particles

The given information are the masses of the objects, the normal unit vector of the line of action $\mathbf{n}$, the coefficient of elasticity e, and the initial velocities. First find the impulse by using the velocity components along the line of action, v_{a0} and v_{b0}. Let J be the impulse.

$$J = - (v_{a0} - v_{b0}) (e + 1) / (1 / m_a + 1 / m_b)$$

We get the new velocities along the line of action this way, remembering equal but opposite directions.

$$v_{a1} = v_{a0} + J \mathbf{n} / m_a$$
$$v_{b1} = v_{b0} - J \mathbf{n} / m_b$$

If angular velocities are required because the bodies can rotate, then there are two velocities to consider at the impact point, that from the center of gravity and that due to angular rotation. Here vector $\mathbf{r}$ is the distance from the body's center of gravity to the point of impact.

$$\mathbf{v}_{impact} = \mathbf{v}_{cg} + (\omega \text{ cross } \mathbf{r})$$

Figure 11.2 shows the collision diagram.

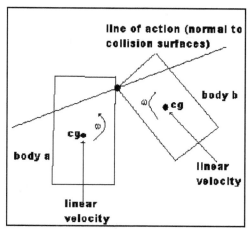

Figure 11.2 Collision of Rotating
Bodies

Again, we first find the impulse J and then find the linear and angular velocities. Let v_r be the relative closing velocity v_{rc} along the line of action, found by subtracting the two velocity vectors and then taking the dot product of that result with the collision normal vector, $\mathbf{n}$, which is the normal line to the collision point of contact. To find $\mathbf{n}$ first subtract the two position vectors to obtain the line of action and then normalize it.

$$\mathbf{v_{rc}} = (\mathbf{v_1} - \mathbf{v_2}) \text{ dot } \mathbf{n}$$

Next, we need the collision points on both objects, each in their own local coordinates. This can be quite tricky to obtain, in the generalized case of non-spherical objects. If we use the race cars from an earlier chapter for example, their shape is that of a rectangle, as shown in Figure 11.2 above. However, since this is our first look at collisions, let's take the simpler case of two spheres or circles in 2D and see how the collision point can be found.

The first object is at position (x_1, y_1) and has a radius of r_1, while the second is at position (x_2, y_2) with a radius of r_2. The two objects have collided and let's call the collision point (x_3, y_3). The collision point lies along the line of action, a line connecting the two centers of gravity. The general equation for a circle is

$$(x - x_0)^2 + (y - y_0)^2 = r^2$$

Further, we can use the point slope equation of a line.

$$y_3 - y_1 = slope * (x_3 - x_1)$$

where the slope is given by

$$(y_2 - y_1) / (x_2 - x_1)$$

The point (x_3, y_3) is on the circle perimeter of both circles.

Game Programming Theory

Substituting, we get

$(slope * (x_3 - x_1))^2 + (x_3 - x_1)^2 = r_1^2$ or just

$x_3 = x_1 + sqrt (r_1^2 / (slope^2 + 1))$

$y_3 = y_1 + slope * (x_3 - x_1)$

From this global coordinate collision point, we can get the local coordinates of the collision points by subtracting each object's position vector from it, yielding the two vectors, $\mathbf{cp_1}$ and $\mathbf{cp_2}$.

$J = - (\mathbf{v_{rc}}) (e + 1) / s$

where s is

$s = 1 / m_a + 1 / m_b$

    $+ \mathbf{n}$ dot $[(\mathbf{cp_1}$ cross $\mathbf{n}) / \mathbf{I_a}]$ cross $\mathbf{cp_1}$

    $+ \mathbf{n}$ dot $[(\mathbf{cp_2}$ cross $\mathbf{n}) / \mathbf{I_b}]$ cross $\mathbf{cp_2}$

We can then find the new velocities this way.

$\mathbf{v_{a1}} = \mathbf{v_{a0}} + J \mathbf{n} / m_a$

$\mathbf{v_{b1}} = \mathbf{v_{b0}} - J \mathbf{n} / m_b$

The new angular velocities are found this way.

$\omega_{a1} = \omega_{a0} + (\mathbf{cp_1}$ cross $J \mathbf{n}) \mathbf{Icg_a}$

$\omega_{b1} = \omega_{b0} + (\mathbf{cp_2}$ cross $- J \mathbf{n}) \mathbf{Icg_b}$

Pgm11b Illustrates Both Linear and Angular Collision

We need to see these effects in action. Consider rolling metal balls, constrained to stay within a rectangular box. That is, when they hit the sides, they bounce back as pool balls on a pool table. For the most part, this sample uses 3D objects, although they are shown only in 2D as circles. In order to show rotation, I have created an origin line from the center outward, rather like a needle on a dial. The position of the needle represents the current orientation, whose position is dependent upon the objects angular velocity, constrained to the x-y plane.

One sphere is user-controlled. That is, the four arrow keys provide an instantaneous thrust in the corresponding direction so that the player can move his or her ball. The opponents, grey balls, cannot be controlled with this thrust mechanism. Further, the size, weight, velocity, angular velocity, and initial position are randomly initialized to some starting values.

The menu allows one to start, stop, and choose whether to see only linear collision responses or to include angular components as well. From this launching point, one could begin to construct a pinball type of game. Figure 11.3 shows a screen shot of the balls in motion. The yellow ball is the player controlled ball. Note that the mass of each sphere is proportional to its size.

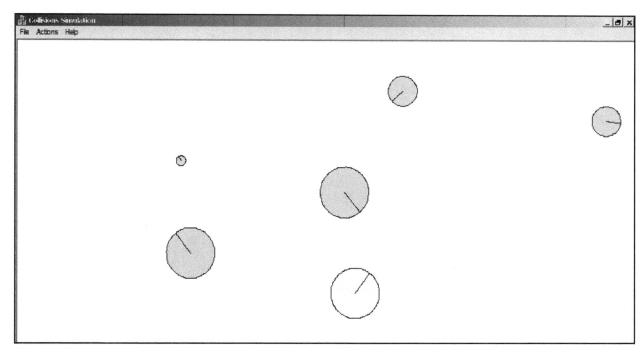

Figure 11.3 Pgm11b in Action

Game Programming Theory

The starting point is to define the points that can be used to orient, scale, and draw the circles. File circle.txt contains the x,y coordinates of a number of points, when connected, draw a circle with the "needle" pointer. The origin point is (0, 0) and its radius is 50 pixels.

Circle.txt
```
0   0
0   50
10  49
14  48
17  47
20  46
22  45
24  44
26  43
27  42
30  40
31  39
32  38
35  36
36  35
37  34
38  33
40  30
42  27
43  26
44  24
45  22
46  20
47  17
48  14
49  10
50  0
49  -10
48  -14
47  -17
46  -20
45  -22
44  -24
43  -26
42  -27
40  -30
38  -33
37  -34
36  -35
35  -36
32  -38
```

```
31 -39
30 -40
27 -42
26 -43
24 -44
22 -45
20 -46
17 -47
14 -48
10 -49
0 -50
-10 -49
-14 -48
-17 -47
-20 -46
-22 -45
-24 -44
-26 -43
-27 -42
-30 -40
-31 -39
-32 -38
-35 -36
-36 -35
-37 -34
-38 -33
-40 -30
-42 -27
-43 -26
-44 -24
-45 -22
-46 -20
-47 -17
-48 -14
-49 -10
-50 0
-49 10
-48 14
-47 17
-46 20
-45 22
-44 24
-43 26
-42 27
-40 30
-38 33
```

```
-37 34
-36 35
-35 36
-32 38
-31 39
-30 40
-27 42
-26 43
-24 44
-22 45
-20 46
-17 47
-14 48
-10 49
0   50
0   0
```

From this set of points, any other circle can be created by scaling each point based on the desired radius other than 50 pixels.

The Ball class begins by defining the usual 3D simulation items, such as the radius, the area, the vector position, center of gravity, velocity and so on. Additionally, I added three vectors to store collision specific information, such as the closing velocity, the closing position, and the normal vector.

ball.h

```
#pragma once
#include "Vector.h"
#include "Quaternion.h"
#include "Matrix3D.h"

const double CoefficientOfRestitution = .8;

class Ball {
public:
  double   mass;
  Vector   centerOfGravity;
  double   radius;
  double   area;
  double   volume;
  Vector   localInertia;
  Vector   normalVector;

  Matrix3D inertia;          // body coordinates
  Matrix3D inertiaInverse;   // body coordinates
```

```
Vector      velocityBody;     // velocity in body coordinates
Vector      angularVelocity;// angular velocity in body coords
Vector      eulerAngles;      // Euler angles in body coordinates
                             // (roll, pitch, yaw)
double      angularPosition;// in degrees
double      speed;            // speed (magnitude of the velocity)

Vector      position;         // position in earth coordinates
Vector      velocity;         // velocity in earth coordinates
Quaternion  orientation;      // in earth coordinates
Vector      thrust;           // current thrust vector

Vector      forces;           // total force on body
Vector      moments;          // total moment (torque) on body
Vector      acceleration;     // acceleration total of plane

Vector      totalLocalForce;

// temp fields for collision calculations
double      velocityClosing;
Vector      collisionNormal;
Vector      collisionPoint;

public:
        Ball ();
        ~Ball ();
void    Initialize (double mas, double rad, Vector velBody,
                    Vector omega, Vector pos);
void    CalculateLoads ();
void    IntegrateEuler (double dt);
Matrix3D MakeAngularVelocityMatrix ();

void    ChangeThrust (bool up, double amount);
void    ChangeDirection (bool left, double amount);

bool    DetectCollision (const Vector& a, double aRadius) const;
double  DistanceSquared (const Vector& a) const;

void    ApplyLinearCollisionImpulse (Ball& e);
void    ApplyLinearAngularCollisionImpulse (Ball& e);
Vector  GetCollisionPoint (const Ball& e);
};
```

The Initialize() function allows us to setup a specific Ball object. As usual there are functions CalculateLoads() and IntegrateEuler(). ChangeThrust() and ChangeDirection() respond to the arrow

Game Programming Theory

keys for the player controlled ball only. The DetectCollision() and DistanceSquared() functions are lifted from Pgm11a and use the sphere method to detect the presence of a collision. Finally, the two new functions handle the two types of collision response, ApplyLinearCollisionImpulse() and ApplyLinearAngularCollisionImpulse(). GetCollisionPoint() is needed only when angular effects are desired.

Finally, note that I assumed 0.8 as the coefficient of elasticity for this demo. Note that using the spherical method for collision detection is a fast method and often used with other more complex methods to see if one is likely, before diving into the more complex coding to ultimately determine if a collision has occurred. We do not need to worry much about penetrating type collisions because the time interval is so small compared to the speeds of the objects. If penetration did occur, it would only be a very small overlap. However, if the time interval were large, one could have two race cars half way inside each other before the collision was detected.

Before we dive into the calculation details, let's examine the higher level, the use of the Ball objects by the MainFrame windows class. Again, you are not responsible for the Windows programming, that is covered in a later course.

The MainFrame class defines the maximum number of points that I used to define a circle object. The MaxEnemy constant is the array size, the number of balls in play. However, always subscript 0 represents the player controlled ball.

```
#pragma once
#include "Vector.h"
#include "Ball.h"

const int MaxPoints = 103;
const int MaxEnemy = 5 + 1;  // [0] is the player
const int Player = 0;         // player index

class MainFrame : public CFrameWnd {
. . .
 char key;
 char specialKey;

 bool linearOnly;

 bool      firstTime;
 Ball      ball[MaxEnemy];
 Vector    circle[MaxEnemy][MaxPoints];
 COLORREF  color[MaxEnemy];

 Vector    basicCircle[MaxPoints];
```

Game Programming Theory

When linearOnly is true, no angular velocity effects are calculated. When the application begins, firstTime is true so that whatever size and position balls the computer generated are used when the menu item to start is chosen. After that, each time the menu start is chosen, a new random set of five balls is generated. Next, since each ball is likely to have a different radius, The circle array holds the scaled set of 103 points that define that ball's circle. The array color holds the color value for each circle, yellow for the player's circle and grey for the enemy's circles. The vector basicCircle hold the inputted point values from the circle.txt file which defines a circle of radius 50. This array is then used to form the different sized circles of the six balls.

Several other functions are needed to get the Ball objects initialized or shown.

```
int  GetRandom (int range);
void InitializeBalls ();
void ScaleCircle (Vector v[], double radius);
void DrawCircle (CDC& dc, const Ball& pos,
                 const Vector circle[], COLORREF r);
void HandleGoingOffScreen (Ball& p);
```

GetRandom() returns a number between 1 and the range number. InitializeBalls() sets each object up, determining its size, location, speed and such. ScaleCircle() is called once the radius is randomly chosen. The scaled circle is then saved and passed to DrawCircle() which must rotate the circle to represent the direction that the ball is now facing. As usual, HandleGoingOffScreen() takes care of objects that collide with the edge of the screen. This time, however, the function makes the balls appear to bounce off the edges, by reversing the velocity.

When the user chooses the Start menu item, the Windows timer is set and when the interval has elapsed, the calculations are done and all objects shone in their new positions. In the constructor, the random number function is given a seed value, based upon the current time on the computer. This way, from execution to execution, the random number sequences are different. GetRandom() calls the rand() function, which returns the next random integer. By moding it with the range and adding one, one gets a number between 1 and the range.

```
int MainFrame::GetRandom (int range) {
  return rand () % range + 1;
}

MainFrame::MainFrame () {
  firstTime = true;
  linearOnly = true;
  srand ((unsigned int) time(0));
  InitializeBalls ();
  . . .
}
```

Game Programming Theory

In InitializeBalls(), the circle.txt file is opened and inputted into the basicCircle array. Next, the player's instance, subscript 0, is setup, always with a mass of 10 slugs and a radius of 50. After that, the enemy balls are initialized. Notice how GetRandom() is used to obtain the radius, position, velocity, and angular velocity if each enemy ball.

```
void MainFrame::InitializeBalls () {
 ifstream infile ("circle.txt");
 for (int i=0; i<MaxPoints; i++) {
  infile >> basicCircle[i].x >> basicCircle[i].y;
 }
 infile.close ();

 ball[Player].Initialize (10., 50., Vector(10, -10, 0),
                              Vector (.2,.2,0), Vector (500, 700, 0));
 ScaleCircle (circle[Player], ball[Player].radius);
 color[Player] = RGB (255, 255, 0);

 for (int j=1; j<MaxEnemy; j++) {
  ball[j].Initialize (10., GetRandom (5)*10,
           Vector (GetRandom (10)*j+5, -GetRandom (10)*j+5, 0),
           Vector (.2*GetRandom(10), .2*GetRandom(10), 0),
           Vector (100*GetRandom(9), 100*GetRandom(8), 0)
          );
  ball[j].mass *= ball[j].radius / 50.;
  ScaleCircle (circle[j], ball[j].radius);
  color[j] = RGB (192,192,192);
 }
}
```

Finally, each ball has its mass adjusted to be proportional to its radius and its actual dimensions are scaled from the basicCircle.

```
void MainFrame::ScaleCircle (Vector v[], double radius) {
 for (int i=0; i<MaxPoints; i++) {
  v[i].x = basicCircle[i].x * radius / 50.;
  v[i].y = basicCircle[i].y * radius / 50.;
 }
}
```

ScaleCircle multiplies each coordinate of the basic circle by its radius divided by 50.

The OnPaint() Window's function is called by the framework whenever the screen needs to be reshown. The dc object, a device context which represents the screen in this case, is obtained and passed to the DrawCircle() function. The loop calls DrawCircle() for each Ball object in the array.

```
void MainFrame::OnPaint() {
 CPaintDC dc(this);
 for (int j=0; j<MaxEnemy; j++) {
```

```
      DrawCircle (dc, ball[j], circle[j], color[j]);
   }
}
```

In DrawCircle(), each point comprising the outline of the ball object must be rotated by the current angular position. Remember that the positive Y axis is downward, which is why I coded 180 – the angular position.

```
void MainFrame::DrawCircle (CDC& dc, const Ball& ball,
                            const Vector circle[], COLORREF r) {
   CPoint a[103];
   Vector v[MaxPoints];
   for (int i=0; i<103; i++) {
    v[i] = GlobalToLocalCoords_2D (180.-ball.angularPosition,
                                   circle[i]) + ball.position;
    a[i].x = (long) (v[i].x + .5);
    a[i].y = (long) (v[i].y + .5);
   }
   CBrush b (r);
   CBrush* ptrold = dc.SelectObject (&b);
   dc.Polygon (a, MaxPoints);
   dc.SelectObject (ptrold);
}
```

The important function is OnTimer(). Every second, the timer goes off and this function gets called by Windows. First, I handle any arrow key request the player may have made, altering the thrust vector for the player's ball.

```
void MainFrame::OnTimer(UINT_PTR nIDEvent) {
  if (specialKey == VK_UP) {
   ball[Player].ChangeThrust (true, 500);
  }
  else if (specialKey == VK_DOWN) {
   ball[Player].ChangeThrust (false, 500);
  }
  else if (specialKey == VK_LEFT) {
   ball[Player].ChangeDirection (true, 500);
  }
  else if (specialKey == VK_RIGHT) {
   ball[Player].ChangeDirection (false, 500);
  }

  key = specialKey = 0;
```

For each Ball, IntegrateEuler() is called to calculate the forces acting on the object and to integrate those forces over a tenth of a second. Experiment with this value and increase it to a full

327

second and observe the impact upon the collisions. While the action is faster, larger amount of movement, we are running the risk of having objects penetrate each other slightly.

After an object has had its new values calculated, it must then be compared to all other objects, checking for potential collisions. Using the spherical detection method, if a collision is detected, then the relative velocity vector is found, along with the normal vector. The local closing velocity and the collision normal vectors are stored in both objects. If the closing velocity is negative, the two objects are moving toward each other, and a collision has occurred. Depending upon the menu choice, either linear impulse is used or both linear and angular impulses are used, being applied to both objects. Once every object has been handled, the final positions are altered if the object has collided with the edge of the screen.

```
for (int j=0; j<MaxEnemy; j++) {
  ball[j].IntegrateEuler (.1);
  for (int k=0; k<MaxEnemy; k++) {
   if (k == j) continue;
   if (ball[j].DetectCollision (ball[k].position,
                                    ball[k].radius)) {
    Vector relativeVelocity =
                       ball[j].velocity - ball[k].velocity;
    Vector norm = ball[j].position - ball[k].position;
    norm.Normalize ();
    ball[j].collisionNormal = ball[k].collisionNormal = norm;
    ball[j].velocityClosing = ball[k].velocityClosing =
                  relativeVelocity * ball[j].collisionNormal;
    if (ball[j].velocityClosing < 0) {
     // is a collision
     if (linearOnly)
       ball[j].ApplyLinearCollisionImpulse (ball[k]);
     else
       ball[j].ApplyLinearAngularCollisionImpulse (ball[k]);
    }
   }
  }
}
for (int j=0; j<MaxEnemy; j++) {
  HandleGoingOffScreen (ball[j]);
}
Invalidate (true);
}
```
The Invalidate() function call forces a complete redisplay of the screen.

Game Programming Theory

Now, let's examine the Ball class coding.

```cpp
#include "Ball.h"

Ball::Ball () {
 mass = radius =  area = volume = speed = angularPosition = 0;
}
```

Remember that the area of a sphere is $4\pi r^2$ and the volume is $4/3\pi r^3$. Further the moment of inertia of a sphere along the x, y and z axes is $2/5\ mr^2$.

```cpp
void Ball::Initialize (double mas, double rad, Vector velBody,
                       Vector omega, Vector pos) {
 mass = mas;
 radius = rad;
 position = pos;
 velocityBody = velocity = velBody;
 angularVelocity = omega;
 area = 4 * PI * radius * radius;
 volume = 4./3. * PI * pow (radius, 3.);
 localInertia.x = localInertia.y = localInertia.z = 2./5. *
                  mass * radius * radius;
 orientation = MakeQFromEulerAngles (eulerAngles.x,
                                     eulerAngles.y, eulerAngles.z);

 // creating an inertia matrix (which is a tensor)
 // that is in body coordinates
 double Ixx = 0, Iyy = 0, Izz = 0, Ixy = 0, Ixz = 0, Iyz = 0;
 Ixx = localInertia.x + mass *
                   (centerOfGravity.y * centerOfGravity.y
                    + centerOfGravity.z * centerOfGravity.z);
 Iyy = localInertia.y + mass *
                   (centerOfGravity.z * centerOfGravity.z
                    + centerOfGravity.x * centerOfGravity.x);
 Izz = localInertia.z + mass *
                   (centerOfGravity.x * centerOfGravity.x
                    + centerOfGravity.y*centerOfGravity.y);
 Ixy = mass * (centerOfGravity.x * centerOfGravity.y);
 Ixz = mass * (centerOfGravity.x * centerOfGravity.z);
 Iyz = mass * (centerOfGravity.y * centerOfGravity.z);

 // Store these in the plane's inertia matrix
 // and find the inverse of the inertia matrix
 inertia = Matrix3D (Ixx, -Ixy, -Ixz,
                     -Ixy,  Iyy, -Iyz,
                     -Ixz, -Iyz,  Izz);
```

```
    inertiaInverse = inertia.Inverse();
}


Ball::~Ball () { }
```

Unlike previous examples, there is very little to do in CalculateLoads(), primarily because the only force acting on the ball is any player controlled thrust.

```
void Ball::CalculateLoads () {
// reset forces and moments:
forces = moments = Vector (0, 0, 0);

// First, find the forces and moments in body space
Vector localVelocity;  // local velocity in body space
double localSpeed = 0; // magnitude of the local velocity
Vector result;
Vector temp;
Vector totalForce;
Vector totalMoments;

// Find the local velocity which includes the velocity due to
// linear motion of the ball plus the velocity due to rotation
temp = angularVelocity ^ centerOfGravity;
localVelocity = velocityBody + temp;
localSpeed = localVelocity.Magnitude(); // the local speed

// accumulate the total forces acting on plane
totalForce += thrust;
thrust = Vector (0,0,0); // reset thrust
totalLocalForce = totalForce;

// Calculate the moment about the CG of this element's force
totalMoments += centerOfGravity ^ result;

// Convert forces from body space to global space
forces = GlobalToLocalCoords_2D (-angularPosition, totalForce);
moments += totalMoments;
}

void Ball::IntegrateEuler (double dt) {
// calculate all of the forces and moments on the ball
CalculateLoads();

// calculate the acceleration of the ball in earth space
acceleration = forces / mass;

// calculate the velocity of the ball in earth space
```

```
velocity += acceleration * dt;

// calculate the position of the ball in earth space
position += velocity * dt;

// Now handle the rotations by calculating the angular velocity
// in body space either by the quaternion or by matrices
// angularVelocity += inertiaInverse * (moments -
//            angularVelocity ^ (inertia * angularVelocity)) * dt;

Matrix3D mAngularVelocity = MakeAngularVelocityMatrix ();
angularVelocity += inertiaInverse *
  (moments - mAngularVelocity * inertia * angularVelocity) * dt;
```

Here I need to determine the new location of the origin point, which is changing because of the angular velocity.

```
Vector ap = angularVelocity * dt;
angularPosition += RadiansToDegrees (ap.Magnitude());
if (angularPosition > 360) angularPosition -= 360;
else if (angularPosition < 0) angularPosition += 360;

// Calculate the new rotation quaternion:
orientation += (orientation * angularVelocity) * 0.5 * dt;

// Normalize the orientation quaternion:
double mag = orientation.Magnitude();
if (mag != 0) orientation /= mag;

// Calculate velocity in body space
velocityBody = QVRotate (~orientation, velocity);
```

I've discovered that the above quaternion approach is not working properly, so I resorted to the 2D method, given next.

```
velocityBody = GlobalToLocalCoords_2D (angularPosition,
                                       velocity);
// calculate the air speed
speed = velocity.Magnitude();

// Find the Euler angles for our information
eulerAngles = orientation.MakeEulerAnglesFromQ ();
}

Matrix3D Ball::MakeAngularVelocityMatrix () {
 const Vector& v = angularVelocity;
 return Matrix3D (0.0, -v.z, v.y,
                 v.z, 0.0, -v.x,
```

```
                    -v.y, v.x, 0.0);
}

void Ball::ChangeThrust (bool up, double amount) {
 thrust.y = up ? -amount : amount;
}

void Ball::ChangeDirection (bool left, double amount) {
 thrust.x = left ? -amount : amount;
}

bool Ball::DetectCollision (const Vector& a, double aRadius) const
{
 double distance = sqrt (DistanceSquared (a));
 return distance < aRadius + radius;
}

double Ball::DistanceSquared (const Vector& a) const {
 double x = a.x - position.x;
 double y = a.y - position.y;
 double z = a.z - position.z;
 return x * x + y * y + z * z;
}

void Ball::ApplyLinearCollisionImpulse (Ball& e) {
 double J = - (1. + CoefficientOfRestitution) *
             velocityClosing / (1. / mass + 1. / e.mass);
 velocity += J * collisionNormal / mass;
 e.velocity += - J * collisionNormal / e.mass;
}

void Ball::ApplyLinearAngularCollisionImpulse (Ball& e) {
 Vector globalCollsionPoint = GetCollisionPoint (e);
 collisionPoint = globalCollsionPoint - position;
 e.collisionPoint = globalCollsionPoint - e.position;
 double J = - (1. + CoefficientOfRestitution) * velocityClosing /
   (1. / mass + 1. / e.mass +
    collisionNormal * (((collisionPoint ^ collisionNormal) /
                      localInertia.x) ^ collisionPoint) +
    collisionNormal * (((e.collisionPoint ^ collisionNormal) /
                      e.localInertia.x) ^ e.collisionPoint));
 velocity += J * collisionNormal / mass;
 e.velocity += - J * collisionNormal / e.mass;
 angularVelocity +=
         (collisionPoint ^ J * collisionNormal) * localInertia.x;
 e.angularVelocity +=
```

332

```
    (e.collisionPoint ^ - J * collisionNormal) * e.localInertia.x;
}
```

In GetCollisionPoint(), when calculating the slope of the line, if the divisor, x, is zero or nearly so, then the line is horizontal.

```
Vector Ball::GetCollisionPoint (const Ball& e) {
 double x = position.x - e.position.x;
 double y = position.y - e.position.y;
 if (fabs (x) < EPS) {
  return Vector (position.x, position.y + radius, 0);
 }
 else {
  double m = y / x;
  double x3 = position.x + sqrt (radius * radius / (m * m + 1.));
  double y3 = position.y + m * (x3 - position.x);
  return Vector (x3, y3, 0);
 }
}
```

Often this simple spherical collision detection and handling method is sufficient for a game. However, if one is dealing with more complex objects, such as biplanes, other approaches can be used. Still many of those first use the spherical method to see if there is any possibility of a collision before launching into the very complex alternate methods, which are run-time execution intensive routines.

Another approach that I use in my WWII game is to have two images of the objects. One image is what the user sees on their screen. In the other image never shown onscreen, I draw each object in a different color. In True Color mode, there are millions of different colors, more than enough to handle a large number of objects. Collision detection becomes very simple. One only needs to check if the current object (which has one color value) is overlaying another object which has a different color value. This method of collision detection is very fast indeed, requiring little calculations to determine if a collision has occurred. However, its drawback is the difficulty of maintaining the duplicate image of the screen drawn in different colors.

Programming Problems

None

Chapter 12 Repeatable, Random Terrain Generation

The handling of terrain deserves an examination. While the terrain could be stored in data files, as it was with the Doom game in its .wad files, often vast amounts of storage space is needed, sometimes more then can fit on a CD-Rom. An answer to saving the terrain on permanent storage is to have a way to have the game program automatically generate any needed terrain. A primary consideration is that for any given section of the game world, the terrain should be re-producible. That is, any time a player visits a section of the game world, the terrain there should be the same as the last visit. Yet another consideration is the actual construction of vast amounts of terrain for a large game world. Usually, programmers' resort to some form of "random" terrain generation. This chapter explores techniques for random, repeatable terrain generation.

The Basic Algorithm

The fundamental method to generate random terrain is to use the random number generator function, rand(). First, one decides upon how many different types of terrain the world should have, such as mountains, hills, forests, plains, and waters, say 5. One then uses the mod or remainder operator, %, to get a number between 0 and less than 5.

rand() % 5

Or if one wants a number between 1 and 5 inclusive, just add 1.

rand() % 5 + 1

Are the numbers really random? Yes, and no. The random number generator requires an initial seed value. If the same seed is used, the same series of numbers is generated. Thus, when random die rolls are required, for example, the current time on the computer is used to guarantee a different series of random numbers are given each time the game is played.

With terrain generation, repeatability is now something desirable. Yet, randomness in the overall results is also wanted. The trick is to use the same seed values from run to run. Here is how it is done.

```
void MakeTerrainRawRandom (char t[][MaxCols]) {
 for (int row=0; row<MaxRows; row++) {
  for (int col=0; col<MaxCols; col++) {
   srand (col + col * row);
   t[row][col] = rand () % MaxColors;
  }
 }
}
```

Game Programming Theory

The array t is just a 2D array holding the type of terrain number, in this case a number between 0 and 4. Often, a large array size is used to encompass the whole world, but only a small subset of that array is shown on the screen, around the player's current location within the game world. The key line is highlighted in boldface. To obtain predictability from execution to execution, the same seed must be used. Here, it is the value of the column number plus the product of the column and row numbers.

This offers us another advantage. Say the game world is an array 100,000 by 100,000 locations or tiles in size. If we were to store the whole world, that would be an array of 100,000 x 100,000 x 1 byte or 10,000,000,000 bytes or roughly 10G, vastly exceeding the amount of memory available for a program, 2G. Yet, assume that at any point in time, only an area of 24 rows of 80 columns must be visible on the screen. Using the above method and substituting in different starting and ending values for the two for loops, one can generate just those rows and columns!

For example, suppose that the world coordinates for which current terrain had to be generated was given by two ints, worldRow and worldCol. Further, assume that from this upper left coordinate, an array of 24 rows of 80 columns needed to be created. The modified function would then be this.

```
void MakeTerrainRawRandom (char t[][MaxCols], int worldRow,
                           int worldCol) {
 int wRow = worldRow, wCol;
 for (int row=0; row<24; row++) {
  wCol = worldCol; // reset starting world column
  for (int col=0; col<80; col++) {
   srand (wCol + wCol * wRow);
   t[row][col] = rand () % MaxColors;
   wCol++; // increment world column
  }
  wRow++; increment world row
 }
}
```

Notice that it is the world coordinates that are used to create the random terrain, always then repeatable for any given location.

Pgm12a illustrates the various methods we are examining in this chapter. The array size is 80x80 because some of the other methods we will discuss require a square array and one whose dimensions are evenly divisible by 4. Here is the start of Pgm12a.

```
#include <iostream>
#include <iomanip>
#include <cmath>
#include <ctime>
using namespace std;
#include "Screen.h"
```

```
// overly large array because algorithms need equal number
// of rows and columns
const int MaxRows = 80;
const int MaxCols = 80;

const int MaxColors = 5;

void DisplayTerrain (Screen& s, const char t[][MaxCols]);

void MakeTerrainRawRandom (char t[][MaxCols]);
void SmoothTerrainByAveraging (char t[][MaxCols], int step);
void SmoothTerrainByCorners (char t[][MaxCols]);
void MakeTerrainByFaultLines (char t[][MaxCols], int numLines);

// these are the terrain colors
// order: mountain, hill, forest, plain, water
const Screen::Color Colors[MaxColors] = {
                    Screen::Black, Screen::Gray,
                    Screen::Green, Screen::Yellow, Screen::Blue};

int main () {
 cin.sync_with_stdio (); // if you want to use cin
 Screen s (Screen::Black, Screen::White);
 s.ClearScreen ();
 s.DrawBox (0, 0, 24, 79, Screen::Gray, Screen::BrightYellow);

 char terrain[MaxRows][MaxCols] = { {0} };

 s.SetTitle ("Terrain Generation - Crude Random Generation");
 MakeTerrainRawRandom (terrain);
 DisplayTerrain (s, terrain);
 s.GoToXY (1, 24);
 s.GetAnyKey ();
```

Once more, I use the simple DOS Screen class for easy display. The DisplayTerrain() function is also simple.

```
void DisplayTerrain (Screen& s, const char t[][MaxCols]) {
 for (int i=1; i<24; i++) {
  for (int j=1; j<MaxCols-1; j++) {
   s.OutputUCharWith (' ', i, j, Colors[t[i][j]], Screen::Red);
  }
 }
}
```

Game Programming Theory

The real problem with this method is that the terrain generated is really random and looks absolutely awful. Figure 12.1 shows the output of this method. Some improvement is definitely needed here.

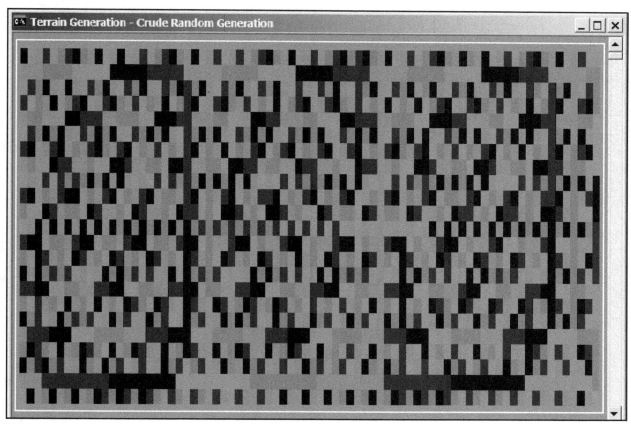

Figure 12.1 Random, Repeatable Terrain

Smoothing by Averaging

Given the raw terrain array, one technique that can be used to improve the results is called Smoothing by Averaging. The idea is to replace each terrain result with the average of its nearest neighbors. The variable in the method is how many near neighbors are used. If 4 are used, for example, then each terrain location's value is replace by the straight average of the square 4x4 around it. That is, we examine the first block of 4x4 and replace all of these 16 values with the average of these 16 original values.

Once more, the coding is simple. The size of the square block to average is passed to the function as the parameter step.

```
void SmoothTerrainByAveraging (char t[][MaxCols], int step) {
 // averages step nearest neighbors
 int row, col, localRow, localCol;
 int average, total;
 for (row=0; row<MaxRows; row+=step) {
  for (col=0; col<MaxCols; col+=step) {
   total = 0;
   for (localRow=row; localRow<row+step && localRow<MaxRows;
         localRow++) {
    for (localCol=col; localCol<col+step && localCol<MaxCols;
          localCol++) {
     total += t[localRow][localCol];
    }
   }
   average = total / (step * step);
   for (localRow=row; localRow<row+step && localRow<MaxRows;
         localRow++) {
    for (localCol=col; localCol<col+step && localCol<MaxCols;
          localCol++) {
     t[localRow][localCol] = average;
    }
   }
  }
 }
}
```

The main() function calls SmoothTerrainByAveraging() three times, using a step size of 4, 3, and then 2. The next three figures show the results. Remember, each one of these begins with the random terrain shown in Figure 12.1 above. We are only smoothing out the final results.

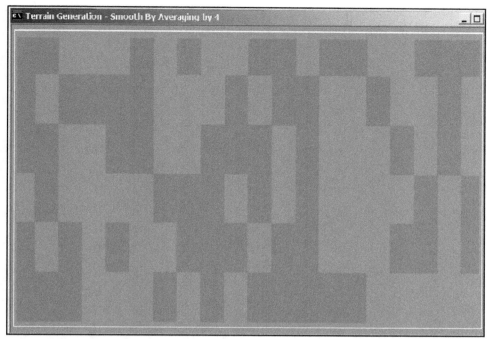

Figure 12.2 Smoothing Out the Random Terrain by Blocks of Four

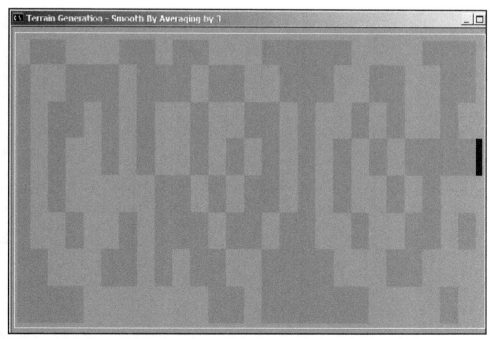

Figure 12.3 Smoothing Out the Random Terrain by Blocks of Three

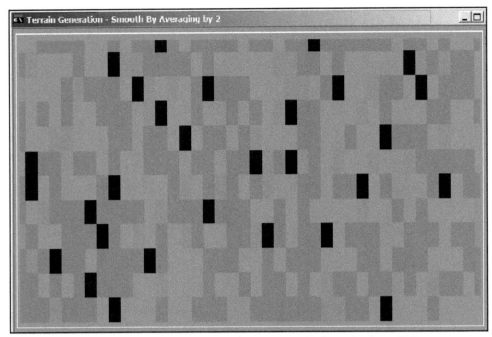

Figure 12.4 Smoothing Out the Random Terrain by Blocks of Two

Notice the tremendous difference that the step size has on the final result. If your game world was very large, then a step size of 4 might work well. However, I find that the step size of 2 looks better in this case of a 24x80 display.

Smoothing by Using the Corner Points

Perhaps the best method for smoothing terrain was created by James McNeill and uses the corners and centers, with a weighted average. The results are shown in Figure 12.5 below and for my money, looks the best of all these.

The method requires a square array whose dimension is evenly divisible by 4. A square subsection is taken from the whole array and a weighted average is made from the 4 corners and the four centers.

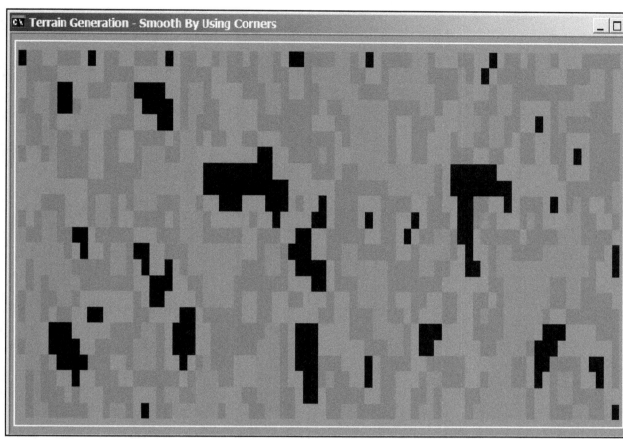

Figure 12.5 Smoothing by Using the Corners and Centers in a Weighted Average

```
void SmoothTerrainByCorners (char t[][MaxCols]) {
 // weighted average of four corner points
 // must be a square terrain array evenly divisible by 4
 int i1, i2, i3, i4, p1, p2, p3, p4, x2, y2, x3, y3;
 int rowOffset = 0;  // start at zero for first row

 for (int squareSize=MaxCols; squareSize>1; squareSize/=2) {
  for (int x1=rowOffset; x1<MaxRows; x1+=squareSize ) {
   for ( int y1=rowOffset; y1<MaxCols; y1+=squareSize ) {
    // Get the four corner points.
    x2 = (x1 + squareSize) % MaxRows;
    y2 = (y1 + squareSize) % MaxCols;

    // load the corner points
    i1 = t[x1][y1];
    i2 = t[x2][y1];
```

341

```
i3 = t[x1][y2];
i4 = t[x2][y2];

// weighted averaging of the four corner points
p1 = ((i1 * 9) + (i2 * 3) + (i3 * 3) + (i4)) / 16;
p2 = ((i1 * 3) + (i2 * 9) + (i3) + (i4 * 3)) / 16;
p3 = ((i1 * 3) + (i2) + (i3 * 9) + (i4 * 3)) / 16;
p4 = ((i1) + (i2 * 3) + (i3 * 3) + (i4 * 9)) / 16;

// store the new smoothed points
x3 = (x1 + squareSize/4) % MaxCols;
y3 = (y1 + squareSize/4) % MaxCols;
x2 = (x3 + squareSize/2) % MaxCols;
y2 = (y3 + squareSize/2) % MaxCols;

t[x3][y3] = p1;
t[x2][y3] = p2;
t[x3][y2] = p3;
t[x2][y2] = p4;
}
}
rowOffset = squareSize / 4;   // set offset for next row
}
}
```

Fault Line Landscape Generation

This technique has a far greater value in terrain generation, because it creates a random series of elevations from −128 to +127, undulating up and down patterns, indicative of terrain features. The method takes two random points within the area and draws a line at a given height between them. The number of lines drawn is the variable commodity.

Once all of the lines have been drawn, one then goes back over each point and alters the number at that location into your terrain value. I chose the largest numbers to represent mountains, and the lowest numbers (close to −128) as representing water. The precise cut-off values used are totally up to you. If you want to have predominately plains and forests, make the range of generated values for them larger than the rest. If hilly, mountainous terrain is desired, allow those two to encompass the largest range of resultant numbers.

Figure 12.6 shows the raw output, while figure 12.7 shows the output after Smoothing by using the Corners has been done.

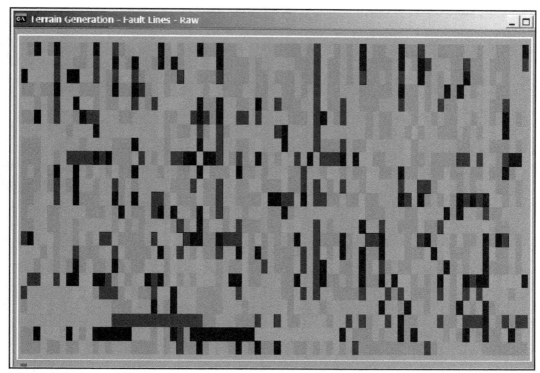

Figure 12.6 Random Terrain Using Fault Line Method, Raw Results

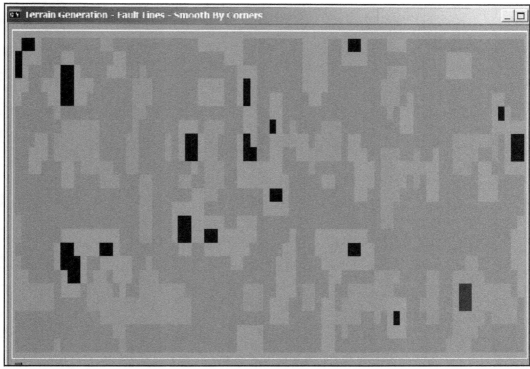

Figure 12.7 Random Terrain, Fault Line Method, Smoothed Using Corners

```
void MakeTerrainByFaultLines (char t[][MaxCols], int numLines) {
 int nCurrentRandomValue; // last selected random value
 int col, row;            // terrain coordinates
 int i;
 double colStart, rowStart, colEnd, rowEnd, colDifference,
        rowDifference;
 const double PI = acos(-1.);
```

For each of the desired lines, a random number determines whether it will be a vertical line, < 50, or a horizontal line. Next, if it is to be a vertical line through all rows, another random number is used to decide in which half of the array the beginning column (and corresponding ending column) resides. The max() function returns the larger of two values, while the min() function returns the smaller of two values. The number of columns to do for each step in row is then determined.

```
 for (i=0; i<numLines; i++) {
  if ((rand() % 100) < 50) {
   if ((rand() % 100) < 50) {
    colStart = rand() % (MaxRows / 2);
    colEnd   = colStart + rand() % (MaxRows / 2);
   }
   else {
    colStart = MaxRows - (rand() % (MaxRows / 2));
    colEnd   = colStart - (rand() % (MaxRows / 2));
   }
   rowStart = 0.0;
   rowEnd   = MaxRows - 1;

   if (colStart < MaxRows / 2) {
    colDifference = (max (colStart, colEnd) -
                     min (colStart, colEnd)) / MaxRows;
   }
   else {
    colDifference = (min (colStart, colEnd) -
                     max (colStart, colEnd)) / MaxRows;
   }
   rowDifference = 1.0;
  }
  else {
   if ((rand() % 100) < 50) {
    rowStart = rand() % (MaxRows / 2);
    rowEnd = rowStart + rand() % (MaxRows / 2);
   }
   else {
    rowStart = MaxRows - rand() % (MaxRows / 2);
    rowEnd = rowStart - rand() % (MaxRows / 2);
   }
```

```
colStart = 0;
colEnd = MaxRows - 1;
if (rowStart < MaxRows / 2) {
  rowDifference = (max (rowStart, rowEnd) -
                   min (rowStart, rowEnd)) / MaxRows;
}
else {
  rowDifference = (min (rowStart, rowEnd) -
                   max (rowStart, rowEnd)) / MaxRows;
}
colDifference = 1.0;
}
nCurrentRandomValue = 0;
```

Once the starting and ending point are fixed, this next block draws in the line between them. The "randomizer" is the sine function, passed the start column or row number. Each point on the line is given its random number between –128 and +127.

```
do {
  if (rowStart<MaxRows && rowStart>0 &&
      colStart<MaxCols && colStart>0)
   t[(int)rowStart][(int)colStart] = nCurrentRandomValue;
  colStart = colStart + colDifference;
  rowStart = rowStart + rowDifference;
  // Apply a sine function oscillating between 0 and 255
  // the sin should be called with values from -pi/2 to pi/2
  if (colDifference < rowDifference) {
   nCurrentRandomValue = (int)
                          ((sin (colStart) * 128.0) + 128.0);
  }
  else {
   nCurrentRandomValue = (int)
                          ((sin (rowStart) * 128.0) + 128.0);
  }
 } while (rowStart<MaxRows && rowStart>0 &&
          colStart<MaxCols && colStart>0);
}
```

Once all lines have been drawn, then you need to replace these values with your terrain numbers, based upon the type of terrain that is to predominate in this section. As the comments indicate, you can replace my choices for cut-off values with those that you desire.

```
// now convert into terrain features
// you can adjust these cut-off values to emphasize
// the most desired terrain feature for this map
const int Plains  = -75;
const int Forest = 0;
```

```
const int Hills = 25;
const int Mtns  = 80;
for (row=0; row<MaxRows; row++) {
 for (col=0; col<MaxCols; col++) {
  char x = t[row][col];
  if (x > Mtns) t[row][col] = 0;
  else if (x > Hills) t[row][col] = 1;
  else if (x > Forest ) t[row][col] = 2;
  else if (x > Plains ) t[row][col] = 3;
  else t[row][col] = 4;
 }
 }
}
```

Don't forget that you do need to then pass the result back through one of the smoothing functions. Further modifications can be made to these algorithms to suit your specific needs.

Handling Location within a World

A somewhat related problem facing games programmers is keeping track of just where in the game universe moving objects are currently located. Often coupled with the location will be the image to be shown on the screen. Sometimes it is sufficient to store only the point location (x, y) of the object. Other times, this is not enough.

I've played a lot of car racing games, such as Crash Bash, with my nephew. As the cars move around the track, the terrain is shown flying by. With the curving race tracks, how can one keep track of where a race car is located?

One of the clever techniques is to subdivide the race track into a series of connected convex sectors. This is shown in Figure 12.8.

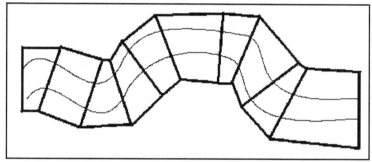

Figure 12.8 A Race Track Subdivided into Sectors

What we desire is a function that returns a double representing the distance through any given sector, where 0.0 means that the car is at the leading edge of the sector and 1.0 means that the car is at the ending or trailing edge of the sector. The algorithm must be fast, since the distance must be computed for each race car each frame, so that we can display the correct image the driver sees on the screen.

Figure 12.9 shows the layout of a sector. The requirements are three. First, the sector must have four sides of non-zero length. Second, the area of the sector must not be zero. Third, the current position of a race car is at point P which must be within the sector or on the leading or trailing edge or any of its perimeter bounding lines.

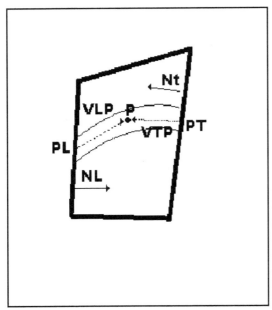

Figure 12.9 The Vectors

Vector N_L is the normal vector to the leading edge and points inward, N_t is the normal to the trailing edge and points inward. Vector V_{lp} represents the position of the car from the leading edge, V_{tp}, from the trailing edge. Point P_L is any point along the leading edge, P_T is any point along the tailing edge.

We can find V_{lp} and V_{tp} by vector subtraction of point vectors.
$$V_{lp} = P - P_L$$
$$V_{tp} = P - P_T$$
The fast, simple solution to find the distance d is given by this equation.
$$d = (V_{lp} \text{ dot } N_L) / (V_{lp} \text{ dot } N_L + V_{tp} \text{ dot } N_T)$$
If P is on the leading edge, d is zero. If P is on the trailing edge, d is 1.0. The global coordinate, P, can be used directly in the equation.

P_L can lie anywhere along the leading edge, just as P_T can be anywhere along the trailing edge. However, if we pick opposite corners for these two, then we can use the equation to calculate the lateral distance as well, since then the same two points lie on the opposite pair of bounding edges! Thus, we can get the distance through the sector and the current size-ways location as well.

When I laid out the track in the above Figure 12.9, notice that adjacent sectors shared the same vertices. At initialization time, all sector's normal vectors can be calculated one time and stored for later us, avoiding runtime overhead. Further, we can get a close estimate of the distance through the sector by using the midpoints of the leading and trailing edges, as long as the sectors are laid out well.

One problem that arises at once is knowing when a point is within a sector or lies outside of the sector. There are numerous solutions to this geometry problem. I've chosen a method that makes use of an interesting property of the closed, convex polygons. If the polygon is convex, one can consider the polygon as a "path" from the first vertex. If a point is always on the same side of all the line segments making up the path, then that point is in the interior of the polygon. In this situation, I am creating the array of points going clockwise around the polygon. The math is this. Given a line segment between vertex point P_0 (x_0, y_0) and vertex point P_1 (x_1, y_1), any other point P (x, y) has the following relationship to the line segment:

$$(y - y_0)(x_1 - x_0) - (x - x_0)(y_1 - y_0)$$

If the result is less than 0, then point P is to the right of the line segment. If the result is greater than 0, then point P is to the left. If the result is equal to 0, then the point lies on the line segment. This is shown in Figure 12.10.

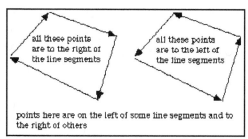

Figure 12.10 Point Results

Putting It All Together, Pgm12b

This example illustrates how a car racing game, such as Crash Bash, can be written. Of course, we are ignoring totally the graphical user interface, concentrating on the physics and geometry of the implementation. In such games, often there is an overview of the race track and the player's position. It is this overview that Pgm12b illustrates.

When the user chooses the Start Race menu item, a timer gives the three second countdown. When the race begins, another interval counter handles the action every tenth of a second, updating the race car and the screen. Additionally, the statusbar shows the current race progress, including the car's current miles per hour, the total distance traveled down the race track thus far, the percentage through the current sector, and of course, the all important total time.

Further, when I play my nephews, I often run off of the track. Sometimes in frustration or desperation, I drive the race track backwards. Hence, whenever the car leaves the sector by running totally off the track, the program resets the car back on the track at the beginning of the sector, so that you can try to navigate it again. If you try to drive the track backwards, another message appears on the statusbar notifying you that you are going the wrong way. As a new sector is entered, the outline of the sector is also shown.

I have arbitrarily capped the top speed of the car to be 150 mph. Figure 12.12 shows the car, a black circle, on the yellow race track, just after starting, only five seconds into the race. The controls are crude. Page Up and Page Down keys alter the speed by 50 with each click, while the Up and Down Arrow keys increment by a smaller amount. The Left and Right Arrows handle turning. No attempt has been made to insert the physics of an actual race car into the game, it is all simulated only.

The starting point for this application was the design of the track and its layout. Again, I used graph paper to draw out the desired track. Next, I divided the track into a number of logical sectors, drawing them on the paper as well. A coordinate scheme was laid out over the drawing, locating the origin point, (0, 0). For each of the sectors, the four vertices were measured and entered into a text file. Always, the upper left corner point is entered first and then the others, going clockwise around the polygon.

Thus, the first action of the program is to load in this scale model of the race track, converting it into a two dimensional array of vertex points. Then, each point was scaled to represent the actual size of the track. In this case, the length of the track along the x axis was twenty squares, which I decided would be a mile, 5280 feet. Dividing 5280 by the number of squares yields the scaling factor which is then multiplied with each vertex number to scale the whole array up to the actual race track.

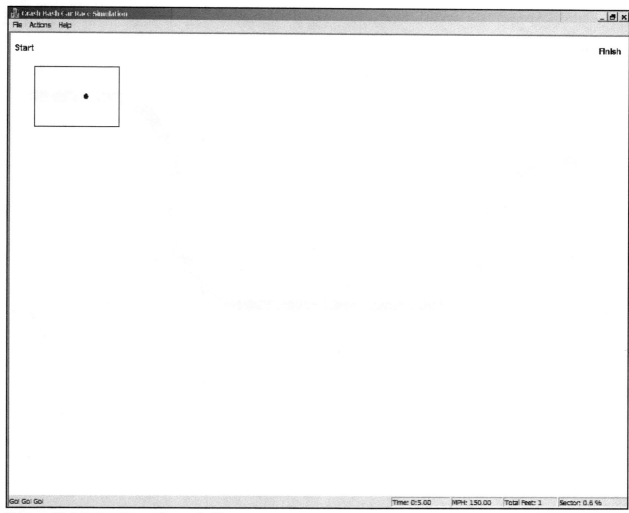

Figure 12.12 The Race Game in Progress

A Track class holds the basic track data and implements the various geometry based functions.

Track.h

```
#pragma once
#include "Vector.h"

const int MaxVertex = 15;
const int MaxCorners = 4;
const double Scale = 5280. / 20.;
const double TrackWidth = 100.;
```

351

```
class Track {
public:
 Vector vertices[MaxVertex][MaxCorners];
 Vector normals[MaxVertex][MaxCorners];
 double vertDist[MaxVertex];
 Vector midPoint[MaxVertex+1];
 double yEndMax, yEndMin , xEnd;

  Track ();
 ~Track ();

 void LoadVertexFile ();
 void Initialize ();

 double DistanceDownTheSector (const Vector& pos,
                                int whichSector);
 bool   IsInThisSector (const Vector& pos, int whichSector);
};
```

The array vertices holds the fifteen sector's four corners. Subscript 0 if the upper left corner with the others entered in a clockwise manner. The 2d array normals holds the four normal vectors to each side of the polygon. The array of doubles, vertDist, holds the total distance across this sector. The array midPoint, one larger than the number of sectors, contains the point which is in the middle of that edge line, representing the centerline of the race track proper.

The LoadVertexFile() function inputs the simple text file, while Initialize() handles the scaling and the initialization of the other arrays. The two new key functions are DistanceDownTheSector(), which returns a number between 0.0 and 1.0, and IsInThisSector(), which returns a bool indicating whether the passed point lies within this sector or not.

```
Track.cpp
#include "StdAfx.h"
#include <iostream>
#include <fstream>
using namespace std;

#include "Track.h"

Track::Track () { }
Track::~Track () { }

void Track::LoadVertexFile () {
 ifstream infile ("vertices.txt");
 if (!infile) {
  AfxMessageBox ("Error: cannot open Vertices.txt", MB_OK);
```

```
  PostQuitMessage (0);
 }
 for (int i=0; i<MaxVertex && infile; i++) {
  for (int j=0; j<MaxCorners && infile; j++) {
   infile >> vertices[i][j].x >> vertices[i][j].y;
  }
 }
 if (!infile) {
  AfxMessageBox ("Error reading in Vertices.txt", MB_OK);
  PostQuitMessage (0);
 }
 infile.close ();
}
```

Initialize() first loops through all the vectors, multiplying each by the scaling factor. Next, the array of four normal lines per sector are found. One subtracts the two points which form that edge, then reverse the x and y values and negate the y value to obtain a normal that is always pointing toward the interior of the sector. Then, Normalize() each vector. Once the four normals are done, the midpoint is found. Once that loop is done and the very last, right most edge midpoint found, the next step is to calculate the total distance across each sector. Finally, for convenience, I calculated once the ending location of the race track and stored those values in yEndMax, yEndMin, and xEnd. After each turn of movement, the car's current position is checked against these three values to see if it has crossed the finish line.

```
void Track::Initialize () {
 int i, j;
 for (i=0; i<MaxVertex; i++) {
  for (j=0; j<MaxCorners; j++) {
   vertices[i][j] *= Scale;
  }
 }
 for (i=0; i<MaxVertex; i++) {
  Vector n = vertices[i][0] - vertices[i][3];
  normals[i][0] = Vector (n.y, -n.x, 0);
  normals[i][0].Normalize ();
  n = vertices[i][1] - vertices[i][0];
  normals[i][1] = Vector (n.y, -n.x, 0);
  normals[i][1].Normalize ();
  n = vertices[i][2] - vertices[i][1];
  normals[i][2] = Vector (n.y, -n.x, 0);
  normals[i][2].Normalize ();
  n = vertices[i][3] - vertices[i][2];
  normals[i][3] = Vector (n.y, -n.x, 0);
  normals[i][3].Normalize ();
  midPoint[i] = vertices[i][0]
              - (vertices[i][0] - vertices[i][3])/2;
```

```
}
midPoint[MaxVertex] = vertices[MaxVertex-1][1]
      - (vertices[MaxVertex-1][1] - vertices[MaxVertex-1][2])/2;
double sum = 0;
for (i=0; i<MaxVertex; i++) {
 vertDist[i] = (midPoint[i+1] - midPoint[i]).Magnitude();
 sum += vertDist[i];
}
yEndMax = midPoint[MaxVertex].y + TrackWidth;
yEndMin = midPoint[MaxVertex].y - TrackWidth;
xEnd = midPoint[MaxVertex].x;
}

double   Track::DistanceDownTheSector  (const   Vector&   pos,   int
whichSector) {
 Vector vlp = pos - vertices[whichSector][0];
 Vector vtp = pos - vertices[whichSector][2];
 double dotLeading = vlp * normals[whichSector][0];
 double dotTrailing = vtp * normals[whichSector][2];
 return dotLeading / (dotLeading + dotTrailing);
}

bool Track::IsInThisSector (const Vector& pos, int whichSector) {
 double d1, d2, d3, d4;
 d1 = (pos.y - vertices[whichSector][0].y) *
      (vertices[whichSector][1].x - vertices[whichSector][0].x) -
      (pos.x - vertices[whichSector][0].x) *
       (vertices[whichSector][1].y - vertices[whichSector][0].y);
 d2 = (pos.y - vertices[whichSector][1].y) *
      (vertices[whichSector][2].x - vertices[whichSector][1].x) -
      (pos.x - vertices[whichSector][1].x) *
       (vertices[whichSector][2].y - vertices[whichSector][1].y);
 d3 = (pos.y - vertices[whichSector][2].y) *
      (vertices[whichSector][3].x - vertices[whichSector][2].x) -
      (pos.x - vertices[whichSector][2].x) *
       (vertices[whichSector][3].y - vertices[whichSector][2].y);
 d4 = (pos.y - vertices[whichSector][3].y) *
      (vertices[whichSector][0].x - vertices[whichSector][3].x) -
      (pos.x - vertices[whichSector][3].x) *
       (vertices[whichSector][0].y - vertices[whichSector][3].y);
 if (d1 <=0 && d2 <= 0 && d3 <= 0 && d4 <= 0)
  return true;
 return false;
}
```

The remaining two functions above implement the geometry equations discussed in the previous section.

Game Programming Theory

The Car class encapsulates the race car, very crudely that is. Two key data members are needed, the car's position and velocity vectors. I also store the sector number in which the car is currently within along with its current mph, distance traveled thus far, and the distance through the current sector. The member previousDownThisSector double is used to help determine when the car is traveling the wrong way, backwards.

Car.h

```
#pragma once
#include "Vector.h"
#include "Track.h"

const double MaxFeetPerSec = 220;

class Car {
public:
 Vector position;
 double mph;
 Vector velocity;

 int    inWhichSector;
 double distanceDownThisSector;
 double previousDownThisSector;
 double distanceUptoThisSector;

  Car ();
~Car ();

 void Initialize (Vector& pos);
 void AdjustSpeed (double amount);
 void Turn (bool left);
 void StopCar ();
 void Integrate (double dt);
 void DetermineResults (Track& t, bool& finish, bool& reset,
                        bool& wrongWay);
 void Reset (Track& t);
 double GetDistanceDownTheTrack () const;
};
```

Initialize() resets the car back to the starting line. AdjustSpeed() and Turn() handle the user interface requests for a change in velocity. Integrate() handled the integration of the forces acting upon the car during this small time interval. However, since there is no physics being implemented, it is a shell that finds the new position, based upon the velocity times the time interval. Once the new position is found, next comes the hard part. We need to find out if the new position lies in the next sector or not. If so, the data stored needs to be updated. Normally, when there is a sector change, it is either +1 or -1 from the current sector.

Game Programming Theory

However, the car could be traveling backwards and the caller must be so notified. The car could have just crossed the finish line, again the caller must be told. Worse still, the car could have "crashed," that is, moved out of the sector, but not forwards or backwards. In the case of a crash, the Reset() function will be called to place the car at the beginning point of the sector with a velocity of zero.

While much of the Car class is simple, a few functions are not. Let's examine the class implementation.

Car.cpp
```cpp
#include "StdAfx.h"
#include "Car.h"

Car::Car () {
  mph = 0;
  inWhichSector = 0;
  distanceDownThisSector = distanceUptoThisSector = 0;
  previousDownThisSector = 0;
}

Car::~Car () {
}

void Car::Initialize (Vector& pos) {
  position = pos;
  mph = 0;
  velocity = Vector (0,0,0);
  inWhichSector = 0;
  distanceDownThisSector = distanceUptoThisSector = 0;
  previousDownThisSector =0;
}
```

Because there is no physics behind the Car, I need to find a way to handle an increase of speed. First, I limit the maximum speed to 150 mph. However, if the car could still be speeded up, I needed a way to handle adding the additional speed. All coordinates are in global, game world values, no local coordinates. This makes adding more speed a real problem, because pushing down or letting up on the gas pedal always acts along the local x axis of the car. My crude solution was to take the current velocity vector and normalize it. If the magnitude of the current velocity was zero, I assume that the car is standing still and add the requested speed to the x axis only. This is a poor assumption. If you run off the road while heading down one of the downward sectors and the car is reset, pressing Page Up now has the car going sideways to the race track! (Consider this to be an additional design feature if you run off the road in the wrong place, tease.)

If the car is moving, then if the normalized x value is zero, the requested speed is added to the y coordinate. If the y value is zero, the requested speed is added to the x coordinate. However, for most situations, part of the requested speed change is added to each axis, proportional to its directional heading. I used the tangent function to find the angle of orientation and then converted the requested adjustment from local into global coordinates and added it to the velocity vector. Alternatively, you can use the sin and cos functions to add the desired amount, which was done in handling the turning request.

```cpp
void Car::AdjustSpeed (double amount) {
 double maxSpeed = velocity.Magnitude ();
 if (maxSpeed + amount > MaxFeetPerSec)
  amount = MaxFeetPerSec - maxSpeed;
 Vector speed = Vector (amount, 0, 0);
 Vector vel = velocity;
 vel.Normalize ();
 if (velocity.Magnitude() < EPS)
  velocity.x = amount;
 else if (fabs (vel.x) < EPS)
  velocity.y += amount;
 else if (fabs (vel.y) < EPS)
  velocity.x += amount;
 else {
  double rad = atan2 (velocity.y, velocity.x);
  double deg = RadiansToDegrees (rad);
  velocity += GlobalToLocalCoords_2D (deg, speed);
 }
}

void Car::Turn (bool left) {
 double maxSpeed = velocity.Magnitude ();
 double amount = 50. * maxSpeed / MaxFeetPerSec;
 if (left) amount = - amount;
 Vector speed = Vector (0, amount, 0);
 Vector vel = velocity;
 vel.Normalize ();
 if (velocity.Magnitude() < EPS)
  velocity.y = amount;
 else if (fabs (vel.x) < EPS)
  velocity.x += amount;
 else if (fabs (vel.y) < EPS)
  velocity.y += amount;
 else {
  double rad = atan2 (velocity.y, velocity.x);
  double deg = RadiansToDegrees (rad);
  velocity += GlobalToLocalCoords_2D (deg, speed);
 }
 maxSpeed = velocity.Magnitude ();
 if (maxSpeed > MaxFeetPerSec) {
```

```
Vector norm = velocity;
norm.Normalize ();
if (fabs (norm.x) < EPS)
  velocity.y = MaxFeetPerSec;
else if (fabs (norm.y) < EPS)
  velocity.x = MaxFeetPerSec;
else {
  double rad = atan2 (norm.y, norm.x);
  velocity.x = MaxFeetPerSec * cos (rad);
  velocity.y = MaxFeetPerSec * sin (rad);
  }
 }
}

void Car::StopCar () {
 velocity = Vector (0,0,0);
}

void Car::Integrate (double dt) {
 position += velocity * dt;
 mph = velocity.Magnitude () / 5280 * 3600;
}

double Car::GetDistanceDownTheTrack () const {
 return distanceDownThisSector + distanceUptoThisSector;
}
```

The DetermineResults() is the really key function in this simulation. It handles the impact of the current movement. One of its primary tasks is to find the new distance down this sector. So to help detect moving backwards, the current value is stored in previousDownThisSector. First, I check for the most likely thing that has happened during the last tenth of a second, the car has moved further down the current sector. Hence, if the car is still in the sector, a new distance down it is found.

If the car is not in this sector anymore, we must find out which one it has gone into, the next or the previous are the only two choices. Again, I checked the most likely possibility first, the car has moved into the next sector. However, the car might be in the last sector, so test for array size before checking to see if it is in the next sector. If it lies in the next sector, increment inWhichSector, obtain the distance down this new sector, and update the total distance traveled.

Similarly, if the car has moved into the previous sector, decrement inWhichSector, and recalculate the respective values. Don't forget to set wrongWay to true!

```
void Car::DetermineResults (Track& t, bool& finish, bool& reset,
                            bool& wrongWay) {
```

```
finish = reset = wrongWay = false;
previousDownThisSector = distanceDownThisSector;
if (t.IsInThisSector (position, inWhichSector)) {
 distanceDownThisSector = t.DistanceDownTheSector (position,
                                                inWhichSector);
}
// not in this sector, so we have a change in sectors
else {
 // first try next sector, if not at the end point
 if (inWhichSector + 1 < MaxVertex &&
     t.IsInThisSector (position, inWhichSector + 1)) {
   inWhichSector++;
   distanceDownThisSector = t.DistanceDownTheSector (position,
                                                inWhichSector);
   distanceUptoThisSector += t.vertDist[inWhichSector - 1];
   previousDownThisSector = 0;
 }
 // no, so try previous sector, if not at the begin point
 else if (inWhichSector - 1 > 0 &&
         t.IsInThisSector (position, inWhichSector - 1)) {
  inWhichSector--;
  distanceDownThisSector = t.DistanceDownTheSector (position,
                                               inWhichSector);
  distanceUptoThisSector -= t.vertDist[inWhichSector + 1];
  previousDownThisSector = 0;
  wrongWay = true;
 }
```

It is possible that the car has attempted to move elsewhere, outside of the current sector. This can be the case if it has crossed the finish line. So the next test is to see if we are at the end and if the car's position lies somewhere on the finish line. If so, set finish to true. For all other cases, the car has effectively crashed! The last test is to compare the current new distance down this sector to the previous value. If it is less than the previous value, the car is going the wrong way.

```
 // here, outside of possibilities
 else {
  if (inWhichSector + 1 == MaxVertex) {
   // see if car is at finish line
   if (position.y <= t.yEndMax && position.y >= t.yEndMin
      && position.x >= t.xEnd) {
    finish = true;
   }
  }
  else reset = true;
 }
}
```

```
  if (distanceDownThisSector < previousDownThisSector)
    wrongWay = true;
}

void Car::Reset (Track& t) {
  position = t.midPoint[inWhichSector];
  distanceDownThisSector = 0;
  velocity = Vector (0, 0, 0);
  mph = 0;
}
```

The MainFrame class handles the Windows programming interface. As usual, you are not responsible for most of this coding. Only a small portion is tied to the actual simulation. Specifically, the class defines the following members.

```
  Track t;
  Car   c;
  bool racing;
  int  countDown;
  double pelsPerFoot;
  double totalTime;
  double mph;
```

Here are the only instances of the Track and Car classes. When the game is underway, the bool racing is true. The member countDown is used to count down from three to zero to start the race. The member totalTime keeps track of the total elapsed time of the race. It begins at 0 and stops when the car crosses the finish line. This member is converted into minutes and seconds and displayed on the status bar each turn. The member pelsPerFoot is used by the drawing functions to convert the feet of the track dimensions and locations into screen pixel locations.

When the window is being initially created as the program is launched, the following get executed, loading and initializing the track and car instances.

```
  t.LoadVertexFile ();
  t.Initialize ();
  c.Initialize (Vector (t.midPoint[0]));
```

When the user chooses the Start Race menu item, a timer is started, which goes off every second, to provide the countdown.

```
  SetTimer (2, 1000, 0);
  countDown = 3;
```

All of the relevant processing is then done from within the OnTimer() function, which is called every time one of the timers goes off, indicating that the preset amount of time has elapsed once again. Two timers are used. Timer #2 is used to count down from 3 to 0, while timer #1 is used to control the race.

```
void MainFrame::OnTimer(UINT_PTR nIDEvent) {
 if (nIDEvent == 2) {
  c.Initialize (Vector (t.midPoint[0]));
  mph = 0;
  totalTime = 0;
  UpdateStatusBar ();
  countDown--;
... here is coding to erase the previous message
  dc.TextOut (avgCharWidth, size.cy - avgCharHeight*4,
              "Get Ready! Three...");
  if (countDown == 2) {
   dc.TextOut (avgCharWidth, size.cy - avgCharHeight*4,
              "Get Ready! Two...");
  }
  else if (countDown == 1) {
   dc.TextOut (avgCharWidth, size.cy - avgCharHeight*4,
               "Get Ready! One...");
  }
  else {
   KillTimer (2);
   SetTimer (1, 100, 0);
   racing = true;
  }
  return;
 }
```

When the counter #2 has counted down to zero, it then sets the main timer #1 to activate every .1 second. When this #1 timer goes off, each .1 second, first, I handle any key presses the user has made during that last tenth of a second.

```
 if (!racing) return;

 if (specialKey == VK_UP) {
  c.AdjustSpeed (10);
 }
 else if (specialKey == VK_DOWN) {
  c.AdjustSpeed (-10);
 }
 else if (specialKey == VK_LEFT) {
  c.Turn (true);
 }
 else if (specialKey == VK_RIGHT) {
  c.Turn (false);
 }
 else if (specialKey == VK_PRIOR) {
  c.AdjustSpeed (50);
```

```
}
else if (specialKey == VK_NEXT) {
 c.AdjustSpeed (-50);
}
key = specialKey = 0;
```

The totalTime is updated and the Integrate() function is called to move the car to it's potential new position. However, because of the various things that can happen, this might not be its new location, such as in a crash or crossing the finish line. DetermineResults() is called to find out if any events have occurred. If any have, they are then handled.

```
totalTime += .1;
c.Integrate (.1);
bool finish, reset, wrongWay;
c.DetermineResults (t, finish, reset, wrongWay);
if (finish) {
 KillTimer (1);
}
if (reset) {
 c.Reset (t);
}
mph = c.mph;
Invalidate (true);
UpdateStatusBar ();
if (wrongWay)
 m_wndStatusBar.SetPaneText (0, "WRONG WAY!!!");
else
 m_wndStatusBar.SetPaneText (0, "Go! Go! Go!");
}
```

Experiment with the race, see how fast you can complete the course. Then, see how goofy you can get, going backwards, running off the race course and such. One detail that I did not implement is an enforced slowing down of a car's velocity when it is off the actual yellow race track portion of the sector. In Crash Bash, if you drive off the roadway, your car gets slowed down noticeably.

Programming Problems

Problem 12-1 Adding the Physics for the Race Car

Modify the Car class to implement the real physics behind a car moving down the race track, handling the forces being applied to it and so forth. It is to be a 2D simulation, not 3D.

Begin by copying the entire Pgm12b folder to another location. Do not try to make a new project, instead, use mine as is. Your changes are most likely going to only be to the Car class, with possibly a function call or two added to the OnTimer sequence.

For your car specifications, search the Internet or books or your experience. Part of the problem is to determine what data about the race car of your choice are needed. Part of the problem is to design and implement the race car physics in a 2D situation. For example, do you need to handle frictional forces? What about curves? Are curves banked? If so, how much? Can the car slide off of the race track? Can the car go into a spin? If you are handling curves, notice that a ninety degree turn is broken into two sectors.

Part of your grade for problem one comes from originality of design and part from how much of the underlying physics of a race car driving a track are implemented. For example, just how does one handle turning the steering wheel in the physics of the simulation?

In this sample program, all units are English. Distances are in feet and time, seconds. Use 32.176 for gravity, if needed.